MORE AUSTRALIAN BIRDING TALES

MORE AUSTRALIAN BIRDING TALES

R. Bruce Richardson

JOHN BEAUFOY PUBLISHING

First published in the United Kingdom and Australia in 2022
by John Beaufoy Publishing,

11 Blenheim Court, 316 Woodstock Road, Oxford OX2 7NS, England

www.johnbeaufoy.com

10 9 8 7 6 5 4 3 2 1

ISBN 978-1-913679-24-8

Designed by Gulmohur
Cartography by William Smuts
Project management by Rosemary Wilkinson
Printed and bound in Malaysia by Times Offset (M) Sdn Bhd

Front cover: Opalton Grasswren © David Adam
Back cover: Author at Port Wakefield, South Australia © James Cornelious
Opposite page: Unk far right in the sailor's cap standing in a Log Canoe,
1930's, Hampton Roads, Virginia.

To my uncle, George R Massenburg, Jr (Unk). You gave me the natural world. You are the main reason I am the man that I am today. I love you and I miss you.

I always will.

The weird go birding. The author exhausted and travel-crazed in Eaglehawk Neck, Tasmania.

"When the going gets weird, the weird turn pro."
Hunter S. Thompson

"When the going gets weird, the weird go birding."
R. Bruce Richardson

Pearl S. Buck wrote about who I was before ever I was born.
The following is me, every word, every thought.

"The truly creative mind in any field is no more than this: A human creature born abnormally, inhumanly sensitive. To him ... a touch is a blow, a sound is a noise, a misfortune is a tragedy, a joy is an ecstasy, a friend is a lover, a lover is a god, and failure is death.

Add to this cruelly delicate organism the overpowering necessity to create, create, create – so that without the creating of music or poetry or books or buildings or something of meaning, his very breath is cut off from him. He must create, must pour out creation. By some strange, unknown, inward urgency he is not really alive unless he is creating."

The contiguous US and Australia are similar in size.

Contents

Prologue / **1**

1. A Birding Sunday / **5**
2. Port Fairy Pelagic and Our Ridiculously Well Travelled Belongings / **11**
3. Letter-winged Kite in Victoria! / **18**
4. Yet Another Port Fairy Pelagic, Victoria / **26**
5. Two Twitches in Victoria / **34**
6. Very Briefly, Health Stuff / **45**
7. Finally Black-breasted Button-quail, Noosa, Queensland / **46**
8. Another Victorian Twitch and a Whale / **57**
9. Aleutian Surprise Old Bar, New South Wales / **64**
10. Two Troopies To Tassie and The Mega Petrel / **72**
11. An Unexpected Journey – Bogey No More / **84**
12. Grey Grasswren, *Amytornis barbatus* 700 / **102**
13. The Nullarbor and More / **118**
14. The Princess Expedition / **132**
15. Tasmanian Boobooks in Victoria, Whales and Other Stuff / **151**
16. Two Twitches / **164**
17. Pelagics and a Rainforest Skulker / **176**
18. Some Very Local Birding: the WTP / **189**
19. More Pelagic Joy Back Down Under the Land Down Under Again / **201**
20. Tassie Again Then Western Australia / **214**
21. Cocos/Keeling Islands / **229**
22. Christmas Island / **253**
23. A Twitch, A Hospital, A Pelagic, and the Pandemic / **270**
24. A Quick Bit on Ageing and Hope / **281**
25. Two Button-quail Tales (Futton-bucking-quail No More!), New South Wales / **286**
26. Serendipity and Alexander von Nordmann's Greenshank, Cairns and FNQ / **302**
27. The Great Grasswren Expedition, Opalton, Queensland and the Birdsville Track / **316**
28. A Longer Dedication Remembering Unk / **339**
29. A Birding Epilogue, The Hudwel Twitch / **347**

Author's Australian Life List Additions / **355**
Glossary / **358**
Who's To Bless and Who's To Blame / **363**
From the Author / **366**

Prologue

If you have already read my first book, *An Australian Birding Year,* this is the second. If I can manage to continue living this wacky, wonderful life that includes Australian adventures, birding expeditions and more, there might even be a third book, making it a trilogy of sorts. And as a friend once joked regarding that, it could be called, *The Lord of the Wings.* We will see. I really am beginning to look more like Gandalf every year.

These are the tales of what happened in the time that followed the year that became a book. If you have ever read and enjoyed a book and thought, I wonder happened next? This is that book. There were changes. There were travels, adventures and there were some very, very cool birds. There were downs as well as ups and I will hopefully hit an interesting and entertaining balance of it all in this once again rather personal account.

I need to travel, bird and write about it. It is what I do. I recently stated that I am an old dog and past learning new tricks but that isn't right. The truth is that I know I am changing, and those changes are a part of this journal. For both good and bad, I am somewhat different than I was a few years ago. I bemoan some of the declines involved in ageing. However, I wholeheartedly approve of some of the changes. For one, I have been able to learn to breathe more fully through my written words and that is a very good thing. I live a not inconsiderable portion of my life in a two-dimensional existence with this screen, tapping out my soul with my fingertips. I write therefore I am.

Of the photos in this book, most are mine, but a few are from my friends and are credited, of course. But this isn't a picture book, most of the photos are just memory photos or photos that I felt enhanced the text. I am a writer and a birder, not a photographer.

I have been told that I write like I talk. I appreciate that. What I write is authentically me and I value authenticity. I am the me that you read in my words. Of course, those words contain many influences that I have connected with over the years. To name just a few, my words are often touched by the words of Patrick O'Brian, Theodor Geisel, Bob Dylan, J. R. R. Tolkien, Jerry Jeff Walker, John Prine, Pearl S. Buck, Anne Morrow Lindbergh, Shel Silverstein, Tom Robbins, early Jimmy Buffett, Marion Zimmer Bradley, Mary Stewart and surprisingly, at least to me, maybe a bit more Hunter S. Thompson than I expected at this point in my life. The weird continues.

As with my first book, I am writing this account first, and foremost, for myself. I want to preserve these memories of the birds, the people, the places and my love of this incredibly diverse and wondrous Land Down Under. I need that for myself, but also to share. To me, sharing is an integral part of living.

The world is different now. My life is different now. The first book was about two people travelling, birding, discovering and appreciating Australia together as a couple. This book is more solitary. That is not my way. No, not if it was ever so. But that is the way that it is for now and that is okay.

This book is not a where-to-find birds in Australia book, though in these tales I happily share information on where and when I found various birds.

From 2017 to now, I added 87 new birds to my Australian bird list, and at the time of writing that list is up to 759. There's a list of my new Life Birds, and the dates and locations where I saw them, at the back of the book.

At the end of *An Australian Birding Year* I wrote a bit about the final move back to Australia in January 2017. My wife, Lynn, and I moved into a very tiny house in Victoria. After living the majority of a year in Troopi (our pop-top Toyota Landcruiser Troop Carrier), that single bedroom house seemed like it would be sufficient for two. We learned that it was not. For financial reasons we have ended up living in what is referred to for marketing purposes as a 'lifestyle village'.

About two years after we moved into that too-tiny house, we were lucky enough to be able to move diagonally across the street into a house that was still quite small but has two bedrooms (and thank you, Dianna). That second bedroom is my study. It can double as a guest room if needs be. I love my study.

There are some truly lovely people who live in this village, but this whole place could not possibly be less 'me'. I will certainly say that inside this little house, amongst our stuff, the antiques, heirlooms and personal items, there is a real home-like connection. There is a 'me' inside this house, particularly in my study. But when I open the door and look outside, I might as well be on f*ing Mars.

Yes, we will wander down paths of joy as well as a few of sadness as I recount these years. I do believe I can find an interesting balance. However, for now I want to move along with these tales. I want to write about some birds and travels. But first...

I will quickly mention spelling and grammar. When I was writing the first book my friends and I had quite a discussion on social media regarding whether I should use Australian English spelling and grammar as opposed to American English spelling and grammar. When all was said and done, the overall consensus was that since Australia is where I live and wrote the book, I should use Aussie spelling. In this book I have also mostly done that. Where I have not it is my mistake (trust me there will be a few). I also capitalise words at my own whims. I feel that Lifer Pie and Lifer deserve to be capitalised and they are when I write them. I am the author. I get to do that. Bird names are capitalised because they should be. A Little Kingfisher is a species, a little kingfisher could be any small species of kingfisher. See how that works? Now let's go birding!

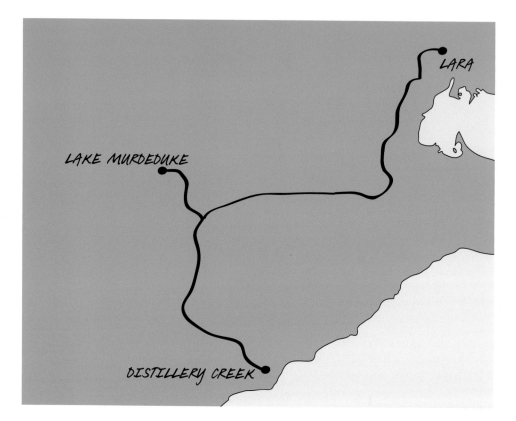

Buff-breasted Sandpiper at Lake Murdeduke, Victoria.

{ 1 }

A Birding Sunday

26 February 2017

It began with a loosely organised outing to Lake Murdeduke, where a group of Victorian birders were gathering to twitch a visiting Buff-breasted Sandpiper.

Lynn and I arrived in Troopi at the lake about 8am. There were already maybe 40 birders there and I don't think anyone was disappointed that day. The main target for everyone was the Buff-breasted Sandpiper. It would be an Australian Lifer for me. There were also sightings of a Ruff. Both of those birds were Australian Lifers for Lynn and she got to see them both. I do not keep her list, but I believe they put her a bit over 650 species seen in Australia. Not a number to be sneezed at. I just realised I have no idea of the origin of that expression. I have never sneezed 'at' anything other than of course, a tissue.

After a delightful morning at the lake, we followed a few good friends: Karen Weil, James Cornelious, Oakley Germech and Alan Crawford, to do a bit of birding over at the Distillery Dam Picnic Area near Airey's Inlet. After a bumpy, dusty ride on back roads over to Airey's, we all arrived in the parking area of the picnic grounds by the little dam there. And it was truly amazing.

This was early afternoon, which is not usually considered a great time for birding, and yet we ended up with 37 species just around

Birders at the twitch at Lake Murdeduke, Victoria.

The little dam at Distillery Creek Picnic Area, Airey's Inlet, Victoria.

the tiny pond area. It was a stationary eBird list! The first big thrill was when James spotted a Satin Flycatcher in the small tree right over the water just after we arrived. There ended up being a male and female together. I have seen them around there before, but always high in the canopy. These birds were at eye level over the dam. Sweet.

For the next three hours we all just marvelled. Not only were the birds awesome, but so was sharing this experience with people who truly get it. These are fun, witty, charming and knowledgeable friends who share this passion for birding and the natural world. There was a wonderful energy that afternoon. I will never forget it.

And then Oakley saw the swift.

One of the dwindling number of land birds that were available to me in Victoria as a possible Australian Lifer was the Fork-tailed Swift, or Pacific Swift as it is called now. Oakley spotted one flying over in the company of some White-throated Needletails. I 'saw' it, but instead of using my binoculars, I tried to photograph it. This produced three photos of empty blue sky and some of the tree canopy. I suppose I will always have to keep reminding myself of my personal birding motto of "Bins first, camera second." I am a birder, not a bird photographer! But as I also often mention, I still like to get a photo when I can. I just cannot, and I will not, allow the photo to be the main focus in my birding. No, that is not an intentional pun, although I do quite like a good pun.

I will quickly relate my very favourite true pun story. Back when I was a full-time touring entertainer, I was doing some shows in Florida with an excellent young comedian and good friend, Matthew Lumpkin. He was opening for me, and we were staying at the same motel, so we were driving to and from the gigs together.

After the gig one night, we drove by a large Barnes & Noble bookstore and very oddly, there were about a half a dozen police cars with their lights flashing arranged around a single vehicle in the carpark. I commented, "That's something you don't see very often, the police surrounding someone at a Barnes & Noble." And

Mr Satin Flycatcher at Distillery Creek Picnic Area, Airey's Inlet, Victoria.

Ms Satin Flycatcher at Distillery Creek Picnic Area, Airey's Inlet, Victoria.

with perfect comedic timing Matthew said, "Maybe they're gonna book him". He is good!

Okey dokey, back to birding. We continued searching through the little groups of needletails that were passing overhead without seeing any with that longer, pointy tail. Eventually the others lost interest and were distracted in part by a beautiful Diamond Firetail, which was sort of unusual for that spot. However, I continued staring up into the sky. I got really good at spotting White-throated Needletails. And then, after about a half an hour with my neck beginning to ache, I saw that longer, pointy tail of a very dark swift. I had it! I kept it in my bins until it was obscured by the treetops. So sweet. I got to feel that warm glow in my chest. A feeling that I cherish. I will often refer to it in the coming pages as a Lifer High. It is the very best, natural and genuine high too.

Lynn and I headed back to Lara and had fish and chips as our 'Lifer Pie' dinner treat. If you have not read *An Australian Birding Year* you might not be familiar with concept of Lifer Pie. So, to explain briefly, it is the self-indulgent treat that you allow yourself to have in celebration of seeing a Life Bird.

Ruff at Lake Murdeduke, Victoria.

The idea began in north-western Ohio at the Black Swamp Bird Observatory's Biggest Week in American Birding with the delicious homemade desert pies at a restaurant called Blackberry Corners. But soon the expression Lifer Pie expanded into representing any sort of treat that you use to celebrate your Lifer. Often for me it has been ice cream or yes, a yummy fish and chips dinner. To others it can be some sort of beverage (especially those containing alcohol for those who imbibe). Whatever it may be, it can still be referred to as your Lifer Pie. It should be fun, and as I said, indulgent. You've earned it. Joy.

As I said, it originated in the USA, but I brought the tradition to Australia where many Aussie birders have embraced it wholeheartedly. That truly makes me smile. So when you get a new life bird, don't forget your Pie!

As I am writing these words, it has been over four years since Lynn and I have birded together. Lynn's journey is her own, and I will not include details, assumptions, judgements or other thoughts about that, or about our relationship in this book. I must mention that she no longer goes birding, since it directly impacts me and these tales. I know that she likes, even loves, birds themselves, but she has no interest in looking for them, or to do any further sort of camping travels. I will leave it there.

Now back to Fork-tailed Swifts for a moment. I want to tell you something that happened only a few weeks later while with my buddy, James. We were at the WTP (the Western Treatment Plant) just doing some general birding when James spotted a nice little flock of those swifts. I saw them well, and after watching them, I even managed some recognisable photos. I was excited to see these birds again and texted Lynn using the dictation function on my iPhone. It produced the best smartphone text mistake I have ever experienced. I sent it without reading what it had written. I just dictated, 'Fork-tailed Swift!' and hit send. Lynn received a very different message, 'F*ck Taylor Swift'.

{ 2 }

Port Fairy Pelagic and Our Ridiculously Well Travelled Belongings

March 2017

Let this sink in for a moment: the crux of our belongings have travelled halfway around the world three times. They have made three trips through the Panama Canal and across the Pacific Ocean. The first was in a 40-foot container going south-west to our new home in Australia, in November 2011. Then a 20-foot container version of our belongings went back to the east coast of the USA in May 2013. Then the final 20-foot container of what was left of our stuff returned to my adopted homeland on 10 March 2017. A few of the details about all of that are covered in the first book. I will say, unequivocally that I will never move back to the northern hemisphere. I certainly hope to visit eventually, there are people and places up there that I love. But I do not plan ever to live there again.

That final container did, for the first time in all of our moves, have quite a few broken and damaged items. We always carried the insurance offered by the removal company (and it was dear), but we had never needed to use it. This time I filed a claim and the company covered everything at the values that I submitted without question. I have no complaints about the insurance. And I am grateful that most of our more cherished and irreplaceable things arrived intact or were at least repairable. The few treasured items that did require repairs were done in the following months. All good.

The two of us and our things did not really fit into that tiny house, but yet we did. No, there was just not enough room, even though I left one of my most treasured possessions in life, my great-grandfather's turn of the century, solid oak, roll-top desk in the US. It was deemed to be too big to bring. If it had only been up to me, I would have brought it anyway. I would have fit it in there somewhere. Somehow.

Regardless, we sorted our things into that tiny house as best we could. With some of our stuff there, at least on the inside, it

In the carport of the much too tiny house our unpacking begins.

became home-like. However, some things that are also precious to me had to be packed away into storage tubs and kept in our dear friend, Carolyn's, garage. I am not sure what we would have done without her generous offer of this space. As I am writing this, we have begun paring-down those stored things. They are being repacked and some will be stored at another dear friend's home. I am very grateful for our generous friends. We have no storage space here. None. I spent my first 60-some years in proper 'houses' with attics, and/or cellars, as well as garages and spare (guest) rooms. There was always space to store stuff. We have none of that here. There is a carport that usually contains the old Prius or Troopi, so there isn't really enough room for storage in there.

I do love to travel and, as I have come to call it, 'the year that became a book' – that year of travelling and birding – was honestly the best year of my life. But every so often, I need to 'land' so-to-speak. And for that I need a home. We have that now. It is far from ideal, but it is a comfortable (little) home and it is in Australia. I am grateful.

Okay, enough of this, let's go on a pelagic birding trip!

Black-faced Cormorant in Port Fairy, Victoria.

Long-tailed Jaeger (without a very long tail), Port Fairy Pelagic, Victoria.

We stayed again at an old, but familiar and oddly comfortable, motel in Port Fairy. I really do like that place. Although as I write this, a year or three ago they upgraded the rooms a bit with new heating and aircon and the prices made quite a jump. But this was back when a double room was still only 85 dollars. I've not done a Port Fairy pelagic in a while, mostly because of the pandemic, but I am sure I will again one day and when I do, I will probably stay at that motel.

We had some wonderful birds that March trip, including a Long-tailed Jaeger, which was an Australian Lifer for me, and of course for Lynn as well. It was definitively identified afterwards from photos. Such can be pelagic birding. Also seen on the trip, was an Arctic Jaeger, which was an Aussie tick for us. It is called Parasitic Jaeger in the USA where we had seen one, but it is the same bird, *Stercorarius parasiticus*.

The seas were very rough through the day and even wearing her patch, Lynn was sick part of the time. I wore my patch as well and gratefully I did not get seasick. Even on that large, seaworthy and stable boat, it was really rocking and rolling out there. Quite a few people were feeling poorly and were happy to be back on firm land. After we docked and said our farewells to friends, Lynn and I headed home.

Over the coming weeks, I occasionally went birding alone. I was able to pop over to the Western Treatment Plant a few times. I am still amazed that it is just across the highway from this house. The WTP is, as my dear friend Asher put it, my 'natal birding grounds'. It is the place where I really first fell in love with birding. I never dreamed that I would live so close to it, and for that, I am very grateful. I also went over to the You Yangs a few times. These lovely 'mountains' are technically a granite outcropping. The traditional owners called them Wurdi Youang. They are also only 10 minutes away. And there are Koalas there! One can go to the Wurdi Youang and with a bit of luck, and lot of looking up, see one of these iconic Aussie treasures. They are definitely worth the neck strain.

Also during this time, I began in earnest writing the first book. It was slow going at times. I was dealing with a lot of depression. And for me, that usually also includes anxiety. A combination that

Arctic Jaeger, Port Fairy Pelagic, Victoria.

I refer to as 'the twins'. They do occasionally come to visit and I have learned to cope with them. Most of the time.

Going back to the laser eye surgery on a tear in my retina in Gosford, New South Wales in chapter 11 of the first book, I still deal with tons of dark cobweb-like floaters swirling through my vision and flashes in the dark. I have referred to floaters as 'tinnitus for the eyes'. I have found it easier to ignore the multitude of 'cicadas' in my ears than junk that floats around in my field of vision. As I write this account in 2021 gratefully, I have gotten much better at ignoring as well as accepting them.

Acceptance has become an important word for me. As has the word, gratitude. Acceptance and Gratitude. Of the two, I find gratitude far easier than acceptance. I can be genuinely grateful and still find it difficult to accept certain aspects of my life. I can be grateful for what I have, while feeling quite bitter about some things that I cannot change, about things that I must learn to accept to have any sort of peace. And I suck at that. Knowing that you suck at something is the first step toward not sucking at it. You may quote me.

A Spotted Parladote is a common but very beautiful little bird.

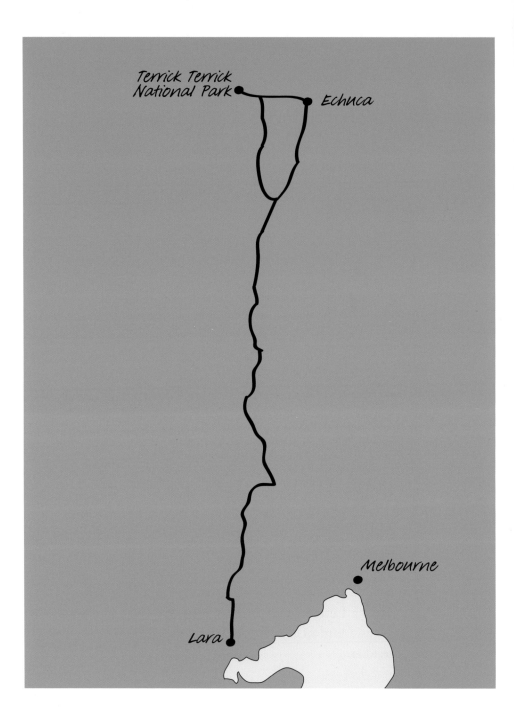

{ 3 }

Letter-winged Kite in Victoria!

27 April 2017

Healthwise, it was a slightly bumpy start back in the land of Oz. Nothing serious, but Lynn had a cough that turned into laryngitis, and then she caught a typically tenacious Victorian cold. Naturally, I soon picked up that cold as well. Also my depression was growing. I felt tired and rundown most of the time. In general, I was not dealing well with some of the changes in my life. And then, Dan Ashdown and Owen Lishmund found the Letter-winged Kite.

Only a month before, I had written a comment on a lovely photo of a Letter-winged Kite posted by my friend and Red Centre birding guru, Mark Carter. I had said that it was "at this point, my number one avian desire". That was the truth. I had long, long wanted to see a Letter-winged Kite. That raptor to me was legendary. It was a bird of Big Years. It was the 800th Aussie tick for my friend and brilliant birder, Jenny Spry. It was a bird of the famous Strzelecki and Birdsville Tracks, a denizen of deserts of the desolate outback. Well, they had found one in Victoria! And it was only about four hours north of Lara.

Dan's report of the kite hit the Facebook Australian Twitchers page at 12:18pm. I saw it very shortly after it was posted. Dan

19

Troopi was a muddy girl.

and Owen are both excellent birders. There was a photo. There was no doubt. There was a Letter-winged Kite in Victoria! It was in something called, the Terrick Terrick National Park Meadows. I Googled the route and location, I considered it. But the clock was ticking and as I said, I was not particularly feeling up to snuff (another expression of questionable origin, and yes, a Letter-winged Kite is nothing to be sneezed at). If I had walked out of the house and gotten into Troopi and driven straight up there, I would not have arrived until at least 5pm. Still, if I had felt better in general, I probably could have pulled it together and dashed up there. But instead I waited, gathered more information, followed the story on social media and packed a few things for a short trip. Several other friends did make the dash that day (Melbourne was an hour or so closer to the spot). They saw and photographed the bird. It was (as they are) gorgeous. I decided to leave first thing the next morning.

The road where the bird had been seen was reported to be muddy and 4WD was said to be advisable, so Troopi and I rolled north at 6am. However there had been a lot of rain down here as well and as I was leaving town, I encountered flooded and closed roads that ended up adding about an hour to my trip. So it was around 10:30am that I finally arrived at the beginning of the road where the kite had been seen.

That road was still soaking wet. The red-clay mud was literally like driving on ice. I rolled carefully down that slippery road to the precise area where the bird had been seen the day before. And there was another vehicle down there and a guy with binoculars! This was a good sign. However, he was also just sort of standing around and not looking in any particular direction. That was a bad sign. I pulled over beside him and asked, "Have you seen it?" There was no need to be more specific, he knew exactly what I was asking. And I received the twitcher's nightmare answer, "Yes, but not for about ten minutes now." Oh, no.

The birder's name was Mark Buckby and he had watched the kite for over an hour that morning. He had last seen it flying off to the west. He spent the next couple of hours looking for the bird with me. His camaraderie and encouragement, in what had become an uncomfortably strong and chilly wind, was much appreciated. He finally packed it in and left the area. The kite had not returned,

Muddy road by the Letter-winged Kite site.

and my heart was heavy and my hands were cold.

I spent the entire rest of that day looking for it with diminishing hope. My friend, Neil Macumber of Birdswing Birding Tours, showed up with a client. They searched with me for a while as well. According to my Fitbit (a little battery-operated pedometer device in my pocket), I had walked over 15 kilometres. The wind was truly howling. For the rest of the afternoon I did not see any raptors, or hardly any birds at all for that matter. Toward dusk the wind lessened slightly and a couple of Black-shouldered Kites showed up, but no Letter-winged was to be seen.

Tired and fading, I grabbed some drive-through fast-food. Then I found a reasonable 'basic cabin' in a caravan park about 15 minutes east in Echuca. I was too tired to camp. I hit the bed early. At first light the next morning, I headed for the Letter-winged spot. As I turned onto the deserted highway, in the distance, I saw one lone vehicle rolling toward me. Even a kilometre away, I knew that camper. Yes, I knew that vehicle well. It was the high-top Troopy of my old friend Robert Shore, the vehicle that had inspired me to purchase my own Troop Carrier. Robert had driven down overnight

My first view of the Letter-winged Kite was perched on the fence.

from his home in Parkes, New South Wales, and I had not even known he was coming. The Universe has its own timing.

The two Troopies headed together over to the area that is officially named 'The Meadows Reserve', although we referred to it as the 'Kite Site'. That has a nice rhyming ring to it. Gratefully, the wind had dropped out overnight. Robert followed me to the spot at the north end of the reserve where Mark had shown me it was possible to jump across the irrigation canal. It was the area where Mark had first seen and photographed the Letter-winged the previous morning. After only about 15 minutes of searching, an elanus type kite perched on the fence behind us.

There were a few Black-shouldered Kites around, but there was something different about this bird and I said as much. Through my bins as well as taking photos and zooming-in on the back of the camera I could see that the eyes did indeed look correct for Letter-winged! Their eye appears as a dark oval shape without the black pointy bit behind that is apparent on the Black-shouldered Kite. I told Robert that I thought we had it. He headed closer for better photos. I was hanging back watching as the bird flushed

There is that glorious black 'letter' mark under the wing.

from the fence. When it did, it lifted its wings and showed that it was without any doubt, a Letter-winged Kite! My heart flew with that bird. I stared at those gorgeous jet-black markings on the under-wing that I had looked for, and hoped for, on so many Black-shouldered Kites over the years. To this day, it remains one of the most beautiful things in birding that I have ever seen. I managed to take a few photos. 'Grateful' does not even come close. Experiencing this bird has stayed one of my best birding memories. It is etched into my birding-heart. I will never forget that kite.

We saw it a few more times. It flew and perched up a couple of times in the brush. Occasionally it was in the company of a couple of Black-shouldered Kites. Simon Starr arrived and luckily, he got good views as well. Soon the bird flew off to the west, just as I heard it had done the day before.

Before it flew off for the last time, I had stopped following it. I had seen it. I had drunk it in. I had beheld the Letter-winged Kite. I just turned and walked back to Troopi by myself. For a few moments, I allowed the elation, euphoria, relief, fatigue, lack of sleep and pure heart's joy of experiencing this magnificent bird flood through me and roll down my cheeks. Yes, there were tears. They were grateful, joyful tears. That would not be the last time they flowed after a successful twitch, and that is a good thing.

To my knowledge, after we saw it that morning, the Letter-winged Kite was never seen there again. Very similar to my experience the day before, my friend Warren Palmer had rolled up and missed it by no more than 15 minutes. Timing is everything. I am so grateful that I had been able to stay up there another day and that I had gotten to see that wondrous bird.

I drove back to Lara that arvo suffused with the blissful feeling of Lifer High. I was at home in time for dinner. I also had ice cream, Murray River Salted Caramel right out of the tub as the first of my Lifer Pie celebrations. I would celebrate that bird for days. Letter-winged Kite in Victoria! Yes!

It looks as if the LWK is chasing a small fish over the fence. I rather enjoyed noticing it. It really looks like a small fish. Maybe it was a Paddock Pollock.

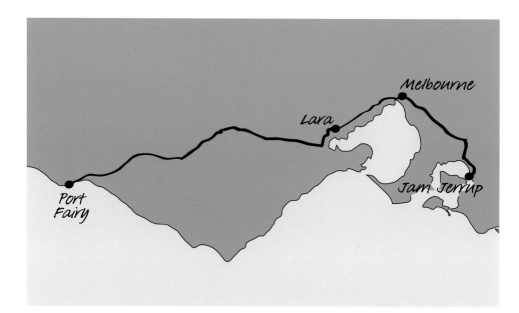

Westland Petrel.

{ 4 }

Yet Another Port Fairy Pelagic, Victoria

16 May 2017

I grew up around water and boats, and I rarely had any issues with seasickness. As I have aged, I've found that I occasionally succumb to what they call, if they are French, 'mal de mer'. When I began to do a birding pelagic or two, I was worried about the possibility of getting sick. I gave the seasickness patch a try and it worked. I use them to this day, and they do prevent seasickness for me. Even though I basically feel like crap while I am wearing one, they prevent the utter misery of full-blown seasickness. I can deal with feeling crap to prevent that. In the past few years, I have learned that the seasickness and queasy-ness in general that I get on occasion, is probably related to what doctors tell me are migraines. I have vestibular migraines and I can get something called migrainous vertigo. I deal with it.

The pain relief that I take for migraines also helps with this migrainous vertigo as well. And seemingly, so does the seasickness patch. I have noticed that when wearing the patches I have never had a migraine and one time, the patch seemed to end a migraine attack.

Before this trip in May of 2017, I had only done six pelagics in Australia. One was out of Wollongong, New South Wales, one from Eaglehawk Neck, Tasmania, one off Broome, Western Australia and three from Port Fairy, Victoria, the most recent had been in March 2017. I had added some good birds to my Life List on pelagics, but there were certainly a lot more birds to see in the sea.   From the very beginning, there was a particular pelagic bird that I had consistently missed. Ever since I became a birder I had been fascinated by the idea of albatrosses. While living at my son and daughter-in-law's in Torquay, Victoria, I would sea-watch off Point Addis. I got my Lifer Black-browed and Shy Albatrosses through my scope from that point. In the wonderful Patrick O'Brian series of books, Dr Stephen Maturin speaks of albatrosses many times in deservedly glowing terms. And I longed to behold what I considered the king of the albatrosses, the Wandering Albatross. It can have a wingspan of up to 11 feet (as can the Southern Royal Albatross). Of all the majestic and magnificent behemoths of the ocean sky, I really wanted to see the Wandering Albatross. I reckon the name had a bit to do with it as well.

Wandering Albatross (Snowy).

Port Fairy is only three hours from Lara and I decided I should do another pelagic there. I contacted my friend, Neil Macumber of Birdswing Tours who runs those trips, and asked about a space on the next one. I was able to get a spot on the Sunday 14 May trip.

I arrived in Port Fairy late Saturday arvo and yes, I checked into that familiar comfortable old motel. It is also less than five minutes away from the boat. I had an early sandwich in my room and then wandered over to the pub to see who was around. I immediately bumped into Kevin Bartram and Scott Baker, good friends through social media and certainly two of Australia's most knowledgeable birders. I chatted with them for a bit. There were a few other familiar faces around as well. As is often the case with Neil's trips, it was shaping up to be a good group of birders. After some more visiting, I retired to my room and carefully applied my seasickness patch behind my right ear and went to bed early.

After a mediocre night's sleep, I was out of bed at 4:30am and began to administer caffeine to the best of my abilities. At about 6:20am, I headed over to the boat. It was just past 7am when we chugged out to the sea. It was a little bumpy out there, but the patches did their job as they do. I am grateful.

We were still within sight of land when I missed what would have been my first Lifer of the day. A Common Diving-petrel appeared, then dove and disappeared. That is what they often do. It would be a couple of years before I got a proper look of those fast, little diving birds. Shortly after the disappearing diving-petrel, a tern was spotted that was later identified from photos as an Arctic Tern. Thus it became my first Lifer of the day, although, I would not know this until a couple of days later and some social media discussion on the ID. Such can be pelagic bird identifications.

We continued out about 40 kilometres offshore to where we were to stop and begin to berley (chum). Almost immediately I heard the word that I had listened for on my past pelagic trips, 'Wandering'! And a young Wandering Albatross came gliding by the boat and into my heart. Although I have seen these birds

Wandering Albatross (*exulans* I think) – look at those wings!

many times since, my first time beholding this graceful, winged giant remains yet another one of the highlights of my birding life. I was thrilled. We saw both 'Wandering type' Albatrosses. Three *exulans* and six *gibsoni*, which are sometimes referred to as the New Zealand Wandering Albatross.

There were a lot of birds! Soon the boat was surrounded by more albatrosses and other sea birds. We had heaps of Shy, as well as Black-browed, Campbell, Northern Royal and Wandering Albatrosses. We had Northern Giant Petrels, Fairy and Antarctic Prions, and Wilson's, White-faced and Grey-backed Storm-Petrels. It was wonderful! But after a while, our large group of birds began to leave us and we spotted a trawler a few kilometres further offshore. Following in its wake was a huge group of birds. We headed over for a closer look.

In amongst the hundreds of birds in the air and on the water behind that trawler, Kevin Bartram noticed a dark petrel. It flew up and by our boat. The word 'Westland' was being shouted. It stayed with us, landing on the water and flying around our boat. It was a Westland Petrel, the first record of a living bird in Victoria. Even

New Zealand Wandering Albatross.

Westland Petrel, the first record of a living bird in Victoria.

The Cape Petrel is black and white gorgeousness.

some hardcore pelagic birders were getting a tick. There was much joy. Lifer High on the high seas.

Speaking of highs, it was a day of seven Lifers for me. They were: Arctic Tern, both Wandering Albatross, Northern Royal Albatross, a stunningly beautiful Cape Petrel, Antarctic Prion and the Westland Petrel. Yes, Westland was the big deal, but my first Wandering Albatrosses stole my heart. The Cape Petrel is pretty damn special and a crazy beautiful bird as well with its striking black-and-white patterns on its back and wings. My Aussie life list was at 685. I was only 15 away from what was to me, a magic birding number.

The long trip back to terra firma seemed shorter than usual. Once back in Port Fairy many of us had a quick coffee and/or a nibble at the coffee house in town before going our separate ways. I drove on back to Lara alone. I had a very large Lifer High glowing in my chest. Thank you, birds.

I have said before that pelagic birding is not my favourite type of birding. I love the sea but I am really not a great pelagic birder. I will not play the age card, although ageing is certainly a part of this book, but I will say that I am not as quick, nor are my eyes as sharp as they used to be. I can find getting 'on' a bird while trying to keep my balance to be a challenge. However, there are so many possibilities when birding at sea, that I happily, and gratefully, continue to do pelagics. Bottom line, I love the sea. I always have, and I always will. I reckon to some degree I still have saltwater in my veins.

There are more pelagics to come.

'Syd', the South Island Pied Oystercatcher

{ 5 }

Two Twitches in Victoria

20-27 June 2017

In early January 2017, while I was sorting the last-minute details for our final move to Australia, a feathered New Zealand visitor arrived on the coast of northern New South Wales. He had already visited Victoria, although when he had, no one had noticed that he was from New Zealand. Still the friendly Victorian bird-banders had given him a silver bracelet and a nice red flag with 1N on it. Many of my Aussie friends dashed to the coast of New South Wales to see him, but I was still in the USA. He had gotten his red leg flag in August of 2016. Since it was again winter, Simon Starr decided to look in the place where this visitor had originally been flagged hoping that he might return. And sure enough, he found the South Island Pied Oystercatcher with its 1N hanging out amongst the numerous Australian Pied Oystercatchers at a place called Stockyard Point by Jam Jerrup, Victoria.

I was birding with some friends in the beautiful Brisbane Ranges on a Sunday afternoon when I heard about this discovery. I considered bolting for the site immediately, but it was over and down on the other side of Melbourne on Western Port Bay and I would not really have been able to get there in enough time to see the bird before dark. So I decided I would go early Monday morning, which I was to discover was not really the best time of day to make that drive.

Anyone who knows me, knows that I am not a fan of big cities and I loathe heavy traffic. For me, there are very few things that are worth driving through Melbourne traffic during the morning rush for, but a South Island Pied Oystercatcher is one of them. A drive that later in the day would have taken about two hours, took over three. I collected my friend, Oakley Germech at a train station near the freeway. He had been one of those who had been with me in the Brisbane Ranges on Sunday. Once I had battled my way out of the congestion around the station, we were gratefully travelling away from the traffic flooding into the city, heading to the twitch. I had expected to be at Jam Jerrup at about 9am. It was close to 10 when we arrived. We had pulled over on the side of the road looking out at the shoreline, when I noticed a vehicle stopped behind us. It was Dave Stabb, who I had first met in January 2011 at the Western Treatment Plant. As birders know, you meet the best people at sewage treatment plants. I had not seen him since

The author at the twitch (photo by Oakley Germech).

then, but we both remembered each other. He remembered me as Bruce from Virginia, where I am originally from in the USA. It was great to see him again, and we remain friends and stay in touch to this day.

I will never forget the first time I met Dave. I was a fairly new birder, and my son-in-law and I were struggling to identify waders at the WTP. I often still struggle to identify waders. Dave and a friend were also there, and he stopped what he was doing to help us to spot, and to correctly identify, a few waders. He found the Stilt Sandpiper for us that was being seen there at the time. We also bumped into Maarten Hulzebosch, who is also truly a great guy and extremely knowledgeable about waders, but that is not why I am telling this part of the story. Dave is very small fellow with a big fluffy white beard. He really is a quite elf-like. I have never asked, but I doubt that he is over five feet tall if that, and I would imagine he doesn't weigh more than 45 kilos soaking wet. Whereas Maarten is all of six feet seven inches tall. Watching them standing beside each other chatting, I turned to my son-in-law and whispered, "I feel like we're in The Lord of the Rings." It still makes me smile to remember that moment.

After checking out a small group of Australian Pied Oyster-catchers from the road north of the parking area, we parked our vehicles and headed out and up the beach to continue searching. Oakley was just ahead of me as a flock of twenty-some oystercatchers flew past us toward the area where we had just been looking. I asked Oakley, mostly joking, "Was it in that group?" And he answered seriously, "I really think it might have been!" Oh, the joys of twenty-year old eyes.

We headed up the beach toward where the flock had landed. Then in only moments, Dave had his scope on the red 1N leg flag of the South Island Pied Oystercatcher. We had it! Dave had identified it first by its flag! Soon Scott Baker, Dan Ashdown, Deb Oliver, David Adam, Mark Hill and others joined us. Everyone was taking photos and rejoicing in the shared Lifer High of a successful twitch. There is nothing else quite like it. Social media soon exploded with photos and joyful postings as more and more birders twitched the oystercatcher. Kevin Bartram, who saw it later the same day, commented on my post asking, "You mean you didn't scare it away?" Later when he had posted about having seen it, I asked him the same question. We joked a bit and then he ended up referring to the bird as 'Syd. Syd the SIPO'. The name stuck and in the general birding world, the South Island Pied Oystercatcher at Stockyard Point was known as Syd. Visiting rarities do tend to acquire nicknames.

The Laughing Gull in Venus Bay, South Australia that stayed around for over a year was known far and wide as 'Chuckles'. The following partial song parody is only amusing if you are familiar with Jim Croce's song, 'Don't Mess Around with Jim'. I have come to understand that although he was massively popular in the USA, Croce was not nearly as well known in Australia. Anyway, here you go, sung to the tune of the original song if you are familiar with it.

Don't Mess Around with Syd
Venus Bay got its 'Chuckles'
Darwin's got its gull.
Stockyard Point got a Pied Oystercatcher
Whose legs are a little small
His bill is long, and his wings are strong
But I reckon that he got lost
And when the twitchers all get together at night,
They call Syd the SIPO boss...

Great, and now I have the original song stuck in my head. That will be there a while.

We actually know some of the history of this visiting rarity. It was banded on 6 August 2016 there at Stockyard Point, Victoria. It was misidentified as an Australian Pied Oystercatcher. It was seen again in that area on 22 August, recorded but still misidentified as an Australian Pied Oystercatcher. Next it showed up at Broadwater

Syd and his 1N flag

Beach in New South Wales in January 2017 where birders did correctly identify "1N" as a South Island Pied Oystercatcher. It was twitched by many in New South Wales. It was seen again in Victoria by Simon on 18 June 2017 and received its official name from Kevin Bartram on 20 June becoming, Syd the SIPO.

Twitch Two! A Little Stint

After Syd was discovered and the word got out, many Aussie twitchers descended on the little hamlet of Jam Jerrup to park at the end of Foreshore Road and twitch the visiting oystercatcher named Syd. Sometimes he would be found close by the carpark, other times he would be out near the sandy point of land over a kilometre to the south. That is the point called Stockyard Point.

It is a very flat area, so the tide makes quite a difference to the size of the 'beach'. At high tide the beach toward the point disappears. At low tide, kilometres of mud flats are exposed, and this can be extremely treacherous. I have seen photos of birders who literally sank up to their waists in it. It is almost like the quicksand in old movies. The waders can be scattered far and wide across those

Jam Jerrup, Victoria.

flats. As the tide rises and covers the mud, many of the waders head toward the sandy point, especially the little waders such as Double-banded Plovers, Red-necked Stints and Curlew Sandpipers. They can arrive in flocks of hundreds. Mostly folks were looking for Syd and did not closely scan the masses of these little waders. But on Sunday, 25 June, Scott Baker and Paul Peake did just that and Scott spotted a Little Stint amongst them! Consulting with Kevin Bartram and others, the ID was confirmed. This was only one week after Syd was first spotted there. The second rarity in the same area in a week. Amazing. The Little Stint was in breeding plumage and stood out fairly well once you found it, but it was also easy to overlook. On 23 June, Geoff Glare took photos of the flocks of waders at the point and later upon close examination, discovered the Little Stint was there in one of his photos.

I had returned to Stockyard Point on Saturday 24th with some birding friends who had not yet seen Syd and I most probably 'saw' the Little Stint as well without knowing it. We did see Syd and we also saw a beautiful Asian Gull-billed Tern. At the time it was a subspecies, but since then there has been a split, and the regular

Gull-billed Tern is now called the Australian Tern and the Asian species is the one now known as the Common Gull-billed Tern. Taxonomy: the fun never ends.

Oh, those lumps and splits. When a split adds a species to a birder's list without them having to go out to see the bird, because they have already seen it as a subspecies, it is referred to as getting an 'armchair tick'. I have had a few of these over the past years. For those of us who keep lists, that is why it is important to try and see the various subspecies when you can. On the reverse side, a species is 'lumped' when it is combined back into another species as taxonomists did with the Adelaide and Yellow Rosellas a few years back. They were all lumped back into being Crimson Rosellas and many birders lost a couple of numbers on their lists. Whereas splits provide us an armchair tick, there is no cute name for the reduction of our lists from a lump. Perhaps an 'armchair dip' would be appropriate.

When Scott's Little Stint discovery hit the social media grapevine, it was about 2:15pm on Sunday. Once again, I seriously considered making the dash immediately, but again I really could

A view of Stockyard Point as the tide rises.

not have gotten there in time. I would have arrived almost at dark. So I planned to go over the next morning. Choosing my departure by the tides (low at 8:30am and high at 3:40pm) I left home at the civilised hour of 9am. My friend Carolyn, who also lives in Lara, went with me. I collected my buddy, James Cornelious as well as our friend Owen Lismund at a train station on the way. Due to the tide situation, we knew that we need not hurry. We needed that tide to rise. We rocked up at Jam Jerrup about 11:30am. The tide was still way out, too far out to have pushed any little waders closer to the point. But it was rising.

A few other birders began arriving and so did some rain showers. We waited a bit longer and headed over to the point at about noon. We had a nice walk down the beach (thank you James for carrying my scope). The tide was still too far out. We could see hundreds of waders way out on the flats. We waited. And sure enough as the water rose, little groups of waders started showing up on the sand spit right in front of us, and then more, and more.

By about 1:30pm we had scores of waders to search through, but still more came. The bird was spotted and then immediately

Little Stint at Stockyard Point, Victoria.

lost when the flock re-shuffled, as they do all too frequently. We all moved to the right to get a better view over a slight rise in the sand. I was standing by James who was scanning with my scope when through my bins, I saw a small and definitely more russet-coloured stint. I got James on it with the scope. He proclaimed, "That's it"! And friends, it was. I had re-found it. Not that that sort of thing is important, but with so many young and more experienced eyes looking, it felt damn good to have been the next one to have spotted it. Yes, it did.

The following day, I celebrated a Lifer Day. Gratefully, there will be a lot more of those as I write these tales. The Lifer Day is an invention all my own. It is the extended version of Lifer Pie. On a Lifer Day, I allow myself a full 'happy day'. Truth be told, it is not something I am particularly good at doing at all. Giving myself permission to be 'happy' for an entire day is no easy task, but I do give it a go. The Lifer Day is now an integral part of my personal birding experience. When I find a new Lifer, I might have a little ice cream or some other Lifer Pie quick treat, but as soon as time can permit, I will do the whole day. Sometimes it can be a week or more after adding the bird to my list. But it is worth the wait and it extends that wonderful Lifer High.

{ 6 }

Very Briefly, Health Stuff

September – October 2017

Now, truly in a long-story-short version (we will be birding again in a few short paragraphs) I need to mention, beginning in September, over the following few weeks I had: a bone scan, two MRIs, a CT scan, a spinal tap (the film was better than the procedure), a chest X-ray, a renal ultrasound and mucho bloodwork. I also began seeing a neurologist who is still my neurologist. His name is Peter and I see him regularly mostly in relation to my migraines. As I mentioned I have migraines.

Thankfully, nothing in all that testing had found the cancer that had originally been suspected after a couple of MRIs, so another MRI of my brain was scheduled in six months time. I had this and they tell me that all is well.

Now I will get back to birding.

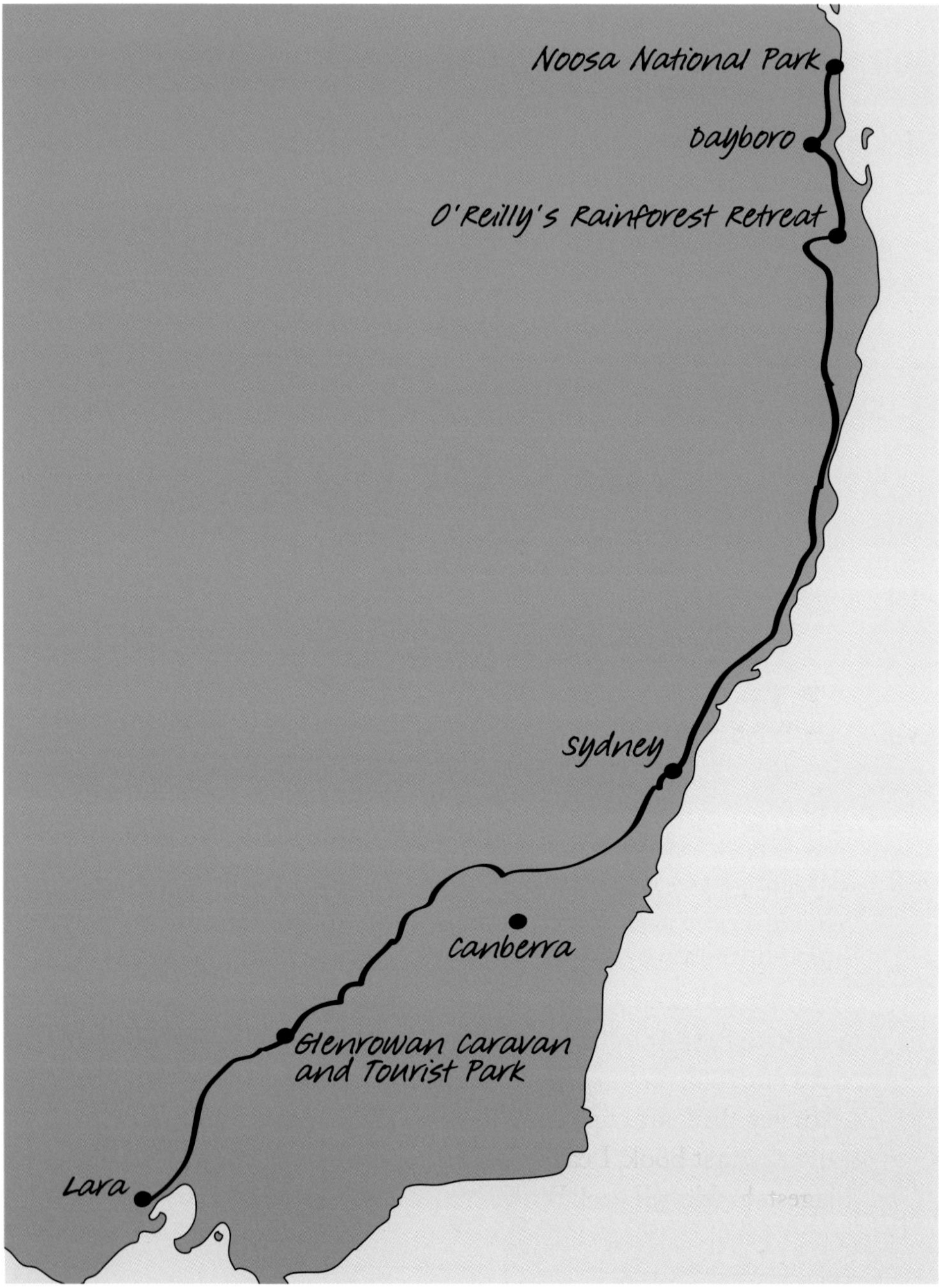

Noosa National Park

Dayboro

O'Reilly's Rainforest Retreat

Sydney

Canberra

Glenrowan Caravan
and Tourist Park

Lara

{ 7 }

Finally Black-breasted Button-quail, Noosa, Queensland

10 November 2017

For my non-birder readers, a Bogey Bird is a bird that has eluded you for an inordinately long time. It is a bird into which you have put a lot of effort and yet you still have never seen it. It is also sometimes called a nemesis bird. Often it is a bird that most of your birder friends have seen, but you have not. A Bogey Bird is usually not a rare bird. Rare birds can be difficult for everyone not just you. A Bogey Bird ends up becoming personal. It is your Bogey Bird.

In the first book, I called the Black-breasted Button-quail my biggest, baddest Bogey Bird. The Yellow-rumped Mannikin was an extremely close second, and in fact I reckon it deserves the honour of first-place bogey. It is a more commonly seen bird than the Black-breasted Button-quail and I had dipped on it repeatedly.

Black-breasted BQ are one of the rarer of the Button-quail (none of which are particularly common). They are beautiful birds and it could be said, not that I ever would, that they are cute as a

Black-breasted Button-quail.

button. And different from many bird species, the female is the real stunner with a beautiful black face and black markings down the breast. The male is a plainer and browner bird, but beautiful as well. They are what is called 'sexually dimorphic'. Their appearance, colouration and even size, differ by sex. Ornithological types refer to the female being flashier as 'reverse sexual dimorphism'. To me, this seems to imply that the male is always meant to be the showier of the two and for it to be the female, that constitutes a reverse of the natural order of things. I am not sure that is fair. There are quite a few cases in which the female is the flashier of the two. This is the case with one of my very favourite birds, the Plains Wanderer. The female is half-again as large as the male and has a beautiful black and white collar above a red breast. The male looks like a small grey-brown combination of a wader and a quail, of course they are neither. Plains Wanderers are the only members of their family. They are unique birds.

Bear in mind that much ornithological terminology originated in the early nineteenth century, which was not necessarily an enlightened time for equality, unless you were a white European. Consider the colours used in some common bird names such as Flesh-footed Shearwater. Whose flesh are we referring to as 'flesh coloured'? Certainly not their black or brown feet. But enough of that. In the spirit of alliteration and rhyme, back to the Black-breasted Button-quail bogey tale.

Lynn and I put in six, full, hard days of scouring every square metre of Inskip Point, Queensland searching for that bird. That was *the* well known spot for them back in July 2016 and we never even had a fleeting glimpse of one. A Black-breasted Button-quail had been seen there by my friend, Mona only four days before we arrived, and I heard that there was one seen a couple of weeks after we had left. A Bogey Bird was created.

In October 2017, my dear friend, Karen Weil went up to Noosa National Park north of Brisbane, Queensland. She went with my good social media friend, birding and photography guide, Matt Wright. They saw and photographed Black-breasted Button-quail. I knew I needed to get up there and try. I mean I really had to do it. The lure of a Bogey Bird is a powerful motivator.

I contacted Matt and my buddy, and often travelling and birding companion, Robert Shore. Robert also needed the Black-breasted Button-quail. It was decided we could meet Matt in southeastern Queensland to look for the bird on 10 November. It is about 2,000 km from Lara to Noosa. I began getting Troopi and myself together for a longish road trip.

The 'twins' came to visit as I prepared to head off alone. 'Separation anxiety' is what it's called by therapists and such. Since I was a child, I have had to overcome it. Nowadays, I almost always manage to do so. I do not mean to minimise it. It is no easy task, and it can be a very uncomfortable process. But I must break free of my comfort zones. They call them comfort zones for a reason. I had travelled for a full year with the comfort and security of having my partner along with me. This is no longer the case. But the road goes on and so will I. Checklists were made and checked and rechecked. Things were gathered, sorted and packed by me alone.

Leaving Monday morning 6 November 2017, I began driving north. I over-nighted in Troopi in the nice caravan park in West Wyalong, New South Wales, then again in Troopi at a lovely, inexpensive and quiet little caravan park in Bendemeer, NSW. The next day, I pressed on to Dayboro, Queensland. Robert and I were meeting at the campground there. Since we had a day before going with Matt, we had arranged to go looking for King Quail with our friend, Marie Tarrant in her local patch on Thursday morning. That would also be a Lifer for us both.

We met her at 6am and began walking the pathways through the tall grassy areas by Lake Samsonvale. After only a half hour or so, and after seeing several Brown Quail, a much smaller, very dark quail flushed off the path. It flew by us calling and then went down into the deep grass where it continued calling. Marie knows that call and that bird. It was a King Quail! John Weigel had told me to be prepared to be satisfied with seeing a 'flying purple potato' and that is what it looked like. Gratefully, I had decent views of said 'potato' as it went past me and down into the grass. We walked further into the tall grasses and listened as it called to another King

Sunset over Dayboro, Queensland.

Quail. It was literally somewhere right around our feet! We heard it repeatedly but did not see it again. Regardless, I was thrilled. Lifer Pie later and a Lifer Day in the future! Thank you, Marie. I absolutely would not have gotten that bird without you.

We went to a café with Marie for some lunch and some form of Lifer Pie. I do not recall exactly what I had, probably ice cream in some fashion. We enjoyed Marie's company for a bit longer and then carried on to a large caravan park in Maroochy River, Queensland. Matt would be collecting us there at 5:30am the next morning. Gratefully, they are not on daylight savings time up there, so to us that would feel like 6:30am. A moot point because I woke up at 3am and could not go back to sleep. Yes, I was excited. The Bogey Bird could be within reach!

True to his word, leaving at 5:30am, Matt drove us to Noosa National Park. It is a beautiful and insanely popular place. We were there before 6:30am on a weekday and it was already a madhouse of people. We eventually found a parking spot as someone was leaving. There were surfers, joggers, beach goers, tourists and hikers in a constant stream going to and fro on the path we had to take. It was about a kilometre and a half up to the trail where we would be concentrating our search. Unbelievably, Matt said that the weekends there are even more crowded. Wow. We wound our way through the throng up to the area where Matt had been consistently finding the Black-breasted Button-quail. There were fewer people on that stretch of track too. It was a long and uphill trudge, but my adrenaline was as high as my hopes.

Once we arrived, Matt said that it could take ten minutes or three hours, but we were where he had been seeing them. We began looking along the 200 or so metres of track. We did not see any. We did see fresh platelets (the round, bare spots in the leaf litter created by their scratching the ground as they feed). We were encouraged. An hour passed, and then two hours, still with no Bucking-futton-quail, and then over three hours passed. I began having a sort of PTSD from my Inskip Point experience in July

Black-breasted Button-quail finally!

2016. I was honestly beginning to stress. This was hard birding. All of my Zen-like beliefs about experiencing the bird, and enjoying the quest were going to hell in a handcart. I just could not dip on this bird again. I continued up and down that track looking. A later check of my Fitbit showed I had walked over 15 kilometres searching that trail. The three of us scattered out along the path as hopes began to somewhat dim to say the least.

Out of the blue, Robert declared, "Well, I think we are going to find it," and stood up. He had been sitting on the edge of the track for a while as I had continued trudging up and down, and up and down the path. I sat down in his spot on the edge of the trail to take a short breather. He wandered off down the trail that I had been searching only moments before. Matt followed along slightly behind him. Less than three minutes later, he burst around the corner saying, "Got them!" I literally began running before I was standing all the way up.

Robert said I looked like one of those cartoon characters whose legs spin in a circle before they start moving. I was literally falling and running at the same time behind Matt toward where Robert had just spotted them. I wish I had a video of that, but thinking about it, maybe not. We quickly rounded a curve in the trail and Matt stopped and said, "Bruce! There!" And I was looking at not one, not two, but three male BBBQ's wandering around on the ground only a few metres off the track. Amazing. Wondrous. Thrilling. They even began scratching in little circles and making platelets! They were right there. They seemed utterly oblivious to our presence as they went about their button-quail ways. It had taken a full four hours, but we had done it. Bogey no more. I was about as happy as it is possible for me to be.

Lifer high flooded me from head to toe and continued to reverberate through me as we walked back to the car. What a feeling. After a nice lunch at a local café, we spent the rest of the day and late into the night doing some more birding and then spotlighting for mammals and owls. By the end of the day, my Fitbit said I that I had walked a total of over 22 kilometres and very little of it was on level ground. My endurance was not nearly as robust as it had been only a year or so before. I was crazy-exhausted, but what a day, what a glorious, glorious day.

I woke up the next morning, tired and actually aching. As we were hanging about the caravan park trying to decide what we might do next, I realised that we were only just over 3 hours from Lamington National Park and O'Reilly's Rainforest Retreat. We could camp a night or two there. Robert thought this was a good idea as well. A magical land awaited just around the corner and that is where we went.

I first visited the amazing O'Reilly's Rainforest Retreat in January 2011. I was a fairly new birder and I was dazzled, stunned and enthralled. It was one the places where I fell utterly in love with Australia and its birds. It will always be a place that is very special to me. Although, as things do, it has changed. It seems to be much more of a high-end tourist location now than the birder's paradise that it felt like back then, but I still loved it. Robert and I spent two nights camped at the Green Mountain Campground right beside O'Reilly's. We were messing about doing some casual birding, just being there and experiencing that wonderful place. That campground was one of the most naturally beautiful camping spots I have ever seen. I understand that it has now been rebuilt as more of a tourist campground. They have 'glamping' tents. I have only seen this new campground online and heard about it secondhand but I might not stay there again. I might just let that original, magical place live safely in my memories. I know this would be a "I liked the old one better" situation. I will write more about that in chapter 11 but curiosity could very well get the better of me someday. We will see.

I needed to be back the end of the week, so after a couple of delightful days, the two Troopies headed back. We drove in tandem for a bit of the journey, stopping at a place called Cunningham's Gap for a delicious piece of the teacake that Robert had purchased

Troopi and an Australian Brush-turkey at her campsite in Lamington National Park.

A very friendly Satin Bowerbird and Robert's hand at Cunningham's Gap.

at a bakery earlier. It was a gorgeous spot with Satin Bowerbirds landing right there on the picnic table trying to grab a bite of teacake. It was quite a special little experience.

After our impromptu lunch, Robert headed off to Parkes and I continued south. For the last night of the trip, I went to Glenrowan Caravan Park because I had heard there were Turquoise Parrots consistently seen there. I rocked up at about 2:30pm and in less than half an hour, I was watching a beautiful male Turquoise Parrot through a fork in a tree as it nibbled on grass seeds. I highly recommend that place as a caravan park and birding spot. It poured with rain later that evening, but I was snug and dry in my Troopi. I was by myself and I was okay. The next morning it was still sprinkling, but between showers I got beautiful views of four more of the parrots. I have returned there several times since and it will be mentioned a few times in the coming chapters. It's only about three hours north of Lara and I always see Turquoise

Turquoise Parrot in Glenrowan, Victoria.

Parrots there. I have also seen Double-barred Finches, Speckled Warblers and Gang-gang Cockatoos among other cool birds. I love that place.

{ 8 }

Another Victorian Twitch and a Whale

10 November 2017

Troopi and I arrived safely back in Lara from our button-quail adventure. On Friday afternoon, I was beginning to write a blog entry about the trip when a Hudsonian Godwit was reported on Reef Island. I had our Aussie Thanksgiving dinner at Josh and Rebekah's, with the other kids on Saturday. It is a tradition that can include others with American origins, and it is a special, family day. We had a wonderful time. But then first thing Sunday morning I was heading over to Reef Island, about two hours away and yet again on the east side of the bay. It was only about 20 minutes past Jam Jerrup where I had seen Syd and the Little Stint.

If you have read my fascinating first book, you might remember that in January 2016, Lynn and I had driven over from Kangaroo Island, South Australia to twitch the mega-rare Paradise Shelduck at Lake Wollumboola, New South Wales. There had been a sighting of a Hudsonian Godwit at the lake as well, but it was not around when we were there. Not as rare as the duck, but certainly a very good bird. I still needed it on my Aussie list.

In Australia we have two godwits that are more common, Bar-tailed and Black-tailed. These get referred to as 'Barwits' and

Reef Island, Victoria – that sandbar connects with land when the tide is lower.

Lifer Selfie for the Hudwit with the legend, Kevin Bartram in the black hat behind me.

'Blackwits'. When the much more rarely seen Hudsonian Godwit shows up somewhere it is referred to as a 'Hudwit'. This was the basis of yet another Kevin Bartram rarity nickname, he called the bird 'Rock'. Rock Hudwit (get it?). Very good name there, Kev.

I collected my friend Owen Lishmund at the Glen Iris Station on the way, and we were on the beach near Reef Island by 10am. My friends Karen Weil, as well as Jannette and Peter Mannis were already there. There were several other birding friends around and more were arriving. I think it ended up being over 15 of us there. You gotta love a Sunday twitch! It was pretty straightforward as to where to look for the little flock of godwits. Reef Island becomes a peninsula at low tide and there was a pile of rocks, and that was where the godwits were hanging out.

I spent some time out on the island trying to get a better angle from which to see the Hudwit behind the rocks. That didn't work. I ended up watching and waiting for the little group of godwits to fly in from their rocky roost to the beach as the tide rose. I was standing with several other birders staring at that pile of rocks. We 'saw' the bird a few times but it kept ducking down with the other godwits behind the rock pile.

One of my favourite moments from the day was my friend Adam Fry's response when most of us were moving back into the beach. We were going to wait there for the godwits to come to us. The tide was rising but they were stubbornly remaining on the far side of those rocks.

Adam said softly, "I really kinda want to see it." Then he glanced toward the beach and back toward the rocks, took a short pause and added, "And I know where it is." And then he glanced back toward the beach and said, "And it's not there." His timing and delivery were movie-dialog perfect. It still makes me smile to remember it. Humour is so much about timing and delivery. I like Adam.

Well, he did see it. We all saw it. The Hudwit finally left the back side of the rocks and was cooperative and was seen, viewed, scoped and photographed copiously. The black underwings were

Hudsonian Godwit showing its lovely black underwing.

Hudsonian Godwit in flight, wings up, with Bar-tailed Godwits.

very apparent when it flapped amongst the other 'wits'. It was a truly successful twitch with good friends and as I have said before, it doesn't get much better than that. Group Lifer High rocks. Yes, it was a wonderful day.

About a week later, on 28 November, I went on another pelagic out of Port Fairy. Birding wise, it was fairly ordinary. It was enjoyable but no new birds for me. Although I did have one amazingly, stunningly wonderful sighting. I saw a Blue Whale.

When I was a child there was a picture book of animal facts in the attic. I do not know why it was in the attic, but that is where I remember looking at it. I spent a lot of time alone in the attic as well as the garage. I spent a lot of time alone full stop. The three facts that I recall clearly from that book were that a rhinoceros' horn is made of hair, not horn, that the Anaconda is the largest snake in the world, and that the Blue Whale is the largest creature ever to live on this planet. I was fascinated by that whale.

I spent a lot of time staring at the illustration of the Blue Whale. I was astounded by the thought of the largest creature ever to have lived; a creature whose heart was the size of a Volkswagen. I

That is a real actual Blue Whale off Port Fairy (photo by Rohan Clarke).

suppose that is something I discovered later after I could read, but it remains connected to those early memories in my mind. And now I had seen a live one in the sea myself, a Blue Whale. It did not disappoint.

When this majestic, massive creature was sideways in the clear blue water of the swell, I was able to briefly comprehend its enormity. It looked to be the size of a train car gliding through the water. My own heart felt like it was the size of a Volkswagen as well. I have included a heavily cropped photo that Rohan Clarke was kind enough to share with me of its back just showing above the water. The photo might look underwhelming, but that is a Blue Whale. I did not even try to take any photos, I just stared at it in awe though my binoculars.

I have beheld a living Blue Whale.

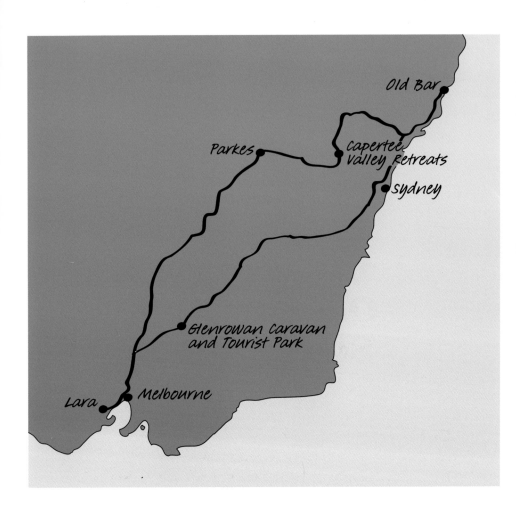

{ 9 }

Aleutian Surprise, Old Bar, New South Wales

12 December 2017

On Monday, 11 December at about 1pm I had been out running some errands. I had just sat down with my laptop when my phone rang. It was Robert. I answered and he just asked, "Are we going?"

And I asked, "Where?"

He said, "Port Macquarie. Australian Twitchers Page. Liam Murphy found Aleutian Terns."

Without even stopping to think I said, "Yes."

They were positively identified as Aleutian Terns. This was a first for Australia! Liam had photographed one the year before but was initially not aware that it was an Aleutian Tern. Studying his photos, he figured out that it was indeed an Aleutian Tern! He had gone back to the same area to look again this year and found a small flock of Aleutian Terns in New South Wales. The Aussie birder world was exploding. Good on you, mate! I consider Liam a dear friend now and I will be birding with him again later in this book. He is one of my favourite people.

I initially told Robert that I could not possibly get there before

Aleutian Terns, firsts for Australia.

Wednesday. It is about 1,300 kilometres to the spot and Troopi is built for off-road power, not highway speed. She drives just fine on the highway, but I keep her down to around 90-95 kph because her diesel mileage, which is already pretty high, goes up quickly above that. I don't just drive by kilometres per hour, I keep my eye on the rpms. I know that around 225k is about 95 kph. That seems to be considered the sweet-spot for many Troopy drivers. The story of how I acquired my 2011 Troop Carrier camper, named her Troopi and some other details are told in the first book. I will just say that I love that vehicle. I even have a heart tattoo with 'Troopi' on it. It is some of my 'birder ink'. I do have quite a few birding related tattoos, though I didn't get my first ink until my 65th birthday in August 2018.

I began pulling it together. The irresistible desire to do the twitch was again colliding with the intense anxiety that I can experience. Even though I was meeting Robert up there, I was heading off alone. I know this about myself. And as I have said and will say again, I deal with it. By 3:30pm I had bought some supplies, packed, fuelled-up and was on my way north.

Since it was a Monday afternoon, I avoided Melbourne and the Western Ring Road. I drove out and around, missing the worst of the city traffic, making it a bit longer but a much more relaxing drive. I arrived at the Glenrowan Caravan Park just after seven. As this book will attest repeatedly, I often return to places that I like and where I feel comfortable. The Glenrowan Caravan Park is certainly one of those places. I had been there only a few weeks before. I settled in and relaxed in the back of Troopi.

Looking online, Google maps said that it was about nine and a half hours from Glenrowan to the twitch location. Nine and a half hours in Google maps time is about 11 hours in Troopi time. As mentioned, Troopi time is determined by the slower speeds that help to keep her diesel mileage more manageable. So if Google Maps says nine and a half hours at the highway speed of 110 kph, then at 90-95 kph it will take about 11 hours. Google maps also doesn't think anyone stops for fuel or the toilet, both of which I do. We would also be taking the Hume Highway into Sydney area traffic. Ugh. I was trying to decide what I was going to do, but I already knew. I was going to go for it and make the drive in one day.

After rising very early (before 4am) as is normal, I was well coffeed and driving Troopi out of the caravan park before 6am. I hoped to get to the little town of Old Bar, and meet Robert and hopefully Liam as well by 5pm. Theoretically, I would still have plenty of daylight left to find and see the terns. Liam had reported at least a dozen there on Monday. It was a long drive, but thankfully there were no unexpected traffic issues. It was just regular Sydney congestion, and I was expecting that.

Somewhere about an hour west of Sydney, I decided to let Troopi go a bit faster, and I did do the last couple of hours driving closer to the speed limit, at least when it was 100 kph. I figured the extra diesel would be worth it. I reckon it was. I arrived precisely at five, and, amazingly, precisely at the same time as Liam and Robert. We all met in Old Bar at the corner of the road into the reserve. The timing of the three vehicles coming together at the same

Troopi waiting in the shade as I waded over to the terns.

time and point was incredible. It still makes me smile to see us all arriving together.

Robert had been there earlier that day and had already seen the terns. He had been very thoughtful when we spoke on the phone. Before ever he said that he had seen and photographed them, he said, "You'll get them. No problem. I am sure you will get them." I appreciated that. But I still needed to successfully do that and as someone once said, there are no guarantees in twitching.

We followed Liam to the parking spot, then clamoured down the bank and walked out into the water. The area where the terns were being seen was a half a kilometre or so across a shallow bay that was easily waded. The bottom was firm and only occasionally did the water go above my knees. I had taken the precaution of emptying my pockets just in case it became deeper. As it was, the little waves occasionally splashed upwards, and I arrived on the large expanse of sandbar a bit wetter in spots than I had intended, but I didn't care about that. The twitch was on.

Out on that sandbar, there were two photographers looking toward a flock of terns through their giant lenses. We walked over and asked them if they had seen the Aleutians. They said that they had seen two, but those had flown off about 15 minutes ago and had not returned. Oh no. Just no. The next 45 minutes of waiting and looking were slightly stressful. I was wacky-tired from the drive and lack of sleep. I had been running on adrenaline and when the terns weren't there, it was like my adrenaline tap had been turned off. I kept up a good front. Robert wandered off looking along another large sand bank off to our left. However, I stuck close by Liam, and he and I kept an eye on that flock of terns hoping the Aleutians would join them again.

And then Liam said, "I think I have a possible" as he stared through his bins. All my brain was thinking was, "Oh please, oh please, oh please." It is a phrase I have often thought whilst birding. I would not call it an actual prayer, but it is close. We crept toward the terns. And then he said, "Yes, it is!" The bird flew briefly but was quickly joined by a second Aleutian Tern. They landed together and gave us wonderful views for the next half hour or so. They

I waded over to that far sandbar and that is where we saw the Aleutian Terns.

were still there when we walked and waded joyfully back to our vehicles. Twitch success once again and an Australian first too! The epitome of Lifer High was reverberating through me as it does. It was worth every hour and every kilometre of that journey to see and experience these very special birds. Thank you, Robert, thank you Liam, thank you terns. These birds remained in that area for months and many birders made their way to the little town of Old Bar. As I write this in March 2021, the Aleutian Terns are still being seen in that area, particularly in the spring and summer. The local economy has gotten a massive birder boost. I have no regrets about making a dash up there immediately. One never knows how long a bird, or birds, will stay. As it turns out, there was certainly no rush. Not that I would, but I literally could have walked to Old Bar and been there in time to see them.

I stayed the night at the caravan park just around the corner from the reserve. Robert and I spent the evening sharing our Lifer High, downloading photos and charging batteries (literally and

Briefly visiting Capertee Valley, New South Wales.

figuratively). I awoke the next morning before five because I was still so happy and excited. Lifer High is a gift that can keep on giving.

We decided to stop by the Australian Reptile Park to say hi to my friend Robyn Weigel (John Weigel was off on Cocos Island), then we headed out to do a little exploring.

We ended up in Capertee Valley. It is a gorgeous place that I had heard about many times but had not yet visited. However, Robert had a puncture just after we arrived there, and we decided it would be better to head to his house in Parkes. So I spent Friday night at Robert and Judy Shore's. Judy is Robert's wife and also a very dear friend. Then I drove on down to Lara on Saturday. On Sunday I had a wonderful Lifer Day, all day long as best I could. Aleutian Terns, Australian firsts. Sweet.

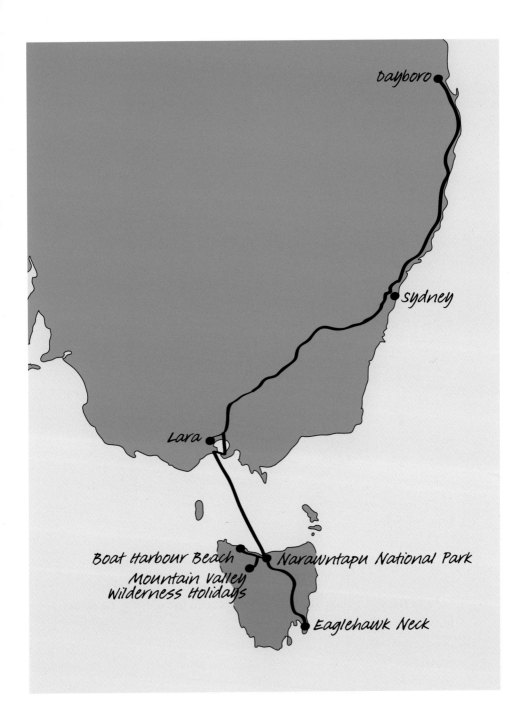

Dayboro

Sydney

Lara

Boat Harbour Beach
Mountain Valley
Wilderness Holidays

Narawntapu National Park

Eaglehawk Neck

{ 10 }

Two Troopies To Tassie and The Mega Petrel

January 2018

I love Tasmania, which is not so unusual since I also love so much of Australia. I truly do. But Tassie is, well, Tassie. When I had the opportunity to get on the 14 January pelagic out of Eaglehawk Neck, I made plans to head to the Land Down Under the Land Down Under.

I learned that there were two places available on the boat, so I contacted Robert and unsurprisingly, he was up for the trip. We made plans to ferry ourselves and our Troopies down to Tassie.

On Friday morning 12 January we boarded the *Spirit of Tasmania* for what is called a day trip. The ferry crossings are either overnight or all day. This was my first day trip on the boat. It was an easy crossing, although mostly rainy and grey. However, the ferry was an hour behind schedule and our arrival at Devonport was close to 8pm. We headed on to what we had heard was a free camping area only 20 minutes south of the ferry. We arrived tired and hungry to a very clearly worded: 'No Overnight Camping' sign. Damn.

We looked online and found another free camp that was

Waiting to board the big ferry, the *Spirit of Tasmania*.

supposed to be about 45 minutes or so further south. After way over an hour of bouncing down winding, rutted, unsealed roads, we finally arrived in the dark at a place called the Liffey Falls Camping Area. It was a beautiful spot, but I could not see that until the next morning. When we arrived it was raining and pitch dark.

After an okay night's sleep, the next morning we had a beautiful ride down the A5 toward Eaglehawk Neck. We saw some of the Central Highlands of Tasmania and it is gorgeous out there. It continued to be rainy and grey, but that did not dull the beauty of the Highlands.

We arrived in Eaglehawk Neck at the Lufra Hotel where I had secured us a room. They call these rooms 'fisherman's rooms'. I mentioned them in the first book, they are less fancy than their regular rooms, but they are clean, comfortable and quite roomy. Personally, I love these rooms and I have stayed in them quite a few times since. I will be mentioning them again in this book several times. I prefer to stay in a cabin or motel room before and after a pelagic so that I can, hopefully, maximise my rest before and after the boat trips.

First thing in the morning we arrived at the jetty to board the Eaglehawk Neck pelagic boat, the *Paulette*. It is a stable, comfortable craft that holds about a dozen passengers. It was a little windy and bumpy, but the seasickness patch was doing its job and I was okay. My first Lifer of the day (yes, there were going to be a few!) was a Providence Petrel that circled the boat a few times. We saw a second one later in the day as well.

Birds of 'Providence' was the name given to them on Norfolk Island, where they are now extinct. About 200 pairs still breed on Phillip Island, which is just 6 kilometres south of Norfolk Island in the south-west Pacific. When a supply ship named HMS *Sirius* was shipwrecked on Norfolk Island in March 1790, there was not nearly enough food to go around in the newly established colony. 'Providence' petrels gave them a food supply to sustain the colony, hence the name. In the year 1790 it is recorded (somewhere) that over 435,000 of these birds were devoured on the island.

Inland of Tasmania on a cloudy, rainy day.

Subsequent harvesting as well as the release of pigs into the natural environment of Norfolk Island saw the extinction of those petrels there by the early 1800s.

After we were set up to berley (chum) we had tons of storm-petrels in the slick, including four little Black-bellied Storm-petrels that came in dancing along the water. They were also Lifers for me. We had a lot of nice birds and then the rock-star of the day, a sighting considered a mega-rarity, glided into view. His name was Juan.

On pelagic birding trips, far more often than I would like to admit, I am thinking, "I'm not sure what that bird is". My pelagic identification skills are fairly lame. I was on the port side of the boat as a petrel that was very light underneath came flying directly toward us. I stared at it and thought, I really don't know what that is. So, as I often do, I pointed and asked excitedly, "What is that?" I had turned to my friend, Paul Brooks who was standing just to my left. Paul organises these trips and his pelagic bird identification skills are truly amongst the best. I will never forget that moment. Paul's face was a blank as his brain tried to assess what he was

My photo of Juan Fernandez Petrel.

The mega-rarity Juan Fernandez Petrel (photo by Robert Shore).

seeing. Still staring at the bird he said, "I… don't… know… Take pictures!" And we did.

After consulting field guides and checking the photos, it was determined that we had undoubtedly seen a Juan Fernandez Petrel. This was only the second sighting ever for Australia! Named for the Juan Fernandez Islands off Chile on which the bird nests, its normal range comes nowhere near Australia. I believe the last sighting had been in 1985 off New South Wales. This was a Life Bird for everyone on board! That is something that does not happen very often in the world of pelagic birding, or terrestrial birding either for that matter. A Lifer for all and from far away South America.

As is often the case off Eaglehawk Neck, we still had some mobile signal and were able to share our joy on social media as well as receiving some enthusiastic confirmations of our sighting. This was exciting stuff indeed!

Oh yes, there was much joy. Organised by my dear friend Karen Dick, most of the group went to the little local café and shared two huge piles of Lifer Chips! In my opinion, Lifer Chips are an excellent version of Lifer Pie. Robert and I also had dinner there

The track into Mountain Valley Wilderness Holidays.

before heading back to the motel. The next day we were going off to the mountains of northern Tassie for a couple of days. I was looking forward to that.

After what will forever be remembered by me, and I am sure others as well, as the Juan Fernandez pelagic, Robert and I drove about four and a half hours up into the mountains of northern Tassie. We were booked to spend a couple of nights in a cabin at Mountain Valley Wilderness Holidays. It is stunningly beautiful up there with Black Bluff Mountain as the backdrop for this idyllic valley setting. It was a wondrous experience just being there in the mountains of Tasmania. I loved it.

It is a private nature reserve and a release area for rehabilitated animals. It is also a wonderful spot to see mammals right in front of your cabin. We did just that. Incredible. From the cosy comfort of our cabin, we watched a Tiger Quoll as well as the iconic, famous Tasmanian Devil come up to within only a metre or two of the front door! We were able to lie on the cabin floor and look at these incredible carnivorous marsupials through the clear glass

A wild Tiger Quoll just outside our cabin door.

A wild Tasmanian Devil.

Boat Harbour Beach, Tasmania.

of the front door. Amazing stuff. We were there for two nights and they visited us both nights, although we did not stay up as long watching them the second night.

Speaking of cool mammals, during the day we did a bit of casual birding around the area. As we walked along the river next to the cabins, we saw another true Australian icon, the Platypus, having a swim. We also saw a Wombat meandering around on the opposite shore. Also iconic, but not quite as famous nor as wonderfully bizarre as the Platypus. I really liked that place. I do recommend it and I hope to return someday if the fates allow. It is the kind of place, and experience, that I long to share.

After those two nights we left that magical valley and without any definitive destinations, just headed off to look around Tassie a bit. One of the most beautiful spots I have ever seen, as well as being a free camp, was in Boat Harbour Beach on the north coast. We spent one night there. They even had proper toilets just a short walk from the camping areas. The water was stunning. The weather was lovely. But still, I was slipping into an unusually massive depression.

Other than my natural tendency for depression and anxiety, there were some situational reasons for it. Yes, I was in a paradise-like place, one of my favourite places, but although my pal Robert was around, I really was travelling alone.

I am not going to get over-dramatic about the solo travel blues. I am not a fan of drama. I prefer comedy and adventure. I need to share. It's one of the main reasons I write. It is what makes social media so important for me. For many reasons, reasons that go all the way back to 'family of origin' issues, sharing makes things real for me. And 'for me' is important to say. I know this is certainly not everyone's way. For me, sharing is at the very core of living life. But that is not how everyone feels. As I write, alone at my desk, I trust that these words will eventually be read and shared. If you are reading this, I thank you with all my heart.

Now I will mention a second portion of my depression. I felt I had let myself down, that I had failed. On Friday, I had been given the option of joining the Sunday pelagic out of Eaglehawk Neck. However, I was booked on the return ferry day-trip departing early Monday morning. I did not feel comfortable coming in from a pelagic and then immediately driving four-plus hours up to Devonport and leaving the first thing the next morning. I chose not to do it. I chose to stay within my comfort zones and that is not something that I usually do. Emotionally, I paid for it. Ironically, comfort zones can become very uncomfortable places.

To make things worse, it turned out that the boat had a phenomenal day (well, no Juan Fernandez Petrel). But if I had I gone, I would have gotten five (yes five) Lifers on that trip and also, I would have hit 700 birds on my Australian list that day. It would have been a huge day. I heard about the trip's success very early Sunday arvo. As I mentioned, there can be mobile signal out there off Eaglehawk. So this news had time to settle into my depressed brain and simmer and stew.

Now, for the positive bit and it is truly positive. As odd as this might sound, in retrospect, as far as reaching 700 goes, I am really

very grateful that I did not do it that Sunday. I would so much
rather have hit that magic (for me) number in the way that I did.
That is coming up soonish in the book. Things do have a weird
way of turning out right. As I look back over my life, there are
many, many moments that seemed initially crushingly bad, but
somehow ended up leading to some of the best and the most
important parts, or changes in my life. But at that moment, there
in Tassie, I could not see it that way. I was deeply depressed and
felt completely hopeless.

On the last night of the trip, I had a phenomenally beautiful
view from my campsite perched high in a caravan park that was
only 10 minutes from the ferry dock. On the ferry, I had another
comfortable crossing, and again I was grateful. I have been very
fortunate in my crossings. I have heard about some very rough
ones and even seen photos. It can get bad.

Not long after I got back, I knew that I needed to get out again.
I decided to make a quick run up to southeastern Queensland in
mid-February (quick is subjective: it is about an 1,800-kilometre
drive one way). I had hopes of seeing an Oriental Cuckoo since

Troopi in a great spot at the caravan park near the ferry.

sightings had been reported in that area recently. But by the time I got up there, it had not been seen for a week or more, and even with the help of my friends, Marie Tarrant and Sue Lee who live near there, I did not see the cuckoo. I was still dealing with the depression and after only birding one morning, I just climbed into Troopi and begin driving back. My first attempt at 'getting back on the horse' had not ended well. Metaphorically, I had been bucked right off. In fact, it seems that the Oriental Cuckoo had departed the area before I arrived. It was not like I had 'just missed it' or anything. There were no other reports of it in the coming days.

But I was determined to keep up my travels and I made plans to leave again in just over a month for another 'solo' trip. Hello metaphorical horsey, I am fixin' to climb on you again.

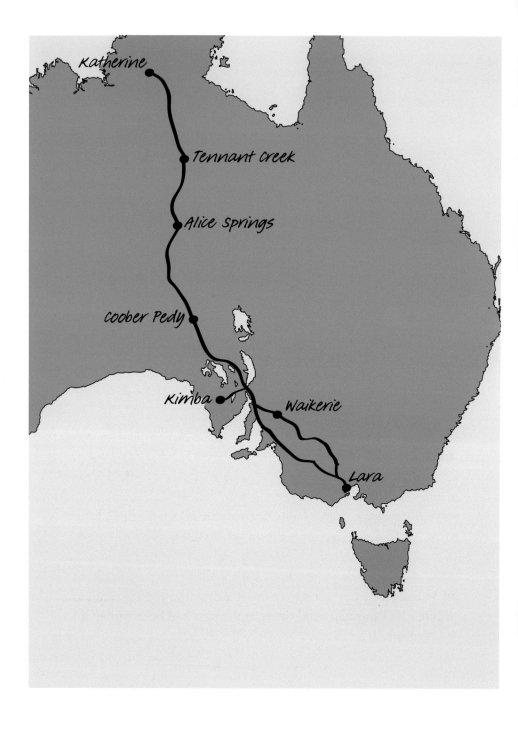

{ 11 }

An Unexpected Journey - Bogey No More

April 2018

My original plan was to meet Robert in Waikerie, South Australia and then head up the Birdsville Track, where we were going to connect with a small group of Victorian birders who were doing a longer trip together. I figured I could get out and back in a few days, and possibly pick up one or two, or maybe even three Lifers. It would be a nice, smallish trip to get myself out again.

As I can do, I pushed through my comfort zones and drove out of Lara first thing in the morning arriving much later that day in Waikerie. It was a long ten-hour drive. The old caravan park where I had stayed several times in the past had been turned into a 'lifestyle village'. I think there is possibly some irony in this, but I am not in the mood to mess about with irony right now. It was no longer a caravan park. However they had built a big, shiny, new caravan park right across the street.

Of course, I liked the old one better. I am at an age where so many things in my life relate to 'I liked the old one better'. Yes, I usually do. I wouldn't mind having that cross-stitched and framed.

Troopi and I were the only passengers on the ferry crossing the Murray at Waikerie at first light.

Just the sentence, 'I liked the old one better'. I would put it somewhere here in my study. My old study in our cottage in Manns Harbor, North Carolina, before we moved into the 'village', was a sunroom with a sweeping view of Roanoke Sound. I would rather be in Australia. Full stop. Never doubt that at any point in my writing. But as far houses go, I truly liked that one much better. I do wish that I could have one like it here. Acceptance.

I have recently become aware of a very old saying that was used upon parting in some Spanish cultures. It is "Que no haya novedad". Which I understand to mean "Let no new thing arise". It is based on the assumption that 'new' things are inherently bad. Based on my personal experiences, I certainly agree with that sentiment in general. Of course, not all new things are bad (vaccines and streaming television come to mind). But as far as most new things go, or particularly 'updates' of things, I almost always liked the old one better.

Regardless, I checked into the new park and had a sandwich (as I do) then set up my Troopi in the dark. It only takes a few minutes to pop the top and settle in, I was cosy as, and even sort of relaxed. Soon Robert rocked up.

We were checking road conditions on the internet and discovered that the Birdsville Track was flooded and closed. That meant I could not get to where I was planning to go from where I was. My plans would have to change. We learned that the group of Victorian birders were going to reverse their trip route, going up through the centre first and coming back down to Birdsville at the end. On the way, they would be stopping in Coober Pedy in two days. There I also had hopes of the Thick-billed Grasswren, a Lifer for me.

Since we were out that way and had a day before we could meet the group in Coober Pedy, Robert and I decided to travel over to the Lake Gilles area of South Australia and have a look for the Copperback Quail-thrush, a bird we both still needed. We could also stay a night in the excellent free camp in Kimba, South Australia. That is the little town of 'Halfway Across Australia' (and 'statue' of the giant Galah) fame that Lynn and I passed through three times in the first book. Despite having coordinates of a very

Beautiful mallee near the large dam on the 'Two Dams Track' Lake Gilles area, South Australia.

recent sighting, we did not find any Copperback Quail-thrushes. After a good night's sleep, we tried for them once again but had no joy. Around mid-morning, we gave up and headed north.

After about a seven-hour drive, I arrived at dusk at the Hutchinson Monument free camping area just south of Coober Pedy. I found a nice spot on the fringes of the Victorian group and popped the top. I had been there before. It's in chapter 23 of the first book, although in 2016 we only birded there, we did not camp. I was tired and I didn't do a lot of visiting. I just said hellos to a few friends and went to bed early. It was a lovely cool evening and I had quite a nice night's sleep. The next morning I was up in the dark, coffeeing and waiting for the sunrise.

Just after first light, and thanks to the younger ears in the group, we saw the Thick-billed Grasswren! I cannot hear them whatsoever (or any grasswrens for that matter). It was heard first and then located. I think everyone in the group who wanted to see the bird, did get to see it. Joy indeed. This was my first Lifer in a while. It was a Lifer for Robert as well. He had arrived a bit later the night before, having stopped for something on the way up. Knowing my

Troopi at the free camp behind the monument just south of Coober Pedy.

Thick-billed Grasswren blending in beautifully. Trust me, it is there.

friend, I am guessing it was food related, but I don't remember.

The Thick-billed Grasswren was the only bird in that region that would be a Lifer for me. The Victorian group was heading north to Alice Springs. I was considering just going back south and on home. It had been a nice trip and I was feeling pretty good. But and it was a big 'but' (no jokes please) there were Yellow-rumped Mannikins being seen very consistently in a specific spot in Katherine in the Northern Territory. And I mean very consistently. The birds were there. Robert had been going on about them. I was painfully aware that they were there. Friends had been posting gorgeous photos of these lovely finches on social media. Of course, Robert thought I should go for them. Robert always says to "go for it" and although it can be annoying at times, I truly appreciate that about him. He can always be relied upon to be that "go for it" voice in my ear and sometimes I need that. In this case, even Lynn encouraged me to go. I am not sure she truly understood how far it was. As I mentioned earlier, those mannikins had been one of two Bogey Birds from the year that became the first book. We had looked in almost all of the 'right places' in Western Australia and the Northern Territory repeatedly to say the least, and never saw one. And now I knew where there were some for sure, or as 'for sure' as one can be about birds. And it was only about 1,900 kilometres north of where I was, bearing in mind that 'only' is one of those words that just means whatever you need it to mean. In this case I needed it to minimise what was actually a long way to drive.

So I decided that I would drive up to the Erldunda Roadhouse, spend the night and then decide whether I would continue north, or head on back. I might decide to drive out to Uluru just because. Anyway, I would have options. The roadhouse would put me 500 kilometres closer to Katherine if I did decide to go and it would be fun going up to where I had stayed before during the year.

I splurged on an air-conditioned room at the roadhouse. It wasn't horribly hot, but it was mid to upper 30's and I was having a Lifer Night to celebrate my Thick-billed Grasswren. It had only been about two years since I had stayed there with Lynn, and it had changed. Prices were higher (or at least it seemed that they were), and the whole atmosphere was more of a "well, where else are you going to go?" attitude. It's a tourist-trap mentality based on not needing to have return business if you can make enough money from someone the first time. Most foreign tourists are only going to be there once. But this is just my opinion. However, it is based on prior visits. There is a reason for the existence of the phrase 'tourist trap'.

Out of curiosity, I just Googled, 'owner of Erldunda Roadhouse' and unsurprisingly, it is the very same corporation that owns, and I think has changed, the Nullarbor Roadhouse in the same way. That is funny, or ironic or something. Really, I suppose it is mostly just sad. Corporate greed spreading into the outback. These are only my opinions.

When I could get the internet there to work, I was looking on Google maps, as I do. I like to sort my options and possible routes on those maps while I am planning trips. I saw that with a pretty good push, I could be in Tennant Creek the next day. That was another place I had stayed before. And then, yes! I could be in Katherine the following day. In two days' time I could be looking at my last (for the time being) Bogey Bird. Just two days of driving up through the beautiful centre of Australia. And I do like it out there. I really do. So of course, I decided to go for it. Just Troopi and me, up through the centre.

On my way to Tennant Creek, my friend, and brilliant photographer and birding guide, Laurie Ross (see the first book, Top End section mostly) passed me going in the opposite direction. He made a U-turn and then caught up with me. It was funny, I did not notice him until he pulled up beside me and there he was. He had a Tracks Birding Tours (his company) T-shirt that he wanted to give me. There we were in the middle of pretty much nowhere, a bit south of Ti Tree, Northern Territory, and he had recognised Troopi and chased me down. It was not much of a chase really considering the speed at which I drive and that it is a 130 kph speed limit out there. After sharing a hug and some smiles, he went on his way to the south and I continued north. That was a very cool experience.

I overnighted in Tennant Creek at the caravan park. It had not changed for the worse, if anything it was better. They had added a couple of new little ensuite cabins that were comfortable as. I hunkered in, had a shower and relaxed fairly well for me. I mentioned this caravan park in chapter 22 of the first book. I had my only flat tyre there during the entire year of travel (and it was a cracked rim, not the tyre). We were very fortunate with our tyres. I fervently believe in, and still use, BF Goodrich all terrain. They have really done well by me, although they are quite dear, in my opinion they are worth it. I was asleep in my comfortable bed early and I was up and out at first light.

My friend, Marc Gardner who lives in Katherine, had given me spot-on directions and a map of the site. Laurie Ross gave me the same gen as well. I rocked up at the mannikin location, which was an almost dry ditch, at about 3pm. It was very hot and humid as it is up there. And as I expected at that time a day, there were no birds around. Finch nap time I reckon. But since I was there, I had to at least have a look and I did. Then I left and took a cabin in a nearby, and rather woebegone, caravan park. The little cabin looked okay, and it wasn't very dear. I took some of my stuff in, turned on the air con and went to the grocery.

I have mentioned that I am a fan of familiarity. I love exploring new areas, but I also love returning to places that I know. I love that even though it is 3,500 kilometres from where I live, I knew that Woolworths in Katherine. We had shopped there several times during the year. These little pockets of familiarity are scattered all across Australia for me. I also know the grocery in Port Augusta, South Australia, and Broome, Western Australia, and Sorell, Tasmania, and Mareeba, Queensland, and Alice Springs, Northern Territory, to mention just a few. They're like having an extended neighbourhood for me. I find genuine comfort in that feeling. I gathered a few items, including a ten-litre box of spring water and returned to the caravan park.

I came back into my cabin and the air con was making a loud 'clacking' sound. I alerted the manager, and he had a look and said that the clacking was a bad thing and gave me a key to another cabin. I gathered up my things, and my groceries, and carried them over to that cabin. The air con in there worked fine. Air con was the main reason I was taking a cabin anyway. It was very humid and in the upper 30's. I made and ate a sandwich as my early dinner and then I went back to the mannikin ditch about 5:00pm.

And finally, in the fading, late arvo light, I saw a pair of Yellow-rumped Mannikins! I had done it! Bogey no more! I had seen all of the finches in Australia. The photos were quite mediocre, backlit and in low light, but that's not an issue for me. Lifer High, joy, relief, and gratitude all shared space in my glowing heart.

Darkness was descending in earnest as I headed back to my cabin to settle in for an early night. I planned to be back in that ditch just before first light. I wanted more looks at these formerly

Finally, Yellow-rumped Mannikin, the true Bogey Bird from the first book.

bogey beauties. As I was fixing to go to the amenities block just after 8pm, I discovered that the sliding door latch had jammed. It would not unlock. I was stuck in the cabin, and it did not have an ensuite. I tried and tried to get the latch to open with no success. It was jammed. I called the number for the park and got no answer. I found an 'emergencies only' number and called it. The manager came. He let himself in using his key. Then he explained, literally as if to a small child, how it was impossible for this simple mechanism to jam. He used to install windows and doors for a living. He demonstrated over, and over, and over how this simple latch locked, and then unlocked. It could not jam. I reminded him that it had jammed. He said that it was not possible as he continued to demonstrate over and over that it could not jam.

And then it jammed.

So, he and I were locked in the cabin together. His own mobile phone was on charge at the office. He had his wife's mobile with him, so he could not call her to come and unlock the door. He finally figured out what his landline number was and rang his wife. In a few minutes, she came to the cabin and opened the door with a key. Leaving the door open, he disassembled the latch. He still did not know how it could have jammed, but he left me a screwdriver to fully disassemble it, should I end up locked-in again. As he was leaving, he stated clearly that if I had any more problems, he would give me a full refund. His suggestion. His words.

Now, pretty exhausted, I went to bed about ten (half an hour later than I had planned). I had just drifted off as something, I am guessing a possum, made a loud scraping and knocking somewhere in the metal walls of the cabin. I bolted out of the bed thinking someone was trying to break in. No one was. I went back to bed and after a while, I drifted off again. Then maybe an hour later, I was awakened by an even louder noise of a similar nature. I was up again in a flash. This time I hurried outside to check on Troopi and the backside of the cabin. Nothing. When I returned, the spring popped out of the latch, and it fell apart in my hands. I was unsure that I could effectively get it locked again. Long story short, I had crap night's sleep in this dodgy place, and I was up and coffeeing by 4am.

Before I got back to the mannikins, there were a couple more dramas that early morning. One was seeing the hairiest *homo sapiens* I have ever beheld. No exaggeration. He was wearing only a towel while brushing his teeth at the sinks in the amenities. This guy was 'circus hairy,' seriously sideshow stuff, and yet bald on top, go figure. I really tried not to stare. I am sure that I was not very successful.

And then back at the cabin, the ten-litre water box exploded as I opened the spout, jetting water from the hole as if from a fire hose, onto me and the cabin floor. Thank God it had not happened in the back of Troopi. I have opened literally scores of those water boxes inside Troopi without a single problem. Regardless, I was still back at the ditch before first light. Then as the sun rose, I saw the mannikins again. Glory.

That was Thursday morning 12 April 2018. I had left Lara on Friday 6 April, planning to be gone for a few days and there I was standing in a ditch in Katherine, Northern Territory, up in

Australia's Top End. I still find that amazingly wonderful.

I went back to the caravan park to turn in my key and see whether the manager really meant it when he had suggested that refund. Since I knew the cabin door would not lock, I had already packed everything before going out that morning. I was carrying the key and assorted parts of the lock mechanism in the palm of my hand as I walked to the office. The manager saw me coming and did not even ask what happened, he just stated rhetorically with a sneer, "How did I know?" And we walked into the office where he said to his wife, "Refund his money" and walked out. Well, this was unpleasant.

He had suggested the damn refund the night before. I had not even brought it up. Now he was gone, and his wife was asking me, "Why are we refunding your money?" And I answered, "Because he said to. It was his idea." And she still asked, "But why." So I asked her, "Don't you remember coming to let us out of the cabin last night? The door lock did not work. It's broken." So she wrote, 'broken lock' in a ledger and gave me a refund. She was scowling. I told her that I had travelled all the way around the continent of Australia for a year and I had never asked for, nor needed to ask for, a refund anywhere. I said my wife and I had been travelling and birdwatching.

And then it all changed. She asked, "You know about birds?" She took her field guide out from the desk and began asking me about Gouldian Finches (everyone talks about Gouldians). And then she was telling me about a bowerbird bower on her property. I finally had to cut this pleasant chit-chat short so that I could get on my way. She had gone from adversarial to almost overly friendly through the bird connection. That was a very nice ending to an uncomfortable situation. And with that refund, I figured I could splurge (okay, splurge again) and stay the night at one of my many favourite places in Australia. I was only about one hour away from Mataranka and beautiful Bitter Springs.

As I left, I stopped at the ditch again about 8:30am. I mean I

Another of the lovely Yellow-rumped Mannikin in the ditch in Katherine, Northern Territory.

had to drive right by it, so of course I looked again and when I did, I had my best views and photos yet. I Facetimed Lynn while standing in the ditch. As I was on the phone with her the mannikins landed right in front of me and she was able to see one over Facetime! That was cool. If only she had been there for real. Regardless, my road goes on.

An Unexpected Journey Part Two: The Return of the Twins
Mataranka is a magical place to me. It is not just the springs, although they are beautiful and very cool. And I mean figuratively very cool. The water in the spring is pretty warm. It is the total vibe of the place that is so cool. We stayed a night in a cabin there when we were in the Top End with friends in August 2012. I loved those cabins then, and as it turned out they had not changed. Yay! I stopped by Woolies again and as I was leaving, I phoned from the carpark and reserved a cabin. I said that I would be there in an hour and asked if they could please start the air con. I rolled into Bitter Springs Cabins and Camping, and by 11am I was inside

my figuratively, and literally, cool cabin. That is a place where I can relax and I was still in the midst of Lifer High, Bogey Bird Lifer High. Heady stuff that!

Before I got too settled in, I decided that I would finally go for a swim in the springs, something I had never done on previous visits. I have had my dive bag containing my snorkel gear tucked behind the driver's seat in Troopi for years. I dug it out and went to the springs. As I said, the water is very warm and it is beautiful down there around the spring, but honestly underwater, there was not a lot to see. I saw a very few tiny little fishes and lots of grey/brown algae covering everything. It was not like snorkelling on a reef with colourful fishes and coral. It was mostly very grey. But it was still quite an enjoyable experience being enveloped in the flowing currents of that warm spring water. Doing things like that alone is not my way, nor would it ever be my choice, but I was there, and I was alone, and I did it. I enjoyed it as best I could, and I was glad that I did it. I often do things because I know that afterwards I will be glad that I have done them. However, I do not really enjoy them in the moment, not doing them alone. But true to form, I

Resting and rejoicing for a night in luxury at Mataranka.

am enjoying the memories as I am working on this third rewrite in December 2021. Oh hell yes, I am very glad that I did that.

After about 45 minutes of leisurely snorkelling in the warm water, I went back to my comfy cabin. I spent the rest of the day just hanging out there. I showered and even took a short nap. I had not taken one of those in a while. Then I had a couple of non-alcoholic beers and a whole lot of pistachios while fiddling with the laptop and my photos of the Yellow-rumped Mannikins. With mobile data, I was able to access the internet, so I had that electronic companionship that helps keep people like me who are the antithesis of loners from losing our minds, or completely losing them anyway.

I had my usual sliced-ham road sandwich and some potato chips on the side. Then I had an ice cream on a stick for my Lifer Pie treat (the first one anyway). They only had one kind at the office/store, and it was a Connoisseur brand Murray River Salted Caramel with Macadamia. That was the go-to brand and flavour of Lifer Pie ice cream on a stick during the year that became the first book. It was perfect and delicious.

I had a lovely evening and the best, and longest night's sleep of the journey. The next morning I drove on to Tennant Creek and stayed in the same little cabin at Tennant Creek Caravan Park again. Like I said, I do like my familiarity, and I was comfortable in that little cabin. I was definitely avoiding the humid heat of the Top End, although I can, at times, enjoy humid heat and I have fond memories of the Top End during our year. But the big difference is that I was sharing the heat and humidity with my partner. So, it was shareable bearable. We did do us some sweating, but we did it together and that was kind of special. Good memories.

In the morning, I drove to Alice Springs. I arrived in Alice, went to its very familiar Woolworths grocery downtown and then I checked into the G'day Mate Caravan Park. I like that park as well. The heat was dropping, and I found a shady spot for Troopi. I took another nap. I took a shower. I was sort of content. Not a feeling that comes easily to me. I like it and I do try to open myself to it, I just don't achieve it often. Content is good.

The next morning I drove down to Coober Pedy for the night. The depression and anxiety twins had stayed quietly in the background for the most part. I had been on a quest, and even alone, questing is something that suits my brain. Now I was two days' drive away from having another try for the Copperback Quail-thrush. It did not have the questing feeling of my dash up to the mannikins. I just wasn't feeling it. The twins were stepping forward out of the shadows.

One of the things that was encouraging the twins was that it was my sobriety birthday the next day. On Monday 16 April 2018 I turned 28 years sober. In recovery, the day that you quit drinking becomes your sobriety birthday. But I wasn't really feeling any sense of accomplishment or joy. I just felt sad and, well, lonely. I spent a night in Coober Pedy in a higher end, but mediocre in my opinion, caravan park. At that point, the twins were pretty much running the show. The park seemed to be full of happy couples travelling together.

Troopi stopped on the 'Two Dams Track' Lake Gilles area, South Australia.

I left early the next morning. Yes, it was my 28th sobriety birth-day, but as is usually the case, no one else remembered it. It has been a lot of years and the significance of the date has faded. It is merely taken for granted that Bruce doesn't drink. How that

Troopi in Murray Bridge being both a camper and a clothes line for my travel towel.

came to be has all but been forgotten. I had a very sad drive down to Lake Gilles. Even though I was rolling through the beautiful, wondrous, rocky wilderness of South Australia, it wasn't getting through. Such can be the twins.

I arrived in the Lake Gilles area and drove to a beautiful spot where I know that the Quail-thrushes were supposedly seen fairly consistently. I birded that area hard for several hours until dusk without joy (literally and figuratively). I decided to drive the 20 minutes into Kimba to that nice free camp for the night.

I slept fitfully and was up before 4am and back out in the mallee before first light. It was unexpectedly drizzly and foggy. Regardless of the wet it was beautiful out there. I birded that area until about 10am at which point I gave up. There had been no sign, nor sound, of a Copperback. Okay, maybe next time. I decided to drive over and stay the night in Murray Bridge, SA, and from there I could reach Lara the next day. I stayed in what was the first caravan park where Lynn and I had camped in Troopi on Boxing Day 2015. I took a powered site and had a shower. Then I made my last road sandwich of the journey. In the morning after a mediocre night's sleep I was driving east before the sun had even begun to rise. I was back in Lara by 3pm.

After 12 days and over 74 hundred kilometres, Troopi and I were parked again at what I referred to as 'the tiny house'. It was a house that was really not big enough for two and certainly not big enough for four when the twins were visiting. But they never move in permanently. Eventually the birds and the bush can scare them off. Sometimes it just takes a while and some determination.

But let us not forget! I had finally seen Yellow-rumped Manni-kins and that was so very, very cool. Bogey Bird no more! I would have a full Lifer Day later in Lara. Although I had certainly had a nice Lifer celebration in Mataranka at Bitter Springs. As I said, Bogey Bird Lifer High is heady stuff. I was able to tap back into it on several occasions in the coming days and that is such a very good thing.

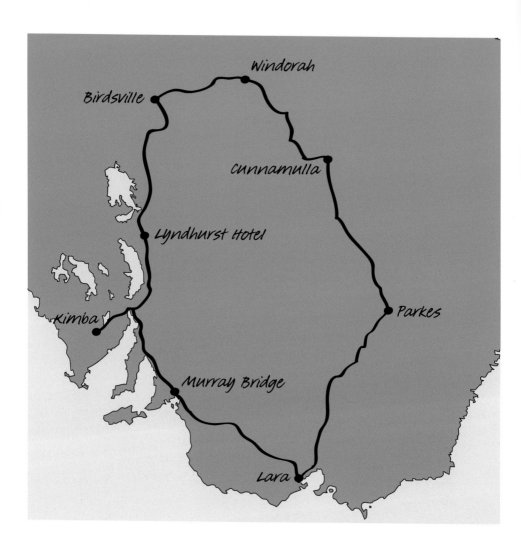

{ 12 }

Grey Grasswren, *Amytornis barbatus* 700

May 2018

I love my bird list. It gives me goals. Pursuing those goals and going looking for new birds has taken me into some of the most incredible, beautiful places in the world. I have seen so much of Australia, and I owe it to the birds. Birds that I hope to add to my list can be that proverbial 'carrot on a stick' leading me on, and then on again. Not that I am all that keen on carrots. I like carrots, but I reckon it should be Lifer Pie on the end of the stick. I reckon carrot cake would work.

In case you are not familiar with the phrase 'carrot on a stick'. It is an old metaphor based on mules being stubborn and not wanting to move. So, some farmer figured out that if he held a carrot, mules are very keen on carrots, on a stick in front of the mule but just out of its reach, it would keep moving forward in an attempt to reach it. I am huge on goals and rewards. Personally, I like to have a 'carrot on a stick' in all things. My bird list is a very tempting carrot for me.

Less than a month after returning from my unexpected solo

journey to the Top End and back, I set off on another adventure. My birding buddy James Cornelious and I left Victoria and drove north. That was on 10 May 2018, and I hoped to add a few birds to my list. James is not only one of my best friends and a great birder, he is also young and has excellent hearing. We were heading up to Birdsville, Queensland, in pursuit of grasswrens. They are literally impossible for me to hear, but not for James.

James and I had been friends on social media before we became friends in the real world. We had birded together a few times, but this was our first proper trip. As this book continues, there will be quite a few more trips with James. We have seen some wonderful birds together. I jokingly, but also in all seriousness, refer to him as my 'hearing-ear boy'. He is an excellent travelling companion as well. There is quite a generation gap between us, James is 42 years younger than I am, yet in many ways we are very much alike.

We drove up to Parkes, New South Wales, and spent the night at Robert and Judy Shore's home. You've often heard about Robert, but I would also like to mention that his wife Judy is one of my favourite people. She is a delightful person, who I do not see often

Troopi and I parked behind Robert Shore's Troopy on the way to Birdsville (photo by Robert Shore).

enough. Robert would be travelling in tandem with us on this trip in his Troopy. So this would be two Troopies to Birdsville. There is something quite comforting about a two Troopy trip. The next morning we began the adventure in earnest. I had booked a site at the caravan park in Cunnamulla, Queensland, where Lynn and I stayed on our way into Bowra Sanctuary during our travelling year. I like that park. The gorgeous Red-winged Parrots perch right in amongst the caravan sites. We had a nice night there and, in the morning, James was out adding birds to his Life List as I was coffeeing in the back of Troopi. He picked up Lifers of Red-winged Parrot as well as Spotted Bowerbird there in the caravan park.

We left Cunnamulla and carried on to Windorah, Queensland, and another caravan park. Thankfully, James and I had an easy drive to the extremely fly-filled town. The flies were pretty bad through much of our trip out there. They are something one just gets used to and thank heavens they do not bite. Robert had stayed at a different accommodation, had taken another route out of Cunnamulla and had gotten a puncture on his way up.

It was on a sunny, pleasant autumn morning on 13 May that we followed Robert out of Windorah and headed west toward the birding-world famous town of Birdsville, and then the equally famous road through the desert known as the Birdsville Track. Oddly, this was a track I had not yet travelled. I was looking forward to this. I had wanted to get over there with Lynn in the last portion of our year of travel, but it was winter and pretty cold out there so we decided against it. Instead we went to see the Laughing Gull in Venus Bay, South Australia, and then to the Flinders Ranges.

After we had been driving west for about an hour, a large bird flew across the track just a few metres in front of our windscreen. It was a Flock Bronzewing! We stopped as it joined about 150 others. Appropriately, it was a flock of Flock Bronzewings! This was a sight I had never beheld. I had seen one bird in the Broome area of WA during the year, but it was just the one and it was flying away from us. James and I got out and marvelled at them. It was

A flock of Flock Bronzewings on the road to Birdsville, Queensland.

another Lifer for James. They are stunning large pigeons. The males have beautiful black and white patterns on their heads. They are more often seen flying and their beauty is not easily noticeable. They usually appear to be big, mostly brown/grey pigeons. But the one that flew across in front of us did give us a good view of that gorgeous head.

James picked up 14 lifers on the whole trip. However they were definitely the best views I had ever gotten of these beautiful birds and as I said, the first time I had seen an actual flock of Flock Bronzewings.

We had continued on only a bit further down the road when Robert came on the radio ahead of us and said, "I think I saw Gibberbirds". He made a U-turn, we stopped, and soon we were all looking at five of these awesome, and sometimes difficult to find, little chats.

This was developing into quite a birdy morning, and we were not even really out there yet! I mean we were out there, but not to the area we were planning to bird. Only about ten kilometres further along, we saw three birds flying on our left. I pointed them out to James just as we all realised ... Grey Falcons! Yes! We had three Grey Falcons flying along beside, then over us. Wow. We immediately drove off the road and marvelled at these stunning, beautiful, rare and very, very special raptors. Truly, wow.

Our first planned stop held my hopes for my first Life Bird of the trip. If I found it, it would put my list at 699. There is a dune line about 17½ kilometres east of Birdsville where my friend Nikolas Haass had Eyrean Grasswrens on his eBird list from November 2017. We stopped and began to bird down this ridge. James and I headed south. He thought he was occasionally hearing them, and we followed his ears. I possibly had a fleeting glimpse of one. We were about three-quarters of a kilometre south of the road and I discovered that I had mobile signal. I called Robert, who was back at the vehicles and also had reception. He said that he had the grasswrens on the ridge just on the north side of the road! We rushed back (as much as we could rush through the deep, soft sand) and soon we were looking at, and taking photos of, at least three Eyrean Grasswrens. Yes!

In the midst of Lifer High I drove us on into iconic Birdsville, Queensland. We were excited for Lifer Pie but were quite

Grey Falcon, a wonderful rare raptor.

Eyrean Grasswren 17 kilometres east of Birdsville.

disappointed to discover that the bakery was closed on Sunday. So we checked into our cabin. Robert's brother-in-law, Chris was travelling with him. He is not a birder and was truly just along for the ride. He needs a ventilator when he sleeps, so he and Robert had been staying in cabins and motel rooms. This was a larger cabin, and we were all able to share it. We considered driving the 90 kilometres south to have our first try at Grey Grasswrens that arvo, but we decided it would be better to wait and go early the next morning. We had a Sunday Roast dinner at the Birdsville Hotel. It was set up outdoors and there were a lot of flies. The food was basic, but good. Then we all settled into the cabin for the night. The next morning we were heading south before first light. The 90 kilometres took an hour and 15 minutes and we arrived at the spot at about 7am. We did a basic search of two locations: one about 90 kilometres from Birdsville and one about a kilometre and a half further. We birded hard in these spots until after 1pm and gave it up. I had seen what could possibly have been a Grey Grasswren briefly and James had heard a few of what possibly could have been Grey Grasswrens, but that was the extent of our success. Not much. We drove back up to Birdsville and arrived just before the bakery closed at 2:30pm.

I had heard about, and I decided that I should try, their Curried Camel Pie. It was absolutely delicious! It remains to this day the best meat pie I have ever had. And yet I had ordered it only to be able to say that I had tried camel. The meat is sourced from a cattle station that also has camels in northern Queensland.

Not too long after our visit, I heard that the Birdsville Bakery had closed. But as I write this in early 2021, I have learned that the Birdsville Hotel has bought it and it has reopened! I have also heard that they plan to serve the same Curried Camel Pie. I planned and I hoped, to go back out there soonish. Read on.

We messed about town, such as there is town to mess about in. Birdsville is pretty small. I went over to the bore area and looked at some of the Pied Honeyeaters that James and Robert found there the day before while I was having a nap. As mentioned in the first book, Pied Honeyeater was my last honeyeater in Australia. They will always be a special bird for me. We had another meal at the hotel and went to bed early. The next morning we packed

Robert Shore's Troopy beside my Troopi at the Birdsville Hotel.

everything up and left in the dark. I had spoken with my friend, Laurie Ross, who had been out there very recently. He suggested we focus on the area about 92 kilometres south. One of the birders who I had originally heard reporting Grey GW's in this spot was my friend-to-be, Bernie O'Keefe. There will be more about Bernie coming in just a few chapters. That was the second area that we had birded the day before. We rocked up in the same spot where we had parked then. It was not even first light yet.

We birded that area for the next couple of hours. For a while, I was looking through the shimmering, rainbow arc of a rather impressive visual migraine, something I occasionally experience. Gratefully, this one did not progress into a proper migraine. They often don't. James thought he heard grasswrens a couple of times, but no joy. We kept on birding. As suggested, we stayed in that area. We worked our way back just behind where we had parked the Troopies. Then James heard Grey Grasswrens. He crept slowly, and he can really creep very slowly when he wants to, toward the contact calls that he was hearing. After several minutes he put his bins up and looked. He turned back to me saying, "I've got them!" Yes!

James listening at the Grey Grasswren site south of Birdsville.

The incredibly beautiful sunset at Lyndhurst on the day of my 700th Australian bird. I will never forget it (photo by James Cornelious).

I will never forget the look on his face. Anyone who has done much birding has seen it, the pure elation that beams from the face of someone who has just seen the bird they were looking for. I knew he had them. Now I needed to see them, and one popped up! I saw it clearly, but literally only for a second. They flew across the track. We headed over, and after about 15 or 20 minutes of searching back and forth with James' ears directing me, I saw a Grey Grasswren perched beautifully on a low branch in a saltbush. I had truly heart-touching views of a Grey Grasswren through my bins. I stared at the black-and-white markings on its gorgeous little head. And then it dropped to the ground in the open under the bush. I swung the camera up in an instant. I was sure I would get a photo. It had been right there, but it was gone. It had disappeared into a hole in the space/time continuum as birds sometimes can do. But I had seen it well, my 700th species of bird in Australia. Once again, as I walked back tears of joy rolled down my cheeks, as well they should.

I had always considered 700 to be *the* goal number of my bird list.

As I am writing this, there are quite a few birders who have gone over 700 and 800 is now often the goal. Mike Carter has broken 900. So has my friend Richard Baxter. However for me, 700 had been the truly magical number. It was a celebration number, even a tattoo-worthy number. It meant a lot to me, and I was so very grateful. Yes, that expression, 'over the moon' was quite fitting for how I felt. I was having an almost overwhelmingly and wonderful Lifer High, Seven-hundredth-bird Lifer High. Joy. Pure, pure genuine joy.

700 Part Two

We had done it. Thanks to James' ears I had seen 700 birds in Australia and the seven-hundredth was the wonderful Grey Grass-wren. It had worked as I had hoped it would. When we began the trip, James and I had discussed that it would be cool to find the Eyrean first so that the Grey GW would be my 700th and that is exactly what happened. Again, such genuine joy. After seeing that wonderful grasswren, the two Troopies headed south down the Birdsville Track. We were going to stop for lunch at the Munger-annie Hotel. It seemed to be a very cool place, and I would not have minded spending more time there but we had decided to press on to Lyndhurst, another iconic place and name. Also, there is no Telstra mobile coverage in Mungerannie, which is a drag and very odd. There is actually another carrier there. Across the vast majority of Australia, Telstra is the preferred network. I was looking forward to sharing the news of my 700th bird. I was still on an almost illegal Lifer High. The joy glowing inside me was wondrous. I am surprised other people couldn't see it radiating from me. What a feeling.

By the way, almost needless to say, the 'twins' were nowhere to be seen during this period of time. They can be very strong and determined, but they are not a match for Lifer High. And they are utterly banished by Seven-hundredth-bird Lifer High.

Before leaving Mungerannie, Phil, the owner of the hotel, put a plug in a small leak in one of Robert's tyres. He ended up having to put a double plug in that tyre and then he would not accept payment for either. Such can be the world of the outback.

Yes, I love it out there and I will return, keep reading and see. The land can be harsh, but it is so incredibly beautiful. The outback is everything you have heard about it and more. It is the 'and more' that has to be experienced to even begin to understand. I will continue to try and capture a bit of what it is with my words. I recommend experiencing it yourself. Make no mistake, it is not for everyone. Some don't get it, but those who do, know what I mean.

We rolled on down the Birdsville Track. I was looking forward to seeing Lyndhurst, yet another iconic spot, however Robert had a puncture. Not in the recently plugged tyre, but another rather worn one had bitten the dust (no pun intended). Yes, the dust was amazing on the dry track and was pretty much coating everything inside our Troopies. You cannot keep that fine dust out. With his tyre changed, we continued on and arrived at the Lyndhurst Hotel on sunset. It was a particularly beautiful sunset too.

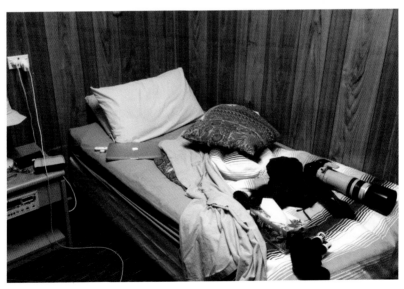

My little, but very comfy, room at the Lyndhurst Hotel.

We took two rooms, a large three-person room and a tiny single room with a small single bed. I was quite happy in the tiny single. There was no ensuite, but I was just across from the door into the amenities building. I was very comfortable that night.

We ate at the hotel. I had fish and chips and it was delicious. I also bought everyone Lifer Pie ice creams on a stick. That Lifer High was still a brightly glowing joy inside me. There was some very mediocre mobile signal on the veranda outside the pub, but it was enough to get 'out'. I was finally able to let Lynn and a few friends about my seven-hundredth. As we know, sharing is very important to me.

I slept quite well, but I awoke even earlier than usual with my chest still filled with joy. I was up and out on that veranda coffeeing just after 4am. I was able to communicate much better online then, since no one else was up and using the limited band width. I watched first light begin to creep into Lyndhurst, South Australia. It was absolutely beautiful. I remember it so clearly and it is a memory that I treasure.

We packed up and headed south-west toward the next possible lifer for Robert and me. James had already seen a Copperback Quail-thrush on a visit to Lake Gilles, South Australia, a while back, but Robert and I both had put quite a few hours looking for it with no joy. The bird was almost attaining bogey status. We were only about five hours from the location and planned to be birding that arvo. And then Robert's Troopy lost a few gears, and then a few more.

He made it to the corner of the A1 outside of Port Augusta just before he had no gears at all. We pushed him over to the side of the road where he called the Auto Club. His Troopy had reached about 600,000 kilometres. It was hard used and had certainly served him well. Robert's Troopy was the inspiration for my Troopi. I had seen first-hand how dependable and durable those vehicles can be and that is what I needed. I had a lot of affection for that old high-top Troopy of his.

But there was nothing else James and I could do to help. So, as Robert and Chris waited for the Auto Club, we pressed on to Lake Gilles to have a look for the Quail-thrush. First, we tried a spot on the road out to the lake that had been recommended to us, but without success. Although James did pick up his lifer Western Yellow Robin. I suggested that we go over on the south side of the main road to what I refer to as 'two dam track' because there are two dams on that track. Clever, huh? This track is about 14 kilometres east of the lake road. I mainly just wanted to show James the area, since the mallee is so beautiful out there. We started down the track and less than 100 metres in from the highway, James spotted a bird running across the ground. We stopped. Then he said those lovely words, "That's the bird." And it was. Number 701! Yes! It was a female. She was soon joined by a male. Then they promptly disappeared. However, James could still hear them making contact calls (of course I could not hear them at all). Once again, we followed James' ears, and had wonderful views of the pair.

We contacted Robert and learned that he was being shuffled around accommodations by the Auto Club in Port Augusta. I

Copperback Quail-thrush on 'Two Dams Track' (photo by James Cornelious).

Slender-billed Thornbill, Whyalla, South Australia, a Lifer for James.

offered to drive over and get him, but instead he suggested that we stay down in Whyalla and try the Conservation Park in the morning. We took a very reasonable and comfortable cabin at the same caravan park where Lynn and I had stayed before when it had been incredibly windy. It was so windy that we had cut our stay short. James and I had a relaxing and very comfortable Lifer Evening. Seven hundred and one! I reckon that is a prime number in more ways than one.

In the morning we drove to the Whyalla Conservation Park in hopes of getting James a Lifer or two. We did get him one. Although the Western Grasswrens were no-shows, the Slender-billed Thornbills were very cooperative for him.

Robert was going to try and catch a ride over to look for the Quail-thrushes, but the dramas with his accommodations continued. Due to reasons I do not recall, most of the rooms in the town were sold out. The Auto Club had to move him and Chris from hotel to motel, not an easy thing as Chris is not fully mobile. We caught up with them at a hotel in downtown Port Augusta that was replete with mid-morning drunken punters. Port Augusta has its own personality. I am okay with it, but some people refer to it as Port Disgusta. We had a short visit then bid them farewell and good luck. James and I headed off for Murray Bridge. One more sleep and back to Lara. At this point, we were both a bit weary (me of course more than James). That particular cabin accommodation in Murray Bridge was one of the nicest in which I have stayed in my travels. I would (and did) return there.

Our entire trip was an impressive nine days of travelling, with two nights in Birdsville. We saw some of the most wonderful birds possible, and the company was excellent. We met some very cool people and experienced some of the most awe-inspiring and diverse of Australia's landscapes. And my Aussie bird list reached and passed 700! I looked forward to more travels with James. He is more than my hearing-ear boy; he is one of my best friends as well as an excellent travelling companion. We do have us some fun.

The badges that Andrew Isles Natural History Books gives free to birders reaching 600 or 700 birds in Australia (and 800, but I do not have that one... yet). These are pinned to the back of the sunshade in front of the driver's seat in Troopi.

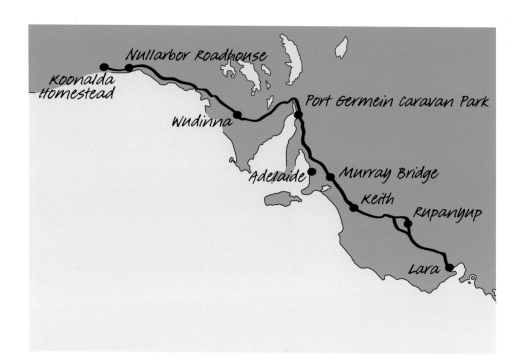

That memorable sunrise in Murray Bridge, South Australia.

{ 13 }

The Nullarbor and More

June 2018

The Nullarbor. That is another iconic name from the outback of Australia. Nullarbor means treeless, although there are more than a few scattered trees out there. I wrote about my initial crossing of the Nullarbor in the first book. I loved it then and I love it now. I find wide-open spaces comforting. As a former agoraphobe that probably should amaze me, except that now, thank heavens, I just consider it normal. I am no longer that agoraphobic person. I am now this person who craves being 'out there'. I am grateful for the many positive changes that I have progressed through during my long life and hopefully for the more to come. I will be a work in progress for the remainder of my days and that is a good thing. I still deal with anxiety and its twin too regularly, but I truly am no longer agoraphobic.

When James and I headed out to the Nullarbor, our Facebook friend, Bill O'Neil referred to us as 'Team Troopi'. I like that. We certainly are a team when we bird. We left on a Wednesday and drove from Lara to Murray Bridge, South Australia, once again availing ourselves of that really nice cabin that I mentioned in the previous chapter. After a very comfortable night's sleep, I remember

Magical sun setting light over the Nullarbor.

that the sunrise was phenomenal. I have seen a lot of magnificent sunrises and sunsets, but only a few really stand out in my memory. I remember that beautiful, glowing scarlet sunrise very well. Both James and I stepped out on the veranda in the brisk morning air and took phone photos of it. I grew up hearing the old nautical saying, 'red sky at morning sailors take warning', but we weren't sailors. We were birders heading west. It was not a warning, but a glowing, glorious send-off for us.

We had a nice and uneventful drive to an unremarkable, yet quite comfortable and reasonable little motel in Wudinna, South Australia. We liked it enough that we stayed there again on the return trip. The next morning, we were out and on the road early, arriving at the Nullarbor Roadhouse midday Friday. Rain was imminent so we decided again not to deal with setting Troopi up to camp. We secured a comfortable, but ridiculously over-priced room at the roadhouse's motel, then bolted for the Koonalda Track.

It is 97 kilometres further west from the roadhouse. We were going out there to look for Naretha Bluebonnets. They are the stunningly gorgeous relative that was once a subspecies of the

Rain on the Nullarbor.

Troopi on the side of the Koonalda Track.

Eastern Bluebonnet. We started down the muddy track with high hopes, but despite searching up and down the track until dark, we did not find any Narethas. But it was beautiful out there. It rained on and off that day, as it did the whole weekend. It truly was a magical rainbow-land. One of my favourite, if not the favourite, photos I have ever taken is from a track by the roadhouse on that rainbow weekend. It is one of the very few of my photos that we have framed and displayed here at the house.

We drove back to our room in the dark, grateful for Troopi's new LED spotties illuminating the wet road in front of us. Travelling back and forth, we would be grateful for them, and for her LED light bar daily.

We were back out at the Koonalda Track the next morning before first light. We spent that entire day going slowly up and down the very wet and muddy track from the old Koonalda Homestead at the end of the track back south six or seven kilometres, and then back north to the homestead. And that is what we did over, and over, and over again. We saw some sweet birds, including Ground

The best photo that I ever lucked into taking. Looking down the track just east of the Nullarbor Road House.

The muddy Koonalda Track.

Rainbows!

The rusty vehicle 'graveyard' at the old Koonalda Homestead.

Cuckoo-shrikes (a lifer for James), which are always a treat, as well as a pair of Stubble Quail wandering around on the edge of the track. We saw several Mulga Parrots that made our hearts jump for a second. They are beautiful, but they were not our Narethas. We knew that they were out there. We just had to keep looking.

The rain showers persisted on and off throughout the day and continued to create some of the most beautifully and intensely coloured rainbows I have ever seen. I have referred to it as the rainbow weekend and it was. The sky and the light in general were as beautiful as I have ever seen anywhere. I will include a few photos. However, our hopes for the bird were beginning to sag. We drove out and around the old Koonalda Homestead with its scores of abandoned, rusting, rotting motor vehicles so many times. I am not sure exactly how or why those vehicles ended up there, but it is an interesting sight. As darkness approached, we headed east to the roadhouse in the rain and dark, again grateful for Troopi's bright lights showing our way.

As usual, the next morning we were up early and out there again. We arrived at the track at first light and began birding. Truly our hopes were not as high as they had been. At this point we had put about 15 solid hours on this less than ten kilometre stretch of track. James had gotten three lifers: Spotted Scrubwren, Redthroat and the Ground Cuckoo-shrike, yet the main target for us both had not even been glimpsed. And then.

At about twenty past ten, we were driving back down the track into one of the small areas of sparse, stubby trees that we had already driven through scores of times before, but this time I saw two birds fly out. They looked light coloured and the right size. They flew low and to the right behind some trees. I quickly drove Troopi around the little curve in the track hoping we would see them on the other side of those trees. As we came round the curve James said, "They landed in the top of that saltbush". It seems I do have some good luck with saltbushes.

I stopped and we both put our bins on them. We had done it. James said those wonderful words, "That's them". For a couple of minutes, they just perched there for us. We stared and took some photos. I am sure that I choked up a little, as I do. A light rain was falling, but there was a bit of sun peeking out. They are one of the

Beautiful Naretha Bluebonnets.

Nullarbor Quail-thrush running across the runway.

most beautiful birds that I have ever seen. It was so worth it. The joy in that instant, that moment in time as we realised that we were finally, after over 18 hours of searching, looking at the bird, our bird, that joy echoed through me for days. Lifer High is a time-release gift that can keep on giving. In the midst of that high, we drove back to the roadhouse where we had lunch. My first Lifer Pie treat was chips and gravy, a big bowl of golden fried chips with gravy! We had done it. We had beheld the Naretha Bluebonnet. Yes, we had!

Yay Team Troopi!

Nullarbor Trip Part Two ~ Another Letter-winged Kite in Victoria. Seriously?

Sunday morning began without rain nor the need to drive 97 kilometres west in the dark. We had gotten our Naretha Bluebonnets. I just took my time, coffeeing at my laptop in Troopi's 'downstairs.' I had not paid the ridiculous price for the mediocre motel room again and we had camped in the Nullarbor Roadhouse's gravel caravan parking area. Grey gravel, it has all the ambience that you might imagine.

A Southern Right Whale and calf in the Great Australian Bight.

My friend, who I refer to as the Alice Springs birding guru, Mark Carter, had been down there only a few weeks before and had given us advice on the Narethas and also suggested looking for the Nullarbor Quail-thrush along the airstrip just behind the roadhouse. That Quail-thrush would be a lifer for James, so as I was coffeeing, he walked over there to have a look. In less than an hour he had returned. He was beaming. He showed me the back of his camera. He had seen and photographed a Nullarbor Quail-thrush! It can be a difficult bird to photograph. I did not get one when Lynn and I saw our Lifer out there together. I took my camera and walked back with James. He quickly refound the bird for us and I even got some recording shots. Sweet.

We packed up and left the roadhouse, then we made a short detour over to The Head of the Bight and paid a small admission fee to park and walk down to the viewing areas and look at the whales. We stopped on the first platform and looked out. There were at least a dozen Southern Right Whales out there. Some were quite far out, but a parent and calf ended up coming in pretty close to the rocky shore. I took some photos. It is a stunningly beautiful view. It was definitely worth stopping, paying the 'cover charge' and having a look. We headed east and stayed the night in Wudinna again, as I mentioned we would. Then we drove over to Telowie Gorge for James to have a look for his Lifer, the Grey-fronted Honeyeater, in the same spot that I saw my Lifer in 2016. He saw at least two and then we both saw our mammal Lifer Yellow-footed Rock Wallaby. That gorge is a beautiful area. Thanks again to my dear friend Kay Parkin who first suggested the spot to me.

After these joys, we went to Port Germein and stayed at the very cool little caravan park there, again revisiting a memory for me from my year of travels with Lynn.

In the morning, as we were leaving the park, James saw his Lifer Black Falcon flying over the small town of Port Germein. There were three Black Falcons in total. I followed them in Troopi through the neighbourhood streets until James got some great views and photos of what had become a Bogey Bird for him.

In the meantime, social media intervened in a good way. Through Facebook we heard that a Letter-winged Kite had shown up that day in Rupanyup, Victoria. Yes unbelievably, a second Letter-winged Kite had wandered down into Victoria. As we know from chapter 2, I had driven up and seen the one in April the year before. That kite had only stayed around for three days. This would be an incredible opportunity for James to add a very special Lifer to his list and a cool sighting for me as well. I will always want to see a Letter-winged Kite when I can.

We altered our route and drove to Keith, South Australia. That would put us about two and a half hours from Rupanyup the next morning. We spent the night in a cabin in the same caravan park where I had stayed previously in 2016, as well as where I stayed when I twitched the Northern Shoveler in 2017. We know I do like familiarity, and they are very comfortable, reasonable cabins. The next morning we were off at first light and heading for the twitch.

We arrived to dense fog. Damn. After a lovely, clear drive over, the whole area around Rupanyup was as foggy as London in an old movie. Our friend, Gary Gale had just arrived as well and the three of us began looking. Gratefully, the fog was beginning to lift. After unsuccessfully scanning the trees along the road where we thought it had been sighted, I decided to ring my friend, Jenn Stephens. She had been one of those who had watched the raptor the day before. She told me that we were looking further east than where she had seen it and suggested we go back down the road a couple kilometres in the direction of town. We did.

As we drove down Rupanyup-Burrum Road, I noticed a 'kite shape' perched amongst the leaves high near the top of one of the tall gum trees. My hearing might be impaired now and my eyes not as sharp as they used to be, but my 'shape recognition' is still pretty damn good. I stopped and said, "I saw something". Gary stopped behind us and watched us get out. James and I walked to an angle where we could see more clearly into the upper branches of the tree. Yes, it was the Letter-winged Kite.

The day before we heard that Black-shouldered Kites had been harassing the bird, and it had flown several times. Our friend, Jenn got some beautiful photos of it in flight. But nothing was bothering

Letter-winged Kite in Rupanyup, Victoria.

Letter-winged Kite perching.

it this morning. It just perched there, occasionally shutting its eyes as it appeared to be nodding off. They are nocturnal after all. Of course, we hoped to see that gorgeous black under-wing 'letter' that goes from its armpit to its elbow, so we waited in case anything happened but it didn't. We stood around chatting and watching that kite for about three hours while it remained quietly perching. We finally just left it there as we had found it. We bid Gary farewell and made the three-and-a-half hour drive on to Lara. A second Letter-winged Kite in Victoria, what a glorious ending for Team Troopi's first official trip.

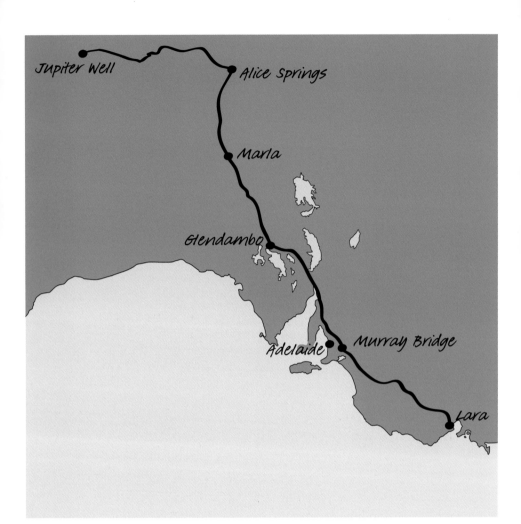

Jupiter Well

Alice Springs

Marla

Glendambo

Adelaide

Murray Bridge

Lara

{ 14 }

The Princess Parrot Expedition

September 2018

Princess Parrots. The name itself is magical to me. They are the parrots Sean Dooley decided not to try for during his Australian Big Year. He said in his book, *The Big Twitch* it was because they live '…about as far from anywhere as you can go and still be on Earth'. But as he also said, 'they are as beautiful as they are rare'. I have referred to them as 'pastel parrot porn'. The subtle shades of pink and green and blue are stunning, heart stopping and breathtaking. They are slender birds with a very long tapering tail that gives them an elegant profile. Even seen in silhouette they are unmistakable. And spoiler alert, we found them. I have a small, framed photo on top of my bookcase to the left of my desk of two of them in flight. But I am getting ahead of the tale.

The trip had been being planned by Bernie O'Keefe for at least a year. I became a part of the trip once again because of my pal, Robert. He had been repeatedly suggesting that I look into it months ahead of the planned September trip. And I am very glad that he did. As I have said, sometimes I do need a bit of a push. Robert can be very good for supplying that push (repeatedly on occasion). But I knew I wanted to do this. I was determined to go on this expedition. And I did.

I loved that Bernie had done so much research and planning. He is a teacher, and he is very organised. I do love organization, especially when someone else is doing it. I can do it, and I can do it pretty well when I have to, and most often I have to, but it does not come easily to me. As I said, Bernie had organised this expedition. We had itineraries, I printed mine of course. We had each other's phone numbers. We had numbers to apply for permits for travelling the original owner lands. We had checklists of supplies and equipment. I also made my own checklists. I have said, I suck at organisation, but most importantly, I know I suck at it. So I have learned coping skills and using checklists is one of the most important ones. I write a lot of things down. Sometimes I need to write 'check the checklist' as an item on my checklist. That's the truth, not a joke.

Of course Bernie had also been in touch with other birders regarding their experiences with these parrots. I also contacted my friend, John Weigel as well as my Alice Springs friend, Mark Carter. I pumped them for all the gen I could get. They both pretty much suggested the same approach to searching. That was to drive very slowly in the early morning, watching and listening along the dunes through which the road passes. One area that had been successful in the past was to the east of the Jupiter Well Camping Area. If the birds are present, it can be possible to hear and/or see them moving along the trees on the dune line. Theoretically, they are mostly active only in the early morning. Although indeed a flock could fly by at any time of day (more regarding that further on).

The Thunderbird Princess Parrot Expedition consisted of four vehicles: Bernie O'Keefe and Glen Pacey in Bernie's Triton 4WD Ute, Robert Shore in his high-top Troopy, David Adam with Bill Twiss in Bill's Prado and me in Troopi. Bernie had come up with the name 'Thunderbird' because he liked it and it sounded cool. It did too. We should have made T-shirts.

I had driven up to Alice Springs alone. On the way I had stayed

Troopi set up in the shade in Marla, South Australia.

in Murray Bridge, South Australia, (not in that nice cabin, but camping in Troopi) and then in Glendambo, South Australia, where I did take a very underwhelming motel room. But it was hot, I was tired, and the room had a bed and aircon. All good.

On my next stop I took a nice little camping spot by a big tree at the caravan park behind the motel in Marla, South Australia. That was better. I had chosen my spot in the late arvo before the campground pretty much filled with caravans and campers. When it became dark, I looked out across the park, and I was amazed at the scores of screens of different sizes lit up around the various sites. More people than ever are now on smart phones, tablets and laptops. They are checking social media, video messaging and streaming television shows and YouTube videos. The mobile bandwidth can only handle so much before it slows to a crawl and that evening it did just that. No worries. I was asleep by 9pm. Then I was up and coffeeing the next morning by 4am. And of course there was plenty of bandwidth then.

At first light, I pulled it together and headed north to Alice

Springs, Northern Territory. As I mentioned earlier, Alice Springs is one of those areas of familiarity for me. I know the grocery, where it is located and the easiest place to park. I was crossing the street from the carpark into Woolworths at exactly the same moment that a Land Cruiser approached the crosswalk. I did the little polite, bounce in my step, that is meant to communicate, "although technically I have the right-of-way, I am not an arsehole, so I will hurry on across the street. Thank you for not running over me," and the Land Cruiser laid on his horn! I turned, ready to be grumpy and was gobsmacked to find myself looking into the face of my friend, Mark Carter! He could have easily run over me just by not applying his brakes. The timing was amazing. The only person that I really know in Alice Springs, and we almost literally bumped into each other.

He parked and we walked into Woolies together. It was great to see him, although he did express his doubts regarding the probability of success for our expedition. Honestly, so had all of the

Troopi and Robert Shore's Troopy at the caravan park in Alice Springs.

knowledgeable birders. Everyone thought it had been too dry and our chances were slim at best. Mark thought that conventional wisdom held that the parrots would be cruising far out in the WA outback looking for better conditions. He also said and I quote, "The over-reliance on dubious 'known facts' has slowed down the learning of reality about several species over the years, Princess Parrots being one of them." He said that the distances, huge landscapes and harsh conditions meant that the conventional ways of studying them don't necessarily work. Mark is a smart guy. I had asked him about this as I was writing this part of the tale.

After visiting with Mark at the grocery, I finished my shopping and drove to the caravan park where I had booked a site. I was meeting Robert there. I ended up in the site behind his and had a nice quiet evening. In the morning we met up with the others to head west and truly begin the expedition.

As we were leaving Alice Springs in the early arvo, we had stopped by the traditional owners offices to personally thank the young woman who had been so helpful to us as we applied for our permits. Bernie had purchased a nice bottle of wine for her from the group by way of thanks. Good touch, that. She had been wonderfully helpful and we had our permits sorted.

We drove west to a free bush camp that was referred to as Kunparrka on the WikiCamps app. It was a fine bush camp. In the previous book, I mentioned that we used that app very often. It was massively helpful. Although the app has updated since then and changed a bit, it still seems to be usable, which is not always the case after 'updates'. I have used it recently with success. Sometimes it seems that things are changed just to change them, and then the app, or device that was already working perfectly fine, no longer works as well as it did. As I have already said, in most things, I usually liked the old one better.

Yes, I should have that sentence cross-stitched and framed. My small office/study is, very thankfully, mostly composed of wonderful, old, meaningful stuff. I've lost many of my treasured life-long processions, but I do have a few left after all of our moves. I had to let go of many personal treasures to make the final move from the proper house on the east coast of the USA to the tiny place. I truly am okay with that. I have to be. I love the things that I have left and when it comes down to it, I truly do have all I need. I love my little, 100-plus year-old writing desk where I am sitting and assembling these words.

Since it is so special to me, I will tell you briefly about the history of my desk. My maternal grandfather worked for the Newport News Ship Building and Dry Dock Company in Newport News, Virginia. I never met him. He died before I was born. As the USA entered the First World War a German ocean liner called, SS *Leviathan* (actually the *Vaterland* in Germany) was seized, then used as a U.S. troop carrier. It was later refurbished at the NN shipyard. Some of the employees there ended up with the old cruise ship furniture. Of those things of my grandfather's I still have two bedside tables, two wing-backed chairs and this small writing desk. It even has a built-in inkwell. I think it was made around 1910. My grandmother called it 'Bruce's little desk' when I was a child. It was in her guest room where I slept-over so regularly that it was called my room.

As I mentioned and justifiably bemoaned earlier, in the last move to Australia, it was deemed that my great-grandfather's large turn-of-the-century, solid oak, roll-top desk was too big to bring back to that tiny house. That roll-top desk had been 'my desk' since my early twenties. Now this little desk has truly become 'my desk.' It is my only desk and as I said, this is where I write.

My old (and yes, I do like it much better) MacBook sits on the raised back of the desk streaming television shows or movies. I 'double screen' when I am working. I have come to understand that it is part of my ADD or as it is usually always referred to now, ADHD brain. It is a fact that I concentrate better when I am partially distracted. Knowing that allows me to accept it and work with it as part of my process. Yes, I write with the 'television' on. I always have. Years ago, I wrote songs with the television on. By the way, I read somewhere that John Lennon also always wrote with the television on. Not that I am comparing myself to him except regarding that practice. Just imagine.

Now back to the expedition. We left our camp at Kunparrka at first light and carried on to Kintore Store, Northern Territory. It is one of the last two opportunities for fuel out there. The store also carried a few groceries and things, convenience-store type stuff, but I really did not need anything. Such is my travelling in Troopi that I have very simple dietary needs. I can happily live for days mostly on sandwiches, almonds and muesli bars, so it is easy for me to stock up. I topped off Troopi's main tank. Diesel was two dollars a litre, which surprisingly was a few cents less than the corporately owned, Erldunda Roadhouse was charging at that time.

We continued west down the unsealed, sand and rock track. It was never a bad drive. There were portions where one could safely roll along at 80 kph. The last stop for fuel was in the aboriginal village of Kiwirrkurra, Western Australia. It's located about 1,200 km east of Port Hedland and about 700 km west of Alice Springs.

Kiwirrkurra Road House supermarket.

What we called John Weigel's spot east of Jupiter Well.

It has been described as 'the most remote community in Australia'. That my friends, is saying something.

Fuel there was a jaw-dropping two dollars and fifty cents a litre. Those who had not topped-up in Kintore Store wished that they had. But it was only 136 more kilometres to the Jupiter Well camping area. We were getting close. After leaving Kiwirrkurra, there were a few long stretches of very soft sand that were better in 4WD and at much slower speeds. But on the entire trip, I was never uncomfortable about the road. Troopi was more than in her element out there. Metaphorically, she barely broke a sweat.

We stopped and had a look around an area that we referred to as John Weigel's spot. It was about 46 kilometres east of the well. He had success with the parrots there during his first Aussie Big Year in 2012. But it was all quiet for us. It was also mid-afternoon. We continued west and soon arrived at the Jupiter Well camping area.

As you turn into the camp, you see the bore pump in the middle of the campground. The water is (I have heard) very drinkable. I can testify that it was delightfully cool and great for bathing, something I did twice while we were there. We had not seen another vehicle since leaving Kintore Store. Nor did we in the coming days except two vehicles that were following each other, pulling small caravans. They just rolled on by us heading east. We had that whole area to ourselves. We were out in the North Gibson Desert. I loved it. I mean I really, really loved it out there. That was living the dream.

I should mention that the weather was very kind to us. It was quite warm in the arvo, reaching the upper thirties, but cooled down beautifully at night to twelve or so. It was really ideal Australian weather. Just the next week my friend Mark Carter went out to the area, and it had gone up over 40. It can get hotter than that out there in the summer and we were only a month away from the first of December, the official beginning of summer.

First thing the next morning we split up into three vehicles. Glen rode with me and Robert hopped in with Bernie. We decided to check out an area Bernie had heard about to the west of the well.

The bore pump at Jupiter Well camping area.

We did, but the habitat proved unimpressive. We decided not to spend too much time there. It was still early-ish, so we headed back to the eastern areas that had more desert oaks and marbled gum trees. These were the areas that I had the most faith in. They were the places specifically mentioned by John and Mark. We passed our camp and rolled along slowly looking and listening as it had been suggested that we do.

We were about 17 kilometres east of our camp when Glen and I saw a small flock of parrots flying on our left. Robert and Bernie had already stopped and jumped out of the ute. As we pulled up behind them, the small flock wheeled and turned flying across the road ahead. Bernie was glowing and had his thumbs up saying, "Princess Parrots!" He and Robert had been closer and had gotten better views than us, but we saw them! We saw Princess Parrots! They were unmistakably long-tailed, elegant and heart stopping. Joy! The little flock of 8 to 10 birds crossed the track in full view, flying south then disappearing over the trees.

David and Bill had been further back, and they rolled up without having seen them. We all headed into the bush hoping they had

Troopi on the Kiwirrkurra Road in the morning light.

Princess Parrots in flight.

landed somewhere close-by. After searching, and searching, and then searching some more, we did not find them. But! On our very first day, at least two-thirds of the expedition had successfully seen these magical parrots. Yes joy, oh yes joy!

Back at camp, Bernie and I used the satellite phone. I called and checked in with Lynn as best as I could, the phone connection was quite poor. But I managed to tell her that we had seen the parrots on our first morning! She even made a little post on social media to that effect, tagging us. Then we had a quiet afternoon as the heat began to build. We searched a bit for lizards and found a few. I am still only learning about reptiles. I saw a few new ones. I also took my first shower under the bore pump. It was a sublime experience.

The next day Bernie suggested that David and Bill take the front spot since they were the only ones who had not seen the parrots. However, we did not see any that morning. Heading back toward camp, we stopped and checked out a large damn where a few of the group decided to sit and watch. Bernie, Glen and I did a bit more driving, continuing to look along the dune line for the parrots. As the early arvo temperatures began to climb, we headed

Enjoying Lifer High during lunch in the Jupiter Well camping area.

back to our shady camp.

I had yet another gloriously refreshing shower under that bore pump. As I worked the handle with one hand, I was pouring water over myself with an old tin can that was there by the pump with the other hand. I will never forget that feeling. It remains the most awesome, unique and memorable shower bathing that I have ever done. The cool, wonderful bore-water gushing out of the pipe with each pull of the handle was the very definition of refreshing. Then I dried-off with my old travel towel. I had used that towel all across Australia during that year of travel that became the first book. Dry and refreshed, I slumped comfortably into a camp chair in the shade. And by the way, I still travel with that towel. It is clean and folded in Troopi as I write these words.

Bernie was grabbing a nap on an air-mattress. He was actually snoring softly. Glen was sitting quietly next to me under the desert oaks when it happened. Twenty-five to 30 Princess Parrots few directly over us at only tree-top height! I shouted, "What the

Centralian Blue-tongue.

Central Netted Dragon.

Troopi parked by the bore pump with my travel towel drying.

f*ck!" (Sadly, that is an exact quote.) At about the same time Glen yelled more appropriately, "Princess Parrots!" It was like watching a formation of miniature pastel bombers passing over us. It was unreal. I will never forget that sight. I could hardly believe my eyes, but of course, believe them I did. Bernie leaped up but he just missed the flock. As I said, they were flying very low, and they were quickly obscured by the treetops. Then only a couple of moments later, another flock of 10 to 15 flew over just as low right behind us. This was around 2:00pm in the heat of the arvo and we had seen two flocks of the parrots flying over the campsite. They were heading south-west.

We ran after them, but evidently they had just kept on flying. Bernie jumped in his ute and took off back to the dam to alert the others. Glen and I continued on foot following in the direction it seemed the parrots had headed. Despite spending a couple of hours walking and doing a lot of searching and a lot of sweating, we did not see them again that day.

At first light the next morning we headed east again. We knew there were parrots around; we just needed for the whole group to see them. About seven kilometres from camp, the lead car with David and Bill stopped. There they were, six Princess Parrots perched! Yes, perched in plain sight on a small, bare tree on the top of the dune line. David took a photo of them there. Oh yes. Joy!

They flew, but they flew down and in just behind the dune line. And soon we found them feeding in a small bush. Everyone took photos and we rejoiced. However, Robert had gone back over to that large dam and was not with us. Bernie tore down there to alert him. Soon he was back with us and again he had excellent views and got photos as well. The great Thunderbird Princess Parrot Expedition was a complete success.

We had done it. We decided that we'd head on back to civilisation. There was a lot of Lifer High flowing through the group as it should. Even though it was already about noon, we started back. The original plan was to camp somewhere on the way to Alice Springs. Then we'd continue on Saturday to the comfortable caravan park there. We headed east. At some point just before Kintore Store, the bull-bar bracket broke (try saying that fast three times) on the

Princess Parrots feeding.

The drawing of my Princess Parrot tattoo on the left and David Adam's photo from which it was traced on the right.

Prado. With some wire and a piece of wood, it was secured well enough to at least stay on the front of the car. They decided to drive straight on to Alice Springs to hopefully have it repaired in the morning. The other three vehicles ended up just pulling over and bush camping by the road sometime after midnight. It had been one very long day indeed.

The next morning we drove about 40 kilometres to Ormiston Gorge and had a look around. It was very beautiful there. It is definitely a place to which I need to return someday and really let it soak in. That morning, I did not truly appreciate it enough. I was still very tired from the drive and after Princess Parrots, everything else was sort of anti-climactic. I did love seeing the Spinifex Pigeons, which I reckon are my favourite pigeon. They were literally running around our feet at the little café kiosk there. But at that point, mostly I was ready to get back to Alice and into a cool comfortable cabin. And I knew I had one waiting for me. We spent a couple of hours at the gorge and then carried on once again to the G'day Mate caravan park in Alice Springs and a much-deserved chill-out.

Summing up, as I said the 2018 Thunderbird Princess Parrot Expedition had been a complete success. The parrots were seen by at least some in the group every day that we were out there and that was beyond anyone's expectations. Bernie O'Keefe did a wonderful job with all of the planning and organising as well as being a true leader in general. With six birders involved, there were stresses and a few dramas on occasion, but he helped the group navigate mostly past any issues that arose. Thank you again my friend. And thank

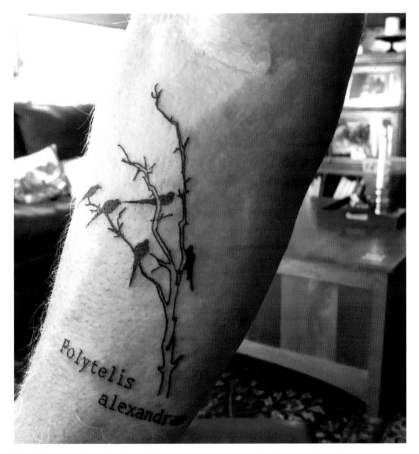

My Princess Parrot tattoo. There were six parrots in the photo but one was obscured and did not work well in the drawing.

you once again, Robert for bringing the trip to my attention and continuing to encourage me to go. As I mentioned, sometimes I need that encouraging push.

After a late arvo chill-out in our cabins that included a nap for me, some of us met Mark Carter for an impromptu celebratory dinner at the pub just around the corner from the caravan park. I think Mark was as almost as excited as we were, if that could be possible. He is a man who is generous with his enthusiasm as well as his knowledge. I do like Mark.

As we were planning the Thunderbird Princess Parrot Expedition, I said that if we were successful, I would get some sort of tattoo to commemorate seeing the parrots. Well we were certainly successful, and I did get the ink.

Using David Adam's photo of the parrots in the dead tree (thank you my friend), I had *Polytelis alexandrae* tattooed on my right arm. The design was exactly what I wanted. It was the second of what would end up being quite a few bird, and birding-related tattoos that Zac at Shinto Gallery in Geelong has inked on me. They are wonderful, permanent reminders celebrating special birds and experiences. I began a Facebook group called 'Birder Ink' where birders can share photos of their tattoos. There are quite a few of us who have them nowadays.

Remembering these experiences to write about them is enlightening for me. The Princess Parrot story was one of the best experiences of my life. I had written 'my birding life', but I should not limit it. It was a wonderful life experience. Full stop. Sure, there were a few dramas and tensions during the trip, but I have honestly forgotten them now. The overwhelming joy of that place, and of those birds, remains clear in my mind above all else. I am so very grateful for that.

{ 15 }

Tasmanian Boobooks in Victoria, Whales and Other Stuff

October–December 2018

Somehow the Tasmanian Boobook, which some call a Morepork, had slipped by me. Earlier in the year, I realised that I did not have it on my list. It had been a subspecies of the Southern Boobook now known as the Australian Boobook, but had been split into its own species and I had not seen one. I had no Tassie trips planned in the immediate future, but I had heard that over the last several years, these owls could be consistently seen at Cape Liptrap Lighthouse in Victoria around mid-October. I talked about it with my buddy, James Cornelious. He had seen them there the year before. Although it was still quite early in October, there had been at least one reliable sighting at the lighthouse on 5 October.

On Sunday 7 October, my friends Murray and Charlie Scott from Brisbane, Queensland were down in Victoria, and James

The Cape Liptrap lighthouse.

and I took them around the WTP. That day of birding ended up including two quite confiding, Orange-bellied Parrots. These previously released birds posed nicely for photos. Murray and Charlie were very pleased, to say the least.

Since James was already down in Lara (he lives in Melbourne), we decided if he stayed the night, we could drive over the next day to Cape Liptrap and see if the owls were around. Team Troopi together again.

It is about a three and a half hours drive to Cape Liptrap. I did not want to drive back late at night, so I decided to book an off-season cabin at Waratah Bay Caravan Park, which is only about 20 minutes from the lighthouse. At least in off-season, I highly recommend this park. The views are wonderful. We had a two-bedroom cabin that was very comfortable as well as being reasonable and having a beautiful view of the sea. I will return sometime.

I had also called my dear old friend, Dave Stabb. He needed the Tasmanian Boobook on his list as well. He only lives about

The view from the deck of the cabin in Waratah Bay.

an hour from the lighthouse and decided to meet us down there at 6pm. I even had time for a short 'granddaddy nap' in the cabin before we left to meet him. This allowed James time to wander off and find lizards, and look at plants and things. James is not only an excellent birder; he is also a genuinely knowledgeable naturalist. I know he often does not have time to look around during our trips as much as he would like. In the future I will try and leave him more time as we travel, and we do have more travels planned, a few of which will be in this book.

On the drive over to the lighthouse a bit before dusk, we had to mind the Wombats crossing the road. We saw several of these delightful creatures, especially in the last ten kilometres of unsealed road. We met Dave at the carpark and walked down the path to the lighthouse. I was surprised at how close it was. It is just a couple of hundred metres of flat, easy, path. Behind the lighthouse there are two picnic tables, one on the left and one on the right. We could sit and wait for the owls. This was looking like it was going to be pretty easy birding.

As we waited for darkness, some 'kids' (late teens, early twenties?

Cloudy at Waratah Bay.

Morepork (Tasmanian Boobook).

I have no clue anymore) arrived carrying stuff including several six-packs of beer. They then set up a small beach-type tent right there on the lighthouse grounds. More came, and then a few more. We were worried that this impending 'party' would be noisy and scare the owls. Even though there eventually was at least a score of them wandering around and hanging out inside that small tent, they were not loud at all. Amazingly, we hardly knew that they were there. I was very pleasantly surprised.

The first owl flew over us just on dusk. We then saw another couple fly by before it was fully dark, including one that I caught in the torch beam giving us decent enough views to tick the bird. Yes! As it became darker, we sat down at the left picnic table (facing the lighthouse) to wait for more. Then as we sat there quietly, a Tasmanian Boobook landed on Dave's head! With absolutely silent flight it landed momentarily on top of his head less than a metre away from James and me. I did not hear or see a thing! I was holding and looking down at my camera. I had tripped and fallen with it earlier (it was not damaged). James was sitting beside Dave and saw the owl land and then take off again. Dave felt it touch lightly on his hat, but that was all. I mean seriously, a wild owl had perched for a moment on his head! Dave, that was so cool.

After sitting a bit longer at the left table, facing the lighthouse, we decided to move to the table on the right side. It seemed the owls were coming in from the left. It was now fully dark. Every so often I'd wander away from the table and shine my torch on the red setting, down along the fence posts and into the trees and brush. On the third or fourth of these wanders there it was, eye shine! Two eyes were peering back at me from a low branch in a stubby tree just off the track. I alerted Dave and James and soon we were looking at a Tasmanian Boobook perching at eye-level. We took a few photos and marvelled at the lovely little owl. Then we let it be.

James and I drove slowly back, losing count of Wombats along the way (nine or ten I think it was) and we were in our comfy cabin by quarter past ten. That is my kind of nocturnal birding. I was happily up at dawn the next morning and after coffeeing and messing about for a bit, we drove on back to Lara. A Lifer Day would be forthcoming.

Moving House Again? Seriously?
Talk about a journey, this next change began just before I landed in hospital for a short stay (not important, I am fine). Out of the blue, there was a woman very interested in buying our tiny house. One-bedroom houses like that are no longer built here in the village. There was a lady who really, really wanted one. No, I never did know why. At the same time, an older two-bedroom house just caddy-corner across the street from ours was up for sale.

This lady had a look at our house while I was in hospital and loved it. She offered top dollar. That made it financially feasible for us to buy the older and under-priced, two-bedroom house. But she needed it to be done quickly. We were moving again, and soon.

But first, Whales! I had already committed to a pelagic trip out of Port Fairy, Victoria with my buddy James for 16 December. It is a trip I am familiar with (that lovely word again, 'familiar').

The head of a Sperm Whale.

The flukes of a Sperm Whale.

I have done it several times. I will not always recount them here unless there was something new and unexpected to report. On this trip we had wonderful, and fairly close views of Sperm Whales. That was truly thrilling to me. The massive square head and long grey back was showing well above the swell. I took photos and etched the memory into my brain and onto my heart as well. It was a wonderful experience. Sperm Whales are the largest of the toothed whales. They are the type of whale that Moby Dick was (although these were the normal grey colour and not white). I will always be in awe of cetaceans. The best of the little boy still within me rejoices in the very idea of these benevolent behemoths. I do love whales.

Now back to the move.

We had moved house six times in eight years. That is far too damn many times, but this was an opportunity that we truly could not afford to pass up and it was the closest move I have ever done. In each of our past moves, we had a removal company handle it all

Moving house again.

from start to finish. This time we only hired professional help to move the largest and heaviest items. So we did not have a proper pack-up by professionals like we have always had in the past. We were only moving about 50 metres away. So on the 19th and the 20th we carried our stuff across the street. The closing was on the 21st. And we got it done. We owe huge thanks to dear friends Gary Gale and Carolyn Edwards for their invaluable help with this move. I reckon they worked harder, and certainly smarter, than I did. They were our only other helpers.

This new house is still a tiny house, but the small extra bedroom makes a massive difference. Sadly, I actually could have brought my old roll-top desk, but I did not think this would ever be a possibility. It is what it is, and I have become very comfortable working at this little desk.

In the 'keeping it real' category, and that is the only category in which I can, and will, write, regardless of the new house and all, my depression during this period continued to be pretty bad. I was also sometimes having several migraines a week. From my neck up, things were not so exactly great.

I continued (and continue to this day) to live with what I have learned are migraines. The medical world knows very little about what causes them or how to treat them. Botox injections were discovered by accident as people were getting them for cosmetic reasons and it was found that they helped with migraines. I get them regularly and they seem to help for me.

Gratefully, for the most part my migraines are not incapacitating. I get what are called vestibular migraines. They can be quite uncomfortable and inconvenient, but I am still able to function for the most part. I do not end up with the excruciating headaches that some migraine sufferers do.

Now leaping forward in time. I am sitting here at the little desk in December 2021. I am working on the last rewrite of this book. I wrote the following on social media recently and want to include it here.

We Are All Philosophers

I am a huge fan of the books of Patrick O'Brian. I have mentioned his character, Stephen Maturin, in my writing as influencing my becoming a birder. Maturin was a naturalist in general, but particularly interested in ornithology. In O'Brian's books, he is often referred to as a 'natural philosopher'.

I very much enjoy some of that old 19th-century phrasing and choose to use a touch of it here and there in my own writing. When I was setting up my Facebook page many years ago, I liked that phrase and in my 'About' section, I said that I was a natural philosopher. Of course, I merely meant that I was very interested in nature. Never in life did I mean that I considered myself to be a proper philosopher. Yet it seems that some people who read that on Facebook took it to mean just that. I found it a little embarrassing actually.

In writing this second book, I wanted to be clear that I am not a philosopher. However, in reflecting on my writing, I found that I certainly do wax a bit philosophical at times. And I began to realise that to some degree, we are all philosophers. We all have our own thoughts on what, and how, we need to live. Yes indeed, we are all philosophers.

A Philosophy of My Own: HPPD

I would like to share some of my own philosophy regarding money. I will start by saying that I do not like money. I loathe the fascination with, the need for and the desire for money (greed) in general. I also know that I cannot live without it. Money holds the keys to escape. Money unlocks the shackles and chains of poverty. Enough money equals freedom as well as security. What is 'enough' is the tricky part. So, I do know that I need it and I do not despise the money itself.

As I have written many times, I am ADHD. I even wrote and recorded a song, 'ADD Cowboy'. Google it and have a listen on YouTube. I am also dyslexic and generally useless with numbers and lists. And a list of numbers might as well be in Sanskrit. I cannot, nor will I ever even attempt to create, much less follow, a budget. My life is what it is and regarding money, I will live in the only way that I can. It is overly simple. If I have the money, I can afford it. If I don't, I can't. If I run out of money completely, I will be broke. Amazingly somehow, throughout my life, the money has managed to come from somewhere. I have lived nearly hand to mouth, gig to gig, royalty check to royalty check, for almost all of my life and I have always survived, for that I am very grateful and very fortunate.

I do not spend money frivolously. That is a bit ridiculous to say because I don't suppose anyone feels that they spend their money frivolously. They spend it on what they consider to be important. This is an example of all of us being philosophers. I do have a very specific money philosophy that I call, HPPD. It stands for: Hours of Pleasure Per Dollar.

I judge any large expense in HPPD. A perfect birding example is my Swarovski EL 10x42 binoculars. I bought them re-conditioned, and fully warranted, in 2009 and they were still very expensive. However, as I write these words, I have had 12 years of birding pleasure with those excellent binoculars. By now, their cost is down to mere pennies or less per hour. It is the same for my digital camera and for my Troopi. Also, into this pile, I will add this machine on which I am writing. Yes, I know what I said about new things but I could not be the writer that I am without a computer. So, I will say that I do appreciate, need and use this 'new thing' for hours on end. I wrote a few magazine articles (remember those paper things?) over 30 years ago on an electric typewriter. White-out was a constant companion.

Bumpy Ain't In It!

As I mentioned, I love the books of Patrick O'Brian and his 19th-century phrasing occasionally does creep into my own writing. Regarding someone being very busy he might say, "Bees ain't in it." Meaning that in a contest of which was busier, although bees might be known for it, whoever he was referring to was even busier. In such a contest, the bees would not even be in the race.

I have occasionally said that a week or a day had been 'bumpy', meaning that my life had not exactly been 'spinning in greased grooves'. Now I have quoted O'Brian and Steinbeck in the same chapter. You might think I'm very well read but I am not. I love books and I do appreciate words deeply, but I am not really particularly well read. My ADHD and tendency to dyslexia can make reading a chore. Long paragraphs are difficult for me. It is why I write my books in short paragraphs. I will break what should really be one long paragraph into two or three, just to keep them shorter and easier to read.

So, no. Life does not always spin in greased grooves for me. It has been particularly bumpy for the several years that are covered in this book. I have in the past, greased those grooves myself with alcohol and other substances. I will not say that doesn't work, but I will state from personal experience that it is not sustainable.

Therefore I will continue to do what I can, as I can, while I can. Doing my best to be who I want myself to be, whether I feel like it or not. It is what I do. And then I write about it. Thank you to the birds and the glorious continent of Australia for feeding this passion that greases my grooves.

Now back to those travels and the birds.

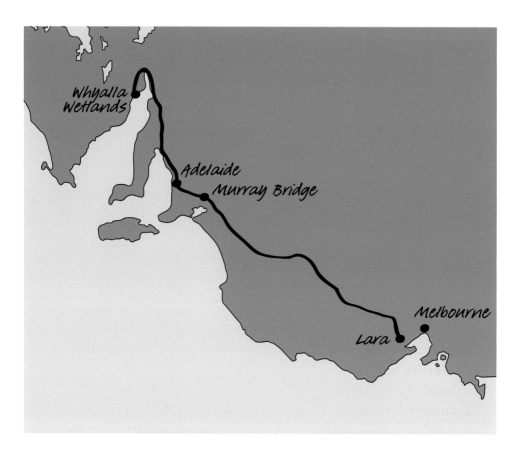

Tuffy with the larger Australian Shelducks.

{ 16 }

Two Twitches

December 2018–January 2019

Citrine Wagtail Twitch, Whyalla Wetlands, South Australia
We were just past the Christmas holidays, and we had just moved house. I was buried in sorting all kinds of things as you might imagine. I had no plans, nor time, to go heading off anywhere. And then Robert Shore (of course Robert) called and informed me that a Citrine Wagtail had turned up in Whyalla, South Australia. I told him that I was not chasing birds right now. I said that trying to get settled into this house must be my priority. So we chatted a bit. I really wasn't going to go for it. I couldn't. It was about 2,200 kilometres round trip, or about 28 'Troopi hours' as I refer to our travel times. As I have said, it takes us longer than the Google map estimates. Long story short, I couldn't do it. No way.

As I am sure you already know by the chapter title, I did do it. But I knew I could only do it if I dashed over and then back to my responsibilities as quickly as possible. My buddy James Cornelious had also called about the bird. He said that he could be in Lara by 9am the next morning. If we left then, we could get to Murray Bridge, South Australia by early evening and then be in Whyalla Wetlands the next morning. It would be a dash. It would be a real twitch, but the bird was kind of a big deal. It is my understanding that the species had only been seen in Australia four times previously: Botany Bay, NSW, on 1 July 1962, Goolwa, SA, on 28 May 1987, on Christmas Island, on 5 May 2009, and Mudgee, NSW, on 24 August 2014.

James arrived on time Friday morning, and we left immediately for the west. We arrived in Murray Bridge early that evening. The really cool cabin that we had stayed in before was booked. So I had checked on another caravan park. I booked an excellent, and more reasonable cabin there. On a twitch, I am on a mission, and when I can, I will opt for comfort and ease. That often means a cabin or motel room if possible. It allows me a simple early-in and early-out. As much as I love my Troopi, she is still not as comfortable, nor as quick and easy as a motel room. I ate a sandwich then checked on social media regarding the bird. It was still being seen. We went to sleep early.

The next morning I was up at 3:30am and we were rolling by 5am. As we had gotten further along, I had spoken with my South Australian friend Eddy Smith. He had seen the bird Friday evening and again early that morning. He said that he would meet us at the park. Cool.

We arrived at the Whyalla Wetlands at 10:05am. The most difficult part of the drive was that last bit. We were hearing that this vagrant rarity was being seen right at that moment. And yet we still had about two hours of travel left, a long two hours of FOMO (fear of missing out). I pushed Troopi up to 100 kph, the actual posted speed limit! She is fine with that, but it does make her quite thirsty.

We finally arrived and Eddy met us in the nice carpark of the well-tended wetland park. We wasted no time in following him over to the north pond where people had been seeing the bird. It was either James or Eddy, I do not recall which, who quickly spotted the wagtail on a little island just in front of us. We had only been there two or three minutes and we were looking at the bird. Sweet. We marvelled. We took photos. We rejoiced. We met other birders. We showed them the Citrine Wagtail. It was a busy little

Citrine Wagtail twitch success!

bird, moving around that pond a lot. We watched it some more. Lifer High reigned as it would. Yes, the dopamine of the Lifer is most intense on a twitch. That's the birding brain chemistry magic.

I got this by Googling 'dopamine':

'The brain includes several distinct dopamine pathways, one of which plays a major role in the motivational component of reward-motivated behaviour.'

Yes, birding is 'the pursuit of that which is elusive, yet attainable, a perpetual series of occasions for hope'. I have those words tattooed on my right arm beside a compass rose. Our hopes had been realised. I absolutely love me some reward-motivated behaviour! Yeah, I am pretty much a big dog that talks. Give me a treat and pat me on the head and I will gratefully follow you anywhere. And it doesn't hurt to tell me I'm a 'good boy' too.

Every birder has their own conception and appreciation of birding. Mine is complex and it is certainly not only about adding the damn tick, that is merely a milestone, a marker. As I have said, it is the carrot on the end of a stick that gives me a direction in which to go. It leads me to new places, new experiences, new people and of course, new birds and they do go on my list.

We left Whyalla before noon and were back in Murray Bridge by about 6pm. I recommend the Golden Chain Murray Bridge Oval Motel (it does have an overly long name though). We had an excellent night's sleep, and I was back in Lara the next afternoon. We had done it all in less than 3 days. Team Troopi, James and I had once again been successful! Yay us, we did it!

Tuffy: An Australian First

Of course, all twitches are memorable, but this one was particularly so. Not only was the Tufted Duck a first for Australia (never seen in Australia or any of its territories ever before), it was only ten minutes from my house! We had lived in Lara for two years, just across the road from the world-famous birding area of the Western Treatment Plant. But there had not been a rarity over there during that time.

I had only recently returned from twitching the Citrine Wagtail in Whyalla, South Australia. After taking a lovely and well-earned Lifer Day on New Year's Eve, I was back to doing house things. I now had a study! A room where I could hang not only my very large, laminated maps, but also my three-foot by six-foot, framed, *Lord of the Rings* mural by Barbara Remington. It was the cover art for the Ballentine Books paperback version of the trilogy in the 1960s. Which is when I first read and fell in love with it. It means a lot to me, and I have never had a place where I could hang it in Australia. As I write these words in 2021, I can glance up from my little desk, and there it is in all its overly colourful glory. I am so glad to have a place for it. It is a part of me. My study is like a little museum of my life, and I love it. These things hold the magic of their past, of my past. The memories live in them as they do in my words. I can touch them, gaze at them, contemplate and remember them.

On Thursday 3 January 2019, I was experiencing the beginnings of a migraine. I had eaten lunch, taken some ibuprofen and was lying down. Then my phone rang. It was James. There are very few people from whom I would take a call when I am lying down with a migraine, my buddy James is one of them.

He said, "I'm at the WTP. Have you heard yet?" I felt a flood of good adrenaline go through me. I knew something must have shown up across the street.

I think I said, "No. I'm just lying down. What's up?"

"There's a Tufted Duck in the T-Section. I am here with Chris Farrell at the pond before the Crake Pond." All I said was, "I'll be there in ten minutes." And I was too.

Therefore, I barely had time for twitcher-anxiety FOMO to build before I was there. I drove straight to the T-Section and over to the pond. In about a minute, I was looking through my scope at the duck. Sweet as. At that point only a small handful of birders had arrived. Soon the birding world would descend upon the T-Section of the Western Treatment Plant. As the afternoon progressed, Rohan Clarke, Alison Nesbit, Tim Bawden, Sue Taylor and many, many others showed up. This was a first, so it was a Lifer for every Australian birder that keeps a bird list. It was glorious fun unfolding

The first Tufted Duck seen in Australia.

across the street. By the way my migraine had disappeared.

I will not attempt to list everyone I saw there that arvo because I am crap with names and I would miss a lot of people. But it was joyful! It was wondrous! The shared happiness emanating from the WTP could probably be seen from space.

Here were more than 50 birders who were all experiencing various states of Lifer High together. It was like being at a large New Year's Eve party with friends that you know well but rarely see. People were smiling, laughing, joking, giggling, hugging, fist-bumping, high-fiving, shaking hands and patting one another on the back. It was the best of what the birding community is about. Sharing. This was shared bird joy. This was shared Lifer High.

There were many of the rock-stars of the birding world. I had the extremely rare opportunity to point to a new Western Treatment Plant bird for my friend Maarten Hulzebosch (he would have seen it on his own of course, but I did get to point to it for him as soon as he arrived). At the time, that put his WTP list up to 233 species. The man is a legend. Dez Hughes, another legend and my dear friend who I refer to as the 'Wader Whisperer', rocked up to see the

Birders' vehicles in the T-section.

Kevin Bartram, Sean Dooley and Mike Carter three legends of Australian birding all looking at a Lifer.

duck. And it was truly amazing that I got to witness Mike Carter, Sean Dooley and Kevin Bartam all getting a Lifer at the same time! These three true Australian birding legends were standing in a row, all looking at the same Life Bird! How wonderful is that?

I heard the phrase, "a bloody first!", multiple times. And to give credit where I think credit is due, it seems that the duck was originally spotted by Michael Dougherty (I believe he was a visiting American no less) and reported to the Facebook Twitchers page by David Parker. Thank you both so very much indeed!

The next day was a Friday and the WTP was closed because there was a Total Fire Ban in the region. It was 44 °C in Lara (111 °F). Therefore we all knew it would end up being a bit crazy over there on Saturday. Robert (who you should know well by now) was driving down from Parkes, New South Wales, and my old buddy Dave Stabb was coming over from his place south-east of Melbourne. Also my friend Eddy Smith was flying in from South

Australia. Our visiting Tufted Duck was definitely an Australian birding celebrity.

Meanwhile, my good friend Karen Weil was in south-east Queensland seeing another visiting rarity, a Buff-breasted Sandpiper. That bird was being referred to as 'Buffy'. She said that when she returned to Melbourne, she hoped to go and see 'Tuffy', which turned out to be the perfect nickname for the Tufted Duck and it stuck. Birders from across the country now called our duck Tuffy. Thank you, Karen.

Over the coming days, I took much joy in looking at Tuffy and sharing him with others. I had seen him enough that I could usually spot him quickly amongst the other ducks (mostly Australian Shelducks, a few Hardheads and Eurasian Coots). Most days, I found him near where he had originally been spotted, in the T-section on pond one or pond two. I wish I had kept track of the number of birders of all ages who looked through my scope for their 'Lifer look' at this wonderful little duck. I saw fresh Lifer High on a lot of faces.

At least on all of my visits the other birders were respecting

Tuffy, the Tufted Duck.

Just some of the people who looked at Tuffy through my scope and yes the little one got a look as well.

The author in the T-section. (At least during this time, the 'T' stood for Tuffy.)

The John Buchan quote and compass tattooed on my arm.

Tuffy's space. I understand one person did try and creep too close
to get that better photo and flushed him, but I had not been
there when that had happened. I am grateful that so many birders
seemingly respected our rare visitor, as well as respecting the other
birders, many of whom were travelling very long distances to see
Tuffy. I watched so many giant lenses pointed at him, and photographers were able to get excellent, although often necessarily
distant shots.

    After the initial sighting and that wonderful, festival-like atmos-
phere on the first day that he was seen, as I said, my continuing
fun came from showing him to others. For me, the joys of birding
are: 1 Seeing the bird myself; 2 Sharing the bird with others;
3 Writing about the bird (which is basically sharing the bird from
my desk in my jammie pants).

    That is one of the genuine joys of birding and life, sharing.

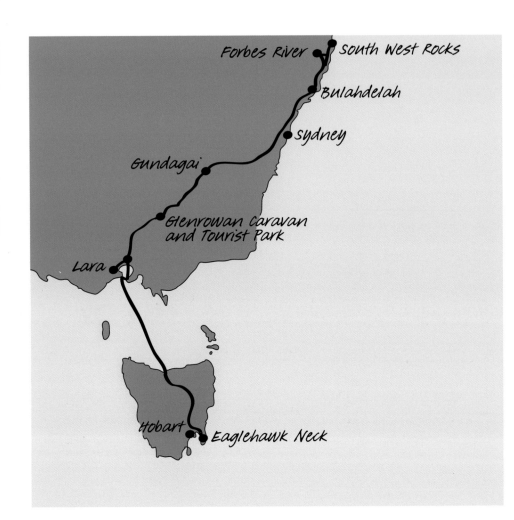

{ 17 }

Pelagics and a Rainforest Skulker

January - March 2019

Robert Shore and I had spots on Rohan Clarke's January pelagic weekend in Eaglehawk Neck, Tasmania. My old friend and I boarded the *Spirit of Tasmania* ferry on Thursday evening for an overnight voyage back to the Land Down Under the Land Down Under. We would be driving straight down to Eaglehawk Neck to our room at the Lufra Hotel for the next few nights. Staying at the hotel, we would not need Troopi's camping abilities, so we took my old Prius. The fuel savings are pretty amazing.

Once again, I was blessed with good weather for a crossing. There is something deeply wonderful about drifting off to dreamland knowing that you are crossing the Bass Strait with the gentle roll of the sea to rock you to sleep.

We arrived in Devonport quite early. The ferry was doing a quick turn-around to return to Melbourne and vehicles began disembarking at 5:30am. For various reasons, I had been awake since 2am. I was seriously sleep deprived. We had an easy and uneventful drive down to Eaglehawk Neck and were able to check in early to our room. I got a nap and I needed it. The next morning we met our friends and other birders at the boat and chugged out to our

177

Sunrise from the parking area on the jetty in Eaglehawk Neck.

first day of birding.

As I mentioned earlier, I am not a brilliant pelagic birder. I try to position myself near an expert (there are always several) and when someone calls a bird and points to it, I can usually get a look at that bird. That's me on a pelagic. I have come to like pelagics more and more over the years. I am always awed by the massive, majestic grace of a Wandering Albatross, or the delicate dance of lovely little storm-petrels as they seem to walk on water by the boat, or the sweet prions darting to and fro just above the waves. Yes, there are certainly some beautiful birds out there and you truly never know what could show up.

When Rohan Clarke called the first Common Diving-petrel, I was close by him, and I was instantly looking at the distant small bird to which he pointed. Yes, I saw it. Not well, but I saw that bird. A half an hour or so later, Rohan called it again and this Common Diving-petrel flew right beside the boat in clear view for us all. Robert even got a few quick 'recording' shots. My camera was in the cabin most of the weekend. My sense of balance (migraine-related it seems) is not what it used to be and jostling for photo position can be difficult. I just wanted to be sure I saw with my eyes the bird that has been identified. Photos are not necessary, although I do like getting one when I can.

The Common Diving-petrel had been my pelagic Bogey Bird. I had repeatedly missed it although I had certainly tried my best. They are often seen on the way out and on the way back in, so I would continue scanning (and scanning, and scanning, and scanning) the sea as most everyone else was hunkered in, particularly on the ride back in. Yes indeed, I was extremely happy to get definitive looks at this small petrel that I have referred to as the 'Button-quail of the Sea', not only because it was a bogey for me, but also because they behave rather like an aquatic Button-quail. They seemingly flush out of nowhere and then disappear quickly when they dive.

My second Lifer of the weekend was Cook's Petrel. It was seen twice, giving us all good views as it flew along the slick and then down the side of the boat. Yay! There would be well-earned Lifer Pie at the little café just up the road from the dock. I enjoyed that small café, and I would eat an early dinner there after the trips. It made my dinnertime about 4pm and I am fine with that. Over the years, my issues with acid-reflux have grown to require an early, and not overly large, dinner. Ideally, I like to have tea, as some call dinner in Australia, between five and six, closer to five if at all possible.

Sadly, that little café has now closed. When I first heard about this, I actually looked online and I called their number. It was no longer connected. It had the most amazing views of Eaglehawk Neck. Their burgers were excellent and their chips were pure gold-en-deliciousness. Sometimes there is a food-trailer in the carpark just above the boat docks that has chips and other food. Eaglehawk Neck is a very small place without a lot of options. The motel does have a restaurant, but they do not even begin taking orders until 6pm. That is too often the case, particularly with pubs in small towns. It is one of the reasons that I regularly arrange to make my

Buller's Shearwater off Eaglehawk Neck (photo by Robert Shore).

own sandwiches when I travel. I can take care of feeding myself within my time frames and I do. I also save a lot of cash since restaurant meals can eat up a lot of money when travelling (no, that was not intended to be a pun, but I'll take it).

The second day began with slightly less bumpy seas, and I brought my camera out for some of it. I took a few photos, but when my third Lifer of the weekend, the Buller's Shearwater, came by I continued looking at it rather than trying to get a photo. The wind blew up on the way in and I was grateful that I no longer had to search the sea for diving-petrels as we bumped and rolled our way back to port. As with so many Bogey Birds, after I had finally seen one, I would see plenty more (although not that weekend). Robert and I stayed for another day at the Lufra Hotel in that comfortable room that I mentioned earlier. We went out that evening in hopes of finding a Tasmanian Boobook (Morepork) for Robert. However, smoke from the small bush fire earlier that day had settled over the area. It was not pleasant. I did see and photograph a lovely pair of Tawny Frogmouths before calling it a night.

On our way back up to the ferry, we stopped for lunch at an interesting restaurant with decor based on the illustrious life and career of Errol Flynn. It was an Errol Flynn museum in a restaurant. Flynn was from Tasmania and is, arguably, its most famous son. I learned a few things about him and saw tons of photos and memorabilia. Errol Flynn was only 50 when he died of a heart attack at a friend's house in Canada. He had lived a notoriously self-indulgent life. My understanding is that Keith Richards (or Keith Moon for that matter) had nothing on Flynn. I have not read his autobiography, but the title, *My Wicked, Wicked Ways,* says a lot in itself.

The ferry trip back to Victoria was gratefully once again on mostly calm seas. I arrived safe and sound, and this time after a decent night's sleep, back in Victoria.

Two Tawny Frogmouths in Eaglehawk Neck.

The Errol Flynn restaurant/museum.

Turquoise Parrot at Glenrowan.

Gang-gang Cockatoo at Glenrowan.

Another Pelagic and the Rainforest

It had been a while since I had climbed into Troopi and headed off alone. I was scheduled to go on a pelagic in New South Wales. I decided to make it a fairly easy drive. So I left on Tuesday arvo, 19 March, and drove to Glenrowan, Victoria. I love that little caravan park and I always see Turquoise Parrots there, as I did this time. I reckon I saw at least 25 in the front paddock. I had fun taking some photos of those stunningly beautiful birds.

The next morning as I was coffeeing, I heard the unmistakable calls of Gang-gang Cockatoos and sure enough there were two in a tree right beside Troopi. I got the camera out again and grabbed a few photos. They are such cool birds. After enjoying the Gang-gangs, I packed up and headed north. I spent one more night on the way at an unmemorable caravan park in Bargo. It was okay as a stopover. The next afternoon I rolled into South West Rocks, New South Wales, and checked into a nice little studio cabin. About 9:30pm, I carefully applied my Scopolamine patch behind my ear and not long after that I was asleep.

Tahiti Petrel off South West Rocks, New South Wales.

The next morning I awoke at 4:30am feeling crap as I do when I wear the patch, but as I have said, they prevent seasickness for me. Feeling crap is worth it. I was at the boat by 6:30am and we were underway at 7am. My friend, Liam Murphy had organised this pelagic. I had first met him at 'his' Aleutian Terns in December 2017 when those terns were very new. As I wrote about in chapter 9, I had dashed straight up there to see them.

The wind was light, as we motored out to the deep waters beyond the shelf and by 9:30 we were drifting and berleying (chumming). Soon we had Providence Petrels and a few other of the usual suspects. I was mostly watching for a white-bellied beauty, and soon it appeared. Tahiti Petrel! Distant at first but then it came in and hung around for an hour or more. Everyone on the boat got cracking views. It is a stunning and easily recognised pelagic bird. I took some photos. Oh, that sweet Lifer High.

The birding slacked off and we headed back a little early. I was knackered. I was more tired than I felt like I should be. I was really beginning to get out of shape. The frequent migraines, my battles with the twins, using food for comfort, and being far too sedentary in general was beginning to take its toll. Anyway, I was tired. I went back to my cabin, showered and had a quiet early evening. I would be meeting Liam in Beechwood, New South Wales at 7am and that meant I needed to leave South West Rocks at 5:30am to be sure I was on time. True to form for me, I was up at 3:30am and on my way before 5:30. I was excited. I was going for that infamous, loud yet invisible, Rufous Scrub-bird. And I was going with someone who had actually seen it.

A few times a year, Liam goes up into the rainforest of Werrikimbe National Park, which is about two hours inland from where he lives in Port Macquarie and has a look for Rufous Scrub-birds. He had given Robert and me the gen on where to look when we went there in October 2017. We heard them ridiculously well in a few spots but did not see them. That is usual for these exceptionally elusive, skulking birds. Liam has only seen them a few times out of more than a dozen attempts.

We rumbled up the rough logging track through the majestic

Brushy Mountain Campground shelter. It has a fireplace.

towering trees of the rainforest, eventually arriving at the beautiful
Brushy Mountain Campground. Robert and I had stayed a night
there on a 2017 visit. It truly is a lovely spot. I was prepared to stay
over if we did not have success that day, although Liam needed to
return to Port Macquarie. We parked behind the charming, and
cool, old picnic shelter with its heavy wooden tables and stone
hearth. Then we hiked up the Loop Walk.

The path slopes up gently, but in my state of non-fitness I was
out of breath in minutes. About five or six hundred metres along,
Liam heard the bird. I heard it too, but I did not know what I
was hearing. He said that the bird was imitating a loud version of
an Eastern Yellow Robin. The bird then did a few more odd calls
before it settled into its own call. It was not far from us, but not
exactly close either. Liam suggested we just stand there on the
track where we had a bit of a view in through the tangles of brush
and trees. There were a few logs lying amongst the various kinds of
thick flora that covers the rainforest floor. There were also leeches.
I flicked a large one off my calf and applied some of Liam's bug
spray. We stood listening and watching. It sounded further off. Then
a few minutes later it sounded closer again. We decided to move
in from the path just a little. We only went four or five metres in,
but it gave us a more elevated view into the area from which we
reckoned the bird was calling. And we stood there, quietly listening
and peering intensely into the underbrush.

After ten or fifteen minutes of this Liam whispered, "On the
log at the base of the tree." Bear in mind that in that area there
were several 'logs at the base of trees' but fortunately we were both
looking in the same spot at the same time. Before Liam had finished the sentence I had a Rufous Scrub-bird in sharp focus in my
bins. Amazing, heart-filling Joy! The bird looked left, and turned
as if to jump off the log, but stopped, turned to the right, stood
for a second, turned back to the left and then disappeared off the
log into the brush. We had had approximately four, full glorious
seconds viewing the bird (one-one-thousand, two-one-thousand,

three-one-thousand, four-one-thousand). Liam said that it was the best look he had ever gotten. We high-fived, fist-bumped and then hugged. Glory. It will remain amongst my top birding moments. I had beheld the endangered, elusive, skulking, seemingly invisible Rufous Scrub-bird. I now have a tattoo of it just above my right wrist, *Atrichornis rufescens*, and a simple drawing that was traced (with permission) from a photo by my dear friend, and brilliant professional photographer, David Stowe.

As we stepped back down onto the trail, Liam said something that I too have often said after getting good views of a target bird. He said, "That bird owes me nothing more". Amen. We let it be. We walked joyously back to the campground. We sat around the shelter, and I even picked up a Lifer mammal in a cute, busy little Brown Antechinus running about. Eventually we left and drove back down to Beechwood to the café there for some sort of Lifer Pie treat. I do not remember what I had; I just know I was very happy. After some visiting and more rejoicing, Liam went

The art in my room at the Mount View Motel.

home and I drove on to stay the night in a very cool little motel in Bulahdelah, NSW. It's called the Mount View Motel. I highly recommend it and I did return later in this book. It was inexpensive, clean, comfortable and it had large Hieronymus Bosch pictures on the walls! In my room was the Garden of Earthly Delights. I have always found Bosch's work beautifully weird and brilliant. I slept well there. Then the next night I stayed in Gundagai before driving on to Lara on Monday. I had been gone seven days and I had added two Life Birds. There would be a good couple of Lifer Days coming soonish. Joy indeed.

{ 18 }

Some Very Local Birding: the WTP

April 2019

As I was going through the photos for this book, I realised that I had seen some very wonderful birds at the Western Treatment Plant that had not been included in this book. In particular I saw quite a few birds over there in April 2019. The proximity of the WTP to where I live is certainly one of the best things about the location of this house. I am literally less than ten minutes from entering the WTP.

It was May 2009 when I first visited the WTP with my step-daughter and son-in-law. That was the month and year that I began to officially keep a bird list. I loved it and I still do. The WTP was closed to birders for most of 2020 and 2021 due to the pandemic and I got out of the habit of going over and just having a look around. I need to start doing that again.

I do not remember many of the details of these little birding sojourns to my natal birding grounds. During this time I was driving over, parking, then doing some walking, mostly to try and get at least a little exercise. I did that daily for a while. I also carried my bins and my camera. I have the date from my photos and that gives me a point of reference for when I saw what.

Black Swan on a nest.

In early April I also began making the occasional drive over at night to look for Barn Owls on the fence posts along the roads around the treatment plant. And I saw some owls over those weeks, usually two or even three in a couple of hours driving slowly along with Troopi's high-beams illuminating the roadsides. I have called Barn Owls 'magic on a fence post' because that is what they look like. I suppose that is why owls were featured in the Harry Potter books and films. I would also occasionally see a Tawny Frogmouth on a post. Beautiful and cool, but magic? Not so much. Although they are always a cool bird to see.

On 14 April, I had gone into the area of the WTP called the T-Section and I saw two birders photographing something. It was a Black Falcon perched on a rock on the far side of one of the ponds. The raptor flushed and was joined by a second falcon. They flew around the pond then over to the fence along the track a hundred metres or so to our left. The two guys decided to try and get closer to the birds for better photos. I had seen the falcons well and did not feel the need to chase after them to get a better shot. So I just stayed there by the pond checking out waders and

In the restricted area of the Western Treatment Plant.

Barn Owl magic on a fence post.

Tawny Frogmouth on a post by the road.

A pair of Black Falcons.

things but soon, the Black Falcons came flying by right in front of where I was standing. The photographers had scared the birds back toward me. I was able to get a few shots of this beautiful pair.

Also in the T-Section is a little spot called the Crake Pond. It is a small area of reeds at the end of a large pond that often has Australian Spotted, Baillon's and Spotless Crakes wandering about. Hence the name, Crake Pond. Of those three, usually for me anyway, the least often seen is the Spotless. But during this month, it seems that I only photographed Spotless. I am sure I must have seen the others as well, but they are not in my photos.

On 18 April, I had gone to have a look for the Lewin's Rail that was being seen with some regularity by the Little River crossing just past Gate Eight. A Lewin's Rail being seen with any regularity is pretty unusual. They are much more often heard than seen. I was successful and using the vehicle as a hide, I was able to take a few photos. My friend Scott Baker was also there looking at the rails. He had heard that there were some Swift Parrots being seen

Spotless Crake in Crake Pond in the T-section.

Lewin's Rail.

on Point Wilson Road and went over to have a look. I stayed by the Lewin's Rails (it turned out that there were two at the spot). Not long after he left, my phone rang. It was Scott. He had found a small flock of the critically endangered Swift Parrots about five minutes away.

I drove out of the WTP and turned onto Point Wilson Road and in less than a couple of kilometres I had parked behind Scott's vehicle on the shoulder of the road. I saw him moving around under the trees and looking up. Soon I was in there and looking with him. We were looking at the parrots. Swift Parrots are beautiful birds that migrate from Tasmania to spend the autumn and winter on the south-east mainland. I was able to get a few photos. That flock stayed in that area for a few days, and I saw them on at least one more occasion.

Driving toward the WTP on Beach Road, just past the little Avalon Airport, there are three large paddocks on the left. In the centre paddock, with a bit of looking, I would often see beautiful Banded Lapwings. These are very cool birds that look as if they are wearing goggles. They were usually a bit far from the road making photographs difficult (with my lens anyway). But I have included one of my better shots here.

Toward the end of April while looking around the Western Lagoons just across the street from the T-Section, I began occasionally seeing Orange-bellied Parrots. Over the coming weeks and months I would see more of these extremely rare, critically endangered parrots. Similarly to the Swift Parrots, OBPs (as they are commonly called) also migrate from Tasmania to spend the autumn and winter on the mainland, but they are even more rare. Only a few years ago, there were thought to be fewer than 50 individuals left in the wild. Yes, less than 50 and in 2012 I had seen three of those at the WTP. That was a huge, early birding moment for me.

There is a breeding and release programme at the WTP now and the OBPs are banded here as well as in Melaleuca, Tasmania, where there is a feeding station and viewing hide. Some of the birds that I saw during this month were recent releases but at least one whose bands were 'Silver Silver C' had made the trip up from Tasmania that year. To think of these precious, little parrots,

Banded Lapwings in their paddock.

Beautiful, critically endangered Orange-bellied Parrots.

Brown Quail in the T-section.

Peregrine Falcon flying over the Western Lagoons.

Brolga in the Western Lagoons.

Brown Thornbill.

Zebra Finch on a wire.

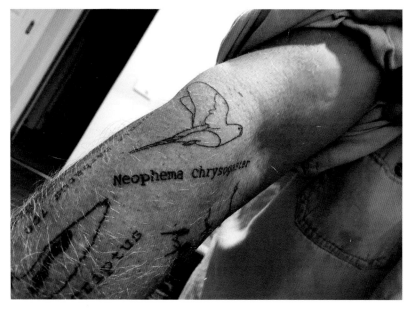

My Orange-bellied Parrot tattoo.

barely larger than a sparrow, crossing the Bass Strait from the west coast of Tassie fills me with wonder and appreciation. I love those parrots and I have a tattoo of one on my right arm. It was traced from my own photo of one of the three OBPs in 2012 with its scientific name, *Neophema chrysogaster* under it. All of my tattoos are monochromatic but I had my tattoo guy add just a touch of orange on its belly.

I've included a few more photos of birds from April 2019 in my neighbourhood at the Western Treatment Plant.

Sunrise heading out into the Tasman Sea.

{ 19 }

More Pelagic Joy Back Down Under the Land Down Under Again

June 2019

Great Shearwater and Southern Fulmar Joy

It had been an odd few weeks in my body (where I spend the majority of my time). I was having a chest cold and dealing with migraines. I went on a Port Fairy trip on 19 May. It was a lovely time out at sea but produced nothing unusual about which to write and no Lifers.

Then Richard Webber, a birder acquaintance on social media, put together a Saturday and Sunday double-header out of Eagle-hawk Neck for 1 and 2 June. I contacted Robert and James, and we got on it. This would be James' first visit to Tassie. Flights were booked and reservations were made for that room at the Lufra Hotel. In the meantime, my migraines were showing up with too much regularity as they can, but I was determined. I left Melbourne's Tullamarine Airport Friday and flew down to Hobart. Many thanks to my friend, Jillian Cornelious (James' mom) for being our airport chauffeur.

As our plane was landing, a little flock of Tasmanian Native-hens (or 'Turbo-chooks' as they are often called down there) ran along a ditch beside the landing strip. James got his first Tassie Lifer while he was still on the plane!

We made a quick stop at the Woolies in Sorell as we do. That is yet another of those groceries across the country that feels like a neighbourhood store to me. The below quote is included in the beginning of the first book and is one of my favourite things that I have written. When I write something I like, I do not consider it my particular brilliance. It is that I have been fortunate enough to be writing when the words happened. My job is to catch them as they flow through and guide them into my text. I think these words from the first book were a particularly good catch.

'The more my heart is spread out across this amazing country, the more heart I have. It is not like my heart gets divided up into smaller and smaller pieces between all of these many places. It is like I have more and more heart. For every piece I leave in another spot, that piece is added to, not taken from, my heart.' Eaglehawk

Rainbow ending on the little harbour at Eaglehawk Neck.

Rainbows over the Lufra Hotel and James taking a photo.

Neck, Tasmania, has certainly added to my heart.

We collected our hire car, and drove down and checked into my favourite room at Lufra. It was rainy and sunny, and rainbows abounded. It is such a beautiful area that the rainbows just seem appropriate. That evening James and Robert went out to have a look for a Tasmanian Boobook and found one! Now Robert had a Lifer to start his weekend as well. Sweet.

Saturday morning I awoke early and began coffeeing hard. As I have mentioned, the seasickness patch makes me feel crap. By 7am, we were on the *Paulette* and chugging out to sea with some old friends and some new. In only about an hour we had our first beautiful Southern Fulmar! It was my first Lifer for the trip and one for many others on board. Joy abounded. We had not even reached the Hippolyte Rocks and we had one of the main target birds of the trip!

There I was in a boat on the Tasman Sea off the rugged, post-card-gorgeous coast of Tasmania yet again. I reckon that above all the things that I owe birds is that they lead me to so many breath-takingly beautiful, wonderful places that I would not experience

Southern Fulmar.

Southern Fulmar and a Shy Albatross.

Grey Petrel on the left and Blue Petrel on the right, the US Civil War set of petrels (photo by Robert Shore).

otherwise. Birding is so much more than making a list of species.

We continued into the offshore waters and began to berley (chum). Over the next few hours I added three more Lifers! Along with the Southern Fulmar (we saw three more of them offshore), we had both Blue Petrel and Grey Petrels. We had seen the US Civil War set of petrels! The Blue and the Grey, just wow. But the heartstopper for me was a massive and elegant giant that glided in on its long dark wings, literally with a smile on its bill, Sooty Albatross! I had long wanted to behold this beautiful albatross. It did not disappoint me. It made passes by the boat and at one time was joined by a second Sooty. Glory.

We rode back in close to the coast hoping to see a Humpback Whale that had been reported by a fishing boat earlier, but it was not around. However, we had some glorious, close views of that rugged, rocky shoreline. It is stunning.

The next day began similarly, feeling crap from the patch, coffeeing hard, and chugging out of the harbour at 7am with much anticipation for another great pelagic day. This time we headed more to the north and once out into offshore waters we began to berley. We had Southern Fulmars again with a total of four through the day. About 9:30am James spotted a Great Shearwater coming in and then flying by the boat. In moments everyone was on it. This was one of the most hoped-for birds. It was a visiting rarity that had been seen on a previous Eaglehawk trip on 19 May (although it was suggested by some that this was not the same individual). We had all beheld a Great Shearwater. Joy again indeed.

It poured with rain and the wind kicked up, but the *Paulette* is a very stable boat and we continued to bird. Time moved on and all too soon we were on the way back in. As we got closer inshore, we began to see quite a few of those 'Button-quail of the Sea', Common Diving-petrels. As mentioned earlier, it had been my pelagic Bogey Bird until the Eaglehawk Neck trip the previous January. Now I was seeing them on either side of the boat including one little 'raft' of about a dozen with their heads poking up out of the water like little turtles. Then they flushed and flew low across the surface before diving and disappearing. Turtles never do that. I even managed a few photos. They are special little birds and certainly a bogey no more.

As we had done the day before, after the trip most of us went to the Havinabite Tucker Spot café just down the road (yes, the one that has now closed). Karen Dick, who is for me the current godmother of Eaglehawk Neck Pelagics, ordered two great piles of chips as the boat docked so that they were hot and ready for us when we arrived. As I have said, I also usually eat my early dinner there and that is what I did. The next morning we took our time going to the airport (our flight wasn't until 3pm). James was able to pick up several Lifers. It was rainy, but on and off it was quite sunny and again we were treated to lots of rainbows. Beautiful. We returned our hire car at 12:30pm and hung out at the airport waiting for our flight. We took a group selfie with the airport Tasmanian Devil statue before boarding out flight back to Victoria.

The smiling Sooty Albatross.

Great Shearwater (photo by Robert Shore).

My former pelagic Bogey, a Common Diving-petrel or as I have referred to them, the Button-quail of the Sea.

Hope and a Soft-plumed Petrel

A friend of mine recently wrote, 'Everyone needs an escape route'. There is much wisdom in that simple statement. Without an escape route and without an awareness of the possibility of hope, there is not much point in living. 'Hope' is the spark that runs the internal engine that keeps me alive, extinguish it for too long and I would be done. I am older and a bit slower but I will definitely continue to be 'escaping' and getting out into the natural world. It is not possible for me to sit and play cards. I will never do that. Old or not, I actually hate card games. It may well be an ADHD thing, but my brain gets no enjoyment whatsoever from playing cards. I have, on occasion, given them a try but without any joy. I am also not big on board games. It might be learning the rules that I do not like, or the reliance on the 'luck' in rolling dice. Unsurprisingly, I also have no interest in any sort of gambling. I reckon that's okay. I have enough tendencies toward vices, it's good that gambling is not even close to being in the mix. It is no temptation to me at all.

As I have mentioned earlier, I have John Buchan's quote

regarding 'a series of occasions for hope' tattooed on my right arm. As well I should. Hope is what feeds and sustains my heart.

Whenever I go off in search of a new bird (or more), I have hope. My love of birding is made of that hope. I may end up in the desert, or the Great Southern Ocean, or in rainforests, or a sewage treatment plant, wherever birds lead me there is beauty and wonder. All brought to me by hope.

My regular birding buddies, Robert and James, and I had experienced a phenomenal trip out of Eaglehawk Neck on 1 and 2 June and I heard that they had another excellent trip down there on 8 June. Robert arranged with Karen to organise a mid-week double header on Tuesday 18th and Wednesday, 19th June. We returned again to Tassie, and we were excited. Anticipation of a possible Grey-headed Albatross or any number of other possibilities fired up my internal hope-engine. The weather, however, had different ideas.

On Tuesday the winds blew hard from the north, and it was very rough. As I have said, the *Paulette* is a stable boat and I always feel safe on her. The patches were also doing their job and they were getting quite a workout. Sadly, two of the other participants ended

Left to right: Karen Dick, Peter Vaughn and Robert Shore.

Some of the gorgeous, rugged coastline around Eaglehawk Neck.

Soft-plumaged Petrel (photo by James Cornelious).

Inside the little Havnabite Café and my new stubby holder.

up 'lying on the deck sick'. Not good.

The absolute high point of the morning for me was finally getting wonderful views of a Soft-plumaged Petrel! It was certainly one of the birds that I was hoping to see. There is that word, hope. I had missed seeing one on 2nd June although some others on the boat had gotten distant views. This time I saw it very well. James even got a good shot of it! With his permission, I will include it this book.

We began our trip back to the jetty early at 11:30am since one of the seasick birders had become very ill. For me it was actually a rather enjoyable rollercoaster-like ride. We went in toward the lee of the shore where the seas were a bit less. We were back at the Havnabite Tucker Spot before 3pm. Since I love that place, I had wanted to add a stubby-holder from there to my little collection of birding-travel related stubby-holders. I asked about this on a previous visit, but I was told that they don't sell them anymore. However, the lady remembered me asking and had found an old one and just gave it to me. She would not take payment for it. That was so very nice of her. It has joined my other birding trip souvenir

The wonderful view from the little cafe.

stubby-holders. They are much less expensive than T-shirts, and they are useable reminders and memory preservers. I do have a few now.

The weather forecast got worse. Wednesday morning began with gale-force winds. We had some hope that the front might move through quickly and we gave it a go. We motored out through 4-metre swells toward the Hippolyte Rocks. However with 6- to 8-metre swells reported beyond the rocks, the *Paulette* turned back for the harbour. We again met at Havnabite for lunch and a meet-up before the group went their separate ways. I mainly napped that afternoon. The patches do sort of knock the stuffing out of me, but as I have so often said, they can be worth it.

All in all, it was a good trip for me. It was great seeing some old friends and once again, making some new friends as well. Such is birding.

An important note on hope: I work hard to embrace rather than avoid 'don't get your hopes up' thinking. Getting your hopes up can be a wonderful thing. And if those hopes do not come to fruition? I have still had the period of time when they were alive in my chest. And that is such a good thing. Go ahead, get your hopes up. Let yourself live.

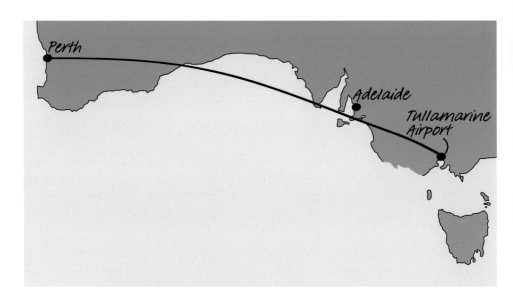

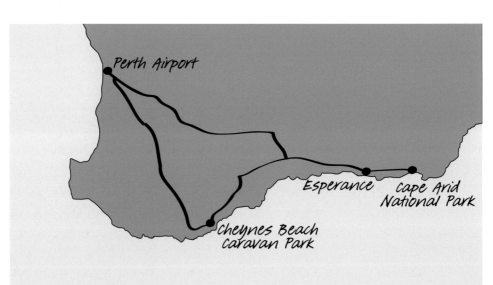

{ 20 }

Tassie Again Then Western Australia

September 2019

A Little of Tassie and a Lot of Western Australia

This chapter starts on Monday, 2 September with a flight from Melbourne, once again to Hobart, Tasmania. Several of us were to do another double-header pelagic out of Eaglehawk Neck on Tuesday and Wednesday. The weather was beautiful on Tuesday and that usually bodes poorly for birding, and it was a bit pedestrian out there. We had a white-morph Southern Giant Petrel that was truly stunning to see, but nothing else noteworthy or unusual to write about.

The next day, we had a bit more wind, but it was still northerly. It seems that a south-west wind is preferred for the pelagic birds there. Around 11:30 that morning Peter Vaughn, our young, knowledgeable main 'spotter' on the boat (he is now a dear friend as well), called our attention to a darkish-headed albatross. He said that he thought it had a 'Salvin's look' and suggested taking photos. Many of us, even including me, did as he said. Unfortunately, while we were still out there, the bird was dismissed by some as just another immature Shy Albatross. We went on about our day. So again, no Lifer Pie for me.

The author holding on and James holding his bins (photo by Murray Scott).

Wings of a Shy Albatross and a Cape Petrel. I like this photo.

That evening I put my photos on the laptop, and I had a better look at that dark-headed albatross. It did look different to me. I decided to post a couple of my mediocre, but fairly clear shots on the Seabirds and Pelagics Facebook page for opinions. Long story short, over 90 comments and much discussion later, it was definitively determined to be a first-cycle Salvin's Albatross. As is sometimes the case, the first impression was right. Peter had correctly identified it as such when he initially saw it. I had gotten a Lifer! However by then it was after 10pm. Lifer Pie or a Lifer Day would wait.

The next day we drove up to Hobart and flew back to Melbourne. I was home in Lara in the late arvo. I had one night there and then I was going to Western Australia with my new good friend, and fairly new birder, Alan Stringer. I was grateful for his sorting of the flights, a task that in the past I had found quite daunting. I have since become much better at it. I have flown more often, and I have needed to become at least somewhat comfortable with booking flights. It is still a daunting task for my ADHD brain.

We were to fly to Perth at 6:15pm arriving there at 8:35pm western time (or 10:35pm to our Victorian body clocks), but our flight was delayed. Now we were to depart at 7:05pm and arrive at 9:25pm (11:25 to us Victorians). When all was said and done, our baggage collected and transport to the motel sorted, it was almost 11pm Perth time. The motel was close to the airport, but still took extra time because the shuttle had some issues. I finally got into my sparse, but okay motel room and was asleep about midnight.

We had a flight to Esperance at 9am. The shuttle was leaving at 7am, so I was up at 5am. We met Mike Carter at the shuttle. 'The' Mike Carter as I referred to him upon our initial meeting in my first book. Mike is a wonderful guy and at that time had seen more birds in Australia than anyone else. He was also 85 years old. This trip was based on going for the elusive and endangered Western Ground Parrot in Cape Arid National Park with him and Tony Palliser. We would be birding there for three days with

My Lifer Salvin's Albatross.

those legends. How could we dip? Well, spoiler alert, we could.

The small turbo-prop plane was on time, and we arrived in Esperance mid-morning. Tony hired a 4WD for us and we were off to Cape Arid before noon. It is over an hour just to get to the beginning of the very rough, muddy track into the park. What we had heard was that the optimum Western Ground Parrot birding area was another 40 to 45 kilometres down that track. It takes at least an hour and a half to get out there from the beginning of the park. The first day we did not go that far, but we still trudged determinedly through over ten kilometres of the scrubby habitat where the parrots supposedly live. My energy reserves were already down from lack of sleep but I certainly gave it a good go. I got my Lifer Western Fieldwren. It was a split from Rufous Fieldwren. I put that Lifer Day away for later with the Salvin's Albatross Lifer Day. It's good to have Lifer Days saved up!

The next morning we birded in another section of the park that had been recommended to Tony by our mutual friend, Nigel Jackett. Again we did a hell of a lot of walking with no success. We trudged about 12 kilometres. I had my Fitbit in my pocket.

I was whupped and all I was trying to do was to keep up with an 85-year-old. I had lost some weight over the winter by working at eating smaller portions and as importantly, making wiser food choices. I do love my chips, both the crispy bagged ones, as well as what my US friends call French fries.

The following morning we were leaving Esperance at 4am. I was up well before 3am as usual. I coffeed hard and of course, I was ready on time. In life I am ridiculously punctual. I am almost always early (which can be a good or a bad thing). We were hoping to hear the parrots calling at first light or before. We arrived out there on first light and heard nothing. We birded hard all day, again without success. Well, we had dipped on Western Ground Parrot as you do. If I were to go back, which I reckon I will do one day, I would rather drive Troopi over and camp out well into the park thus being able to wake up in best habitat while it is still dark and listen for them.

Tuesday morning we did a bit of local birding in the heat around Esperance. It was odd to be in shorts and sweating after winter in Victoria. We walked the flats of the world-famous Pink Lake. Well,

Western Fieldwren at Cape Arid National Park.

another spoiler alert: it is not pink! Not at all. It hasn't been pink for donkey's-years. There is a sign with an explanation regarding the salt content, and how and why that changed, and why it's not pink anymore. Even though tons of things are named 'Pink Lake' this and 'Pink Lake' that, all around Esperance there is no pink-coloured lake anymore.

After that bit of birding and sightseeing, or sight-not-seeing in the case of the 'Pink' Lake, we took our extremely muddy 4WD hire car to the carwash and then to the airport. When we got there, we found that our vehicle had a 100-kilometre limit with additional charges per kilometre after that. So it turned out our car hire was very dear indeed. Thank goodness we were splitting the cost between four of us.

We flew back to Perth together where Alan and I bid a fond farewell to Mike and Tony. Yes, we had dipped, but we had dipped with legends. It had been a great time in general.

I was collecting our bags while Alan found us an economy hire car. For some reason, it was very busy at the car hire places, but he prevailed. Then we drove about 25 minutes east to a lovely

At Cape Arid National Park searching for Western Ground Parrot.

Lovely view at the point by Cheynes Beach.

motel in Armadale called the Heritage Country Motel. I highly recommend it. I had a nice, comfortable night's sleep before we headed off to Cheynes Beach Caravan Park where we had a cabin booked. For birders it is a famous place specifically for three big skulkers: the Noisy Scrub-bird, the Western Bristlebird and the Western Whipbird.   I wrote about this famous caravan park in chapter 17 of *An Australian Birding Year*. Lynn and I had seen the Scrub-bird and the Bristlebird, but we had not even looked for the Western Whipbird in February 2016, since we had just seen one less than a month before on Kangaroo Island. But then the IOC (International Ornithological Congress) split it. The one that she and I had seen over in South Australia is now called the White-bellied Whipbird, and the one in the far west is called the Black-throated Whipbird. Seeing that bird was a part of the reason for me to do this trip.

We arrived Wednesday late arvo and dashed out to give the Whipbird area a go with no success. They are considered to be

Up behind Cheynes Beach Caravan Park.

morning birds, but we had to look. Then since it would be a Lifer for Alan, we gave the Noisy Scrub-bird a try down by the beach at dusk but also without success. We resolved to be out at the Whipbird area before first light. We were there at 5:30am in the dark. We learned that, at least while we were searching, the Whipbirds did not call until about 7am. In general they were not calling very much. However, that first morning we did hear one calling a few times. And then at about 8am it gave a long, clear call. It was repeating what I referred to as the 'hot for teacherrr' call. It brought to my mind a song by Van Halen and if I can relate a call to something, I have at least some chance of remembering it. The bird was close to us. We were standing there with two other birders and although we all heard it clearly, none of us could get an eye on it. After it gave one last long call, it was silent. I was nervous about dipping and decided to add a third night to our booking there.

That evening Alan got to see the classic Noisy Scrub-bird run-across. We listened as it called and called and then went quiet for maybe five minutes. I whispered to Alan that when they stop calling like that, I had heard that it means that they are on the move. So that means, watch the track. Just moments after I said that the small brown, black and white bird dashed across the track! It was just about in the same exact spot where I saw my Lifer run across that track in 2016. Yes, in the same place three and a half years later. I doubt it was the same bird, but it sure was the same spot.

Friday morning at 5:30am, we met up with Jo, a new birder acquaintance also staying at the caravan park. We went to the area where we had heard the Black-throated Whipbird the day before. It was oddly quiet. I am not sure that we even heard the bird that morning at all. Certainly not the clear 'hot for teacherrr' call. A Western Australian birder who had visited there multiple times, speculated that perhaps the birds had settled down and begun nesting. I don't know why they were being difficult, but I added a fourth night to our reservation.

In the meantime, Alan was picking up Lifers. Spotted Scrub-wren, Western Spinebill and Red-capped Parrot to name a few. He had only begun compiling his life list the previous January. He can be a lot of fun and has become a good friend. Friday afternoon a very cooperative Western Bristlebird hopped out on the track

Carnaby's Black-Cockatoos at sunset behind the caravan park.

and posed for photos. Skulker? Not so much while we were there. It turned out to be one of the most co-operative birds of the trip.

Saturday morning began grey and drizzling rain. I decided to leave my camera in the cabin. We walked further up the left track, maybe a kilometre or more and back with no joy. We were again back in our usual spot, within 100 metres from where the track splits when Alan heard the Whipbird do a portion of its call pretty far out, but in front of us. Alan has good ears. We walked into the scrub following Kangaroo paths across to the righthand track. It did the partial call again in the scrub in front of us maybe 50-60 metres in. Continuing to follow Alan's ears, we walked toward it and stood scanning the brush with our eyes and our bins. Then I saw a bird perched on a bush only about 20 metres in front of me. I brought my bins up to my eyes and I was looking at the olive-grey back of a Black-throated Whipbird! There was no doubt. I said quietly, "I've got the bird!" as it turned and then dropped down.

Literally with tears in my eyes, I turned and gave Alan a hug. But now we had to find it again for him to see as well. After about ten minutes of looking, it revealed itself again to us. This time it

Western Bristlebird on the track behind Cheynes Beach Caravan Park.

My Lifer Pie ice cream on a stick as Alan Stringer looks on.

perched out even more in the open on a dead branch about a metre off the ground by a small group of trees in front of us. It was not calling. I said softly, "On the stick to the left of the trees." And Alan replied almost instantly, "Got it!" And we both had it. The bird turned to us in full view. It preened for perhaps three seconds, fanning-out the underside of its lovely tail. We saw the black throat and its little crest. It was giving us an incredible show. I whispered, "Take a picture." And to his credit, Alan said, "I am just looking at it." We probably had about eight excellent seconds of viewing this skulking, and yet still very mobile bird. They move around their areas a lot and yet I never saw this one fly. After it put on its short show for us, it dropped down and was gone again. As I say, that

Brush Bronzewing at Cheynes Beach.

bird owed us nothing more. It had displayed itself completely to us, front, back and under. The Lifer High was glorious. I had tears again. We spent the rest of the day celebrating. I had ice cream on a stick and a crazy-delicious burger and chips made by our new friends D and Kosta from the food truck parked by the office of the caravan park. I remain in touch with D through social media to this day. I really liked them both.

I also loved the staff at that caravan park. I have made several friends there, genuine friends. These are people with whom I also remain in touch and who I hope to see again. There is an energy exchange between individuals when genuine connections occur that is precious. It is life affirming and life sustaining. Making such connections is at the core of genuine sharing.

We had ended up staying for four nights and left the caravan park on 15 September. We drove back to that motel where Alan and I had stayed when we were on the way to Cheynes Beach. We made a stop for lunch, and I had the best toastie I have ever had. It was at the Riverside Roadhouse in Bannister, WA. It was honestly the best toasted sandwich I have eaten to this day. It was

Still the best toastie I've ever had.

a chicken, pesto, cheese, spinach and mayo toastie on thick bread that they bake there. As I write this, my mouth is actually watering. Damn, it was delicious.

We got a good night's sleep before flying back to Melbourne. We dipped on the ground parrot, but it was an excellent adventure nonetheless.

Arrving at Cocos/Keeling Islands.

{ 21 }

Cocos/Keeling Islands

30 November–6 December 2019

The build-up to going was huge for me. I first realised that I could, and then that I actually would, go on Richard Baxter's Christmas/ Cocos birding tour on 24 September 2019. My friend, Damian Baxter, Richard's son, who you may have met in chapter 16 of *An Australian Birding Year* in Perth, Western Australia, posted on Facebook that a spot had come open on his dad's December tour. Messages were quickly exchanged, and I was in. Then began the mental, emotional and even physical shitstorm as the unhealthy parts of my brain attempted to work their insidious sabotage. I was determined not to allow them to succeed, and they did not. I am not saying it was an easy process, it was not, but I did it.   And I am so very glad that I did.

I made checklists. I read Richard's and Lisa's checklists. Lisa is the facilitator of the tours on Cocos and Christmas Islands. Her company is Indian Ocean Experiences and wonderful experiences they are! She knows her stuff. I highlighted things on their lists. I ordered a cool Overboard brand dry-bag backpack. I ended up loving it and use it regularly to this day and later, after I had returned, I ordered their 2-litre waist pack (bum-bag). I use that regularly as well.

And yeah, I worried. I fretted. I talked with friends who had done the trip. I made more lists. Although I had lost some weight, I worried about my fitness level, which really did need work. I worried about my older guy 'waterworks' issues (and as I edit this text in the spring of 2021 three surgeries later, they are still an issue. But I could deal with it then and I deal with it now). I worried about my migraines. I worried about worrying. Which is really just another way to say anxiety. I wanted this trip so badly that I all but worried myself sick that something would prevent me from going. It did not. I saw my neurologist, Peter and had the painful Botox injections in my noggin that do seem to be of at least some help with the migraines. I was doing everything I could to make sure I could go. And now I have done it. I went and I will attempt to write an interesting and fun account of that trip.

The morning of Thursday, 28 November 2019 I drove my Troopi into the Long-Term Parking at the Melbourne Airport. Then I rode their shuttle to the terminal. I was checked-in, through security, and relaxing at the gate over 2 hours early, exactly as I prefer to do. The flight was on time, and I flew the four and a half hours to Perth drifting off occasionally into a sleep-like state as I 'listened' to a Patrick O'Brian audio book in my earbuds. I find the voice of the reader, Patrick Tull incredibly soothing, and as I have mentioned many times, I love the Aubrey/Maturin series of books by O'Brian.

Arriving in Perth in the late arvo, I caught the shuttle to the motel. I had an okay night's sleep and in the morning, I caught up with a few friends on the tour who had also overnighted at the motel. Now I was no longer travelling alone. One of my anxiety battles is about travelling alone and making a mistake. Yes, screwing-up is one of my biggest fears. I understand that about myself. I have learned coping skills that usually work okay for me. Again, it doesn't mean it's easy, but it means I can do what I need to do.

Soon we were on our flight to Cocos. Once again, I did my

best to drift off and let time flow past while listening to the words of Patrick O'Brian and the voice of Patrick Tull. I do not recall exactly how long that flight was. I know we made a short stop somewhere in the outback of Western Australia before we headed west over the Indian Ocean. We arrived on Cocos in the early afternoon. We were met by the legendary Richard Baxter. He would be our leader for the next two weeks. Richard is ideal for what he does. His knowledge and information network for these islands is unparalleled. Make no mistake; there is no one who is more knowledgeable regarding the birds and birding of the Cocos and Christmas Islands than Richard Baxter. He is a natural leader, and I would say this even if I did not like him, but I do like him. However, he is not there to be liked; he is there to find the birds for birders to see. And he delivers.

We dropped our bags at our motel and went to the grocery. I dashed madly about the small, very limitedly stocked store grabbing things. I discovered to my dismay that they do not sell peanut butter. I use peanut butter on bread or crackers as my go-to easy, fast meal. Not really a preferred meal, but it provides energy and

Out in front of the motel on Cocos.

protein and can be made in seconds. Soon we were back at the motel to leave our groceries and then we were off birding.

I want to say again and again, that I adored Cocos. In only one week, I merged with those islands and they became a part of me. I can feel them in my heart as I sit here at my desk in my study writing these words.

The sand beneath my feet on Cocos felt a little different. The grass under my toes felt a little different. The sun shone a little different. The vibe there was unique, but still it felt familiar. A part of my heart was transported back to Sanibel Island, Florida in the early 1960s. That was when a young boy felt the massive joy of loving a place and feeling that place seem to love him back. I felt like I had also melded with Cocos as I had with Sanibel, only this was almost 60 years later. I began writing this hoping I could at least partially capture the vibe of Cocos in words. But I gradually realised that words will not do it. It may be that Cocos is more of a melody than a lyric. It is a beautiful, soothing, joyful, calming, melody. I can close my eyes and 'hear' it. I can feel it inside me. Universe willing, I am going to return in the not-too-distant future.

I was messaging with a friend early on my visit to Cocos and I had not mentioned much about any Lifers, or numbers. He commented "What about new birds? How many?" I don't remember exactly what I said to him. What I do remember very well was telling Richard about it later and saying that I was coming to understand that living the experience was the more important thing on Cocos. And he said, "Yeah, the vibe becomes more than the number." That concept is golden. That is it. The vibe is more than the number. That is Cocos. And that is my birding philosophy in general now as well. The number is only a milepost, not the road. My Life List is a map that goes on and on as long as I go on. It is not a destination at which to arrive.

I was there with people who are truly Australian birding legends. I was in the Cocos Islands with Richard Baxter, Jenny Spry, Darryel Biggles Binns, who everyone knows as Biggles, Glen Pacey, Tania

The man himself. Richard Baxter addressing the group.

Ireton and Joy Tansey. Legends all. This is as good as birding gets. I have referred to Jenny Spry as my 'Yoda' because the force is so strong in her. I benefit from just being in her zen-like birding presence. I could go on and on about these people. I'll just say that it was an honour birding with them, and a lot of fun as well.

As I said, we went off birding that first late afternoon. We piled into the four cars. It worked out to four people per car mostly, but folks could always do what they wanted. Mostly they all wanted to bird, but not always in the same group looking for the same birds. Since it was my first visit, quickly Green Junglefowl and White-breasted Waterfowl were added to my 'Cocos newbie' Life List. They are all over the place. I next added a beautiful Javan Pond Heron on the mudflats in front of the palm trees. It had been visiting there regularly for about three years now. On the Cocos Islands almost all bird life is made up of visiting vagrants. There are no resident passerines (songbirds) living on the island, not a single one. So if you see a small bird in a tree, it is a rarity! Or a 'mega' as they get called. It is exciting that any bird you see is truly a potential mega rarity. At the end of that first day I went to bed about nine and slept the sleep of elation and exhaustion that can come with these types of experiences. That is a lovely combination, elation and exhaustion. It is the full body enjoyment of life. It has been too long since I have felt that. Although I know I will feel it again. I will indeed.

We would meet on the veranda in the mornings between 5:30am and 6:00am depending on what the group was doing; therefore I was up by 4am as I would be. The first morning at Cocos was the canoe trip a few kilometres over to South Island to see the Saunders's Terns. These rare terns nest on South Island and they are pronounced 'Saunders-ez' since the possessive 's' is pronounced separately from Saunders. The canoes have little outboard motors. Bill, a new friend to be, shared a canoe with me. I had the first go at driving it. I grew up around boats and I am very experienced at driving a boat with an outboard motor. The issue was that we were there at a time of very low tides (even at high tide) and the motors continuously hit against the bottom. Everyone's did, and occasionally when they hit, they shut off. Most of the motors restarted with a few pulls of the cord. However, ours eventually

Javan Pond Heron.

Looking back from South Island and the colourful canoes (the blue one had the dodgy motor).

would not. It restarted a few times but then it gave up for good. The canoe rental guy came over in his canoe and he could not restart it either. So we were ignominiously towed for the final kilometre or so to the island.

After a short hike through the palms and bush, we emerged onto a large expanse of flats where the Saunders's Terns were. We saw maybe a dozen of them there. Joy. We hung around a bit then walked back to the canoes where we had some fresh coconut, which the canoe rental guy opened with a machete right in front of us. It was just like on the reality show, *Survivor*, except this was real reality and no one was getting voted off. We had a few other nibbles as well. It was a lovely beach island lunch. Then we got back into the canoes. The guy said that he thought he had fixed our motor, but he had not.

We started back across. It was Bill's turn to drive. One birder drives over and the other one drives back so that everyone has a turn. I was sitting in the bow when suddenly water drenched me from the port side. Bill Betts (a great guy and now a good friend)

Saunders's Tern.

was in the bow of Richard's canoe and had thrown a full bucket of water and had nailed me good! Buckets are kept in the boats for bailing purposes and seemingly for water battles as well. We all had dry-bags and my camera and things stayed dry and safe. I, on the other hand, was soaked to the skin. There was a lot of water thrown between boats all in very good fun. It actually felt good. But once again, our damn motor gave up the ghost and we had to be towed the last kilometre or so to the beach.

On the way back to the accommodations we made a stop where Richard knew to look for a Western Reef Heron, which was split from the Eastern Reef Egret a while ago. And I beheld this beautiful bird. It was white and grey and just gorgeous. It was the second Life bird for me on my first full day on Cocos. Richard leads a two-week tour the end of November and then stays on the island until the next tour arrives. He always keeps up with what birds are where. It is what he does and as I said, he does it very well. As I have mentioned, I need to eat early because of my acid-reflux, so I usually skipped restaurant or pub meals with the group. After dinner, we'd all meet back in the great room of the 'house' at the motel. It is where I was staying with Richard, Biggles, Glen and Tania. It has four bedrooms, a kitchen and a bath. We would do the bird-count for the day. Then Richard would give us the schedule for the next morning, which meant to meet on the veranda as before, depending upon who was going where.

The second morning most of us went to the spot where Richard had seen an Asian Brown Flycatcher not long before we had arrived. We gave it a good go, but it was not around. So Richard took those of us who were new to Cocos to the runway where we saw the resident Chinese Pond Heron.

Just after lunch my new friend Bill Betts (the one who soaked me on the canoe trip) and my new friend Bill (who had shared that ill-fated canoe with the dodgy outboard motor with me) and I decided to go have a look again for the Flycatcher. We did not see it, but both Bills distinctly heard a bird calling. Remember, that any passerine is a rarity on the island. The Bills eventually became referred to by the group as Bill 1 and Bill 2 with Bill Betts being Bill 2. We could not find the bird that they were hearing, but they were sure they had heard it. We returned to the motel and told

The beautiful wings of a Western Reef Heron.

Chinese Pond Heron out on the runway.

the others. Soon the group was spread out surrounding that area of trees. I think Bill 2 first heard it again. Then we saw a bird. Bill 2 got a quick photo. It looked to Richard like a *Phylloscopus* type warbler (which could be any one of several very similar looking birds). Then I played the call of the Arctic Warbler *Phylloscopus borealis,* and Bill 2 said, "That's the bird we heard!" Bill 1 agreed that it was the call he had heard as well. And immediately, the warbler came flying at us calling back. Of course I stopped playing it. Because that is what it was, an Arctic Warbler, heard, seen and photographed.

Later that day, on the backside of the runway, I finally saw an Oriental Cuckoo. It had been a sort of a Bogey Bird for me. A bird that is seen on the mainland, but I had not been able to catch up with one. And I had tried a few times. I finally saw it fly across right in front of me. A beautiful bird it is too.

The next day we took the ferry to Home Island. It is called a ferry, but you leave your vehicle on West Island and ride in air-conditioned comfort across the ten or so kilometres of gorgeous, calm blue water. The Cocos Islands are the ring of a large, extinct volcano.

Arctic Warbler on Cocos.

The stunningly beautiful view from Home Island.

Richard and Joy on the veranda where we all met each morning.

We were crossing the crater.

Home island is populated by about 500 Malay people who practise Sunni Islam. They are the friendliest, sweetest people you could want to meet. Their smiles are genuine, and their greetings are warm. Everyone waves to you, and everyone says hello and smiles. The humanity is wondrous, and the island is utterly beautiful. There are no motor vehicles so we walked everywhere. Some of the locals have golf carts.

The famous Oceana House mansion was closed. I understand that it is for sale. Usually a few of the group would have overnighted there, but it could not be arranged this year. I walked all around the house and peered in the windows. It is truly magnificent. The timber-panelled walls are stunning. The antique furnishings are beautiful. The mansion was built in 1887 and seems to float in a dream outside of time. I was with Jenny Spry as I marvelled at it. She has stayed in the mansion on past visits. Maybe it will be open again on my future visit, crossed fingers. Jenny and I were mostly quiet, just soaking in the vibe of the house. It radiates a feeling of reverence. I will never forget what that felt like. Those massively

Oceana House on Home Island.

Looking into Oceana House through a window. It seemed outside of time.

The beautiful view in front of Oceana House.

thick walls seemed impregnable to time. I am not exactly sure what is going on with it now. Looking online in May 2021, there are reviews from people who say they stayed there in December 2020. So perhaps it is open again, but we will see. If the Oceana House is open when I am there next, I will certainly ask Richard about staying there at least for a night. I would love to have that experience.

Anyway, back to birding. Thanks to Biggles, I beheld the stunningly beautiful Blue-and-white Flycatcher. Biggles had been on the Home Island ahead of us and had originally found the bird and then he refound it for us. I got a few backlit photos that did not do it justice. I was thrilled just to see that awesome bird. It stayed visible for us, although always backlit.

We had a lovely afternoon ride back on the ferry and then chased up an Asian Koel that was hanging out at an area called the 'farm'. It proved not to be co-operative for photos, but it was seen well by most of us. My friend, Bill Betts did get a shot or two. His photographic abilities came into play often during the trip.

Speaking of photos, I was having difficulties with my camera, and

I finally figured out that the eyepiece for the new (and expensive) rain sleeve was inhibiting my ability to see through the viewfinder while wearing glasses. I was having a hard time 'getting on' the bird through the viewfinder. Not good. Things were much better once I switched back to the original eyepiece. I was still not a particularly fast shot with the camera, but I could at least manage to get some better photos. And yes, I still believe in, and practise 'bins first camera second'. As I have said ad nauseam, I am a birder, not a bird photographer. Goodness knows there are a lot of those nowadays. But I am very grateful to those who can get the shot and are willing to share them. This book is enhanced by a few of my friends' photos, and I do appreciate it.

Tuesday morning my friend Joy Tansey and I caught the first ferry to Home Island. We were on a mission. Joy had been with Jenny Spry on the first day on the islands when Jenny flushed, and saw, the Chestnut-winged Cuckoo that had been seen sporadically on Home Island. She had been only a few steps behind Jenny and yet had not been able to see it. They searched a lot, but they did not refind it. So Joy and I were going to give that part of

One of my photos of the Blue-and-white Flycatcher. It never was in good light for photographing, but it was such a thrill to see.

the island a good search. We diligently crisscrossed that area for at least four hours without a single glimpse of the cuckoo. It was beautiful there of course, but no cuckoo joy. To my knowledge, Jenny remains the last person to see that bird. We returned to West Island on the noon ferry.

A Yellow Bittern had been spotted the day before, so Tuesday arvo a large part of our birding revolved around searching the areas where it was thought it might have gone. But despite many hopeful eyes scanning the edges of the mudflats, it seems the bittern wasn't around. We certainly gave it a good go.

Later that afternoon, the group had spread out a bit and a couple of us were back at the motel when Biggles drove up honking his horn. Soon we were in his car headed for a tree just up the road where a bird had been heard calling. This tree, standing by itself behind a short chain link fence, was now surrounded by our group. I think by then, we were all there. We scanned the branches. Counting the time before I arrived; that tree was under close surveillance for well over an hour. Every now and then, the 'bird' would make its little squeak (of course I could not hear it,

Searching unsuccessfully for the Yellow Bittern on West Island.

Geoff's boat that took us to Horsburgh Island.

but others could). So we quietly continued to scan the tree with our bins. Finally, Biggles climbed over the low fence to get the last possible angle looking into the tree and soon he saw it … two branches occasionally rubbing together in the light breeze and making a very bird-like sound. We had watched an empty tree for an hour. Such can be birding.

Wednesday morning, a portion of our group caught a ride with Geoffrey Christie in his boat across to Horsburgh Island. Geoffrey and his delightful wife, Pam, live on West Island part of the year. They have a bed and breakfast called the Bird's Nest. After the short boat ride, we were making the trek across Horsburgh to the pond where a rare vagrant Northern Pintail took up residence a couple of years ago. It's not a long walk, maybe a kilometre or less, but you are required to duck (no pun intended whatsoever) under some very low branches on parts of the path. I nailed the thick stump of a broken branch, front-on with the top of my head. I saw stars. I was sure there would be blood, but I guess my wonderful tired old, beat-up hat had protected my scalp. It hurt like hell, but I did not have time for it.

Old ruins on Horsburgh Island.

After a few more minutes of walking, we were at the little lake. When we first arrived, the duck was not around. Richard walked around to the right of us through the bush and soon the Northern Pintail as well as a Pacific Black Duck floated out into the middle of the pond like magic. No he did not release them from a cage on the other side of the bushes (I don't think). There was also a Red-necked Phalarope twirling about in the pond as they tend to do. It is a very cool bird, but the Northern Pintail was the prize. I have seen literally thousands of them in North Carolina, but in Australia, this was my first.

We headed back across the island. I was walking and chatting with Geoff as a group of White Terns went by us chasing a small raptor. Geoff calls those terns the 'Cocos Air Police'. Soon we heard "Japanese Sparrowhawk!" from the others behind us. That bird circled back around, and bins were up, and cameras were clicking. As we were enjoying the Japanese Sparrowhawk, what we all assumed was an Asian House Martin came zooming through our group. That would be a fairly common bird for the islands. However, after examining the photos later, it proved to be quite an unusual bird,

White Terns.

Japanese Sparrowhawk and a White Tern.

but somewhat disappointing for me. It was Cocos' first record of a Tree Martin. A bird I have seen hundreds of times on the mainland. So I still need Asian House Martin. Hopefully, next time.

We headed back to West Island in Geoff's boat for a short regroup, then we prepared to catch the ferry back to Home Island for a bit more birding followed by a wonderful, delicious and gratefully early, Malay dinner at a local restaurant. Yes, the dinner was served at 6pm which is a doable time for my reflux. It was truly scrumptious. The shellfish, which was a small mollusc called 'gong-gong' was absolutely delicious. The fish was as fresh and as good as it gets. I also enjoyed my first 0% Bintang. It is a non-alcoholic malt beverage. I would not call it an NA beer, but it was beer-like, very refreshing and I really liked it. Unfortunately it is not available in Victoria. Again, next time.

Thursday was the Mugimaki day. There was an area on the north end where an Eyebrowed Thrush had been seen on several occasions but I had not yet seen it. I had gone there looking intently a few times. Tania had taken me on a stakeout there earlier in the week, but the bird had not revealed itself to us. Some others in the group

On Home Island as the sun began to set.

The birders at the Mugimaki Flycatcher spot.

had gotten excellent looks at it Thursday morning. I am not sure where I was, but it was not with the group who saw the Thrush. It had posed for them on a stick out in the open. It was in the same area that I had staked out with Tanya. They do move around.

I was back down that track looking, yet again in vain for the Thrush, when word came in of a Mugimaki Flycatcher. It was in the bushes along the main road only about a hundred metres from where I was standing. Bill (another Bill, this one is a friend of Geoff's who was staying, and birding, with him. We were choc-ka-block with Bills) had found it and was making sure we all knew about it. He had even gone by and left a note for us in our lounge room at the motel. Nice guy. Soon we were all gathered along the edge of the road staring into the bushes. Bill Betts called out that it was in front of him, and I saw it well as it flitted about. And boy can they flit. It was working its way around in a tall bush just across the road. Most of us got decent looks and there was much joy. I still had not seen that Thrush and went back to unsuccess-fully looking for it down the track just around the corner from the Mugimaki spot.

A good shot of the 'mega' Mugimaki Flycatcher (photo by William Betts).

The last evening we met for a beach cookout at the spot where we had hired the canoes. It was like being in some sort of a tropical dream. Again the TV show *Survivor* came to mind. It was a lovely evening, and it was not the first, nor by any means the last, time on the island that I let my hair down. I did not wear it back in the regular ponytail. I wore it down and sometimes I still do. Nowadays, I usually put it in a half-ponytail, sort of Jedi style.

And then somehow it was the last morning on Cocos. But our flight wasn't until 1pm, so we had plenty of birding time that morning. The group headed straight for the Mugimaki Flycatcher spot. Having seen the flycatcher well the day before, I went around the corner to continue looking for that Eyebrowed Thrush. I was with Tania again and her amazing ears had picked up on the Thrush close to the road near where the Mugimaki had been seen the day before. She heard it again, but we looked and looked, still without success. Then we joined the others to have another look at the flycatcher. But in the meantime yet another flycatcher, a Narcissus Flycatcher, a bird that had been seen earlier in the week, began putting on a 'show' by flying repeatedly to and fro across a small track going into the bush. I saw it well at least twice in that opening.

The Mugimaki was still being glimpsed here and there too as it worked its way along the line of bushes. Someone called out that it was in front of them and as I moved to their viewpoint, I saw the Mugimaki Flycatcher flitting its way up in the bush, but more importantly for me, at the same moment a larger bird landed on a palm frond out in the open right in front of me. The beautiful Eyebrowed Thrush! Two 'megas' in a single view! I could see them both in my bins! On an island where you rarely ever see a single bird in a tree or bush, there were two rare vagrants in one view. The thrush only perched out for perhaps three beautiful, heartstopping, seconds before dropping down into the bush, but that was enough. Two new birds in one wonderful last morning, on what has become my favourite island in the world (at least in the southern hemisphere).

We gathered our things and were all at the airport and checked in by noon to make the hour flight over to Christmas Island. I was physically leaving Cocos, but Cocos has never left me.

As I let the memories of Cocos play in my head like a sweet mellifluous melody, I realise that I did not even mention the snipe that Jenny found and we all saw well, on our first visit to Home Island. It looked a whole lot like a Common Snipe, but at least at the time of writing, it was never confirmed as such and it is unlikely that it ever will be. She may have made a submission to the Birdlife Australia Rarities Committee. I haven't heard anything regarding that since then.

I also realised that I did not I mention Tony and the wonderful, handmade ice cream at his little café in the airport. He is renowned for his bread amongst the locals. After he found how much I enjoyed his ice cream, he showed me where I could get it from the freezer for myself if he was closed. He said that I could just pay him later. Such is Cocos. What a nice guy and very delicious ice cream.

Another thing about Cocos is the complete lack of crime. I've never felt more safe anywhere. We locked nothing. We left our

Delicious handmade ice cream Lifer Pie.

laptops sitting out on the table. The keys remained in the vehicles. It is the kind of world in which I wish I could live. And yes again, I am determined to go back.

{ 22 }

Christmas Island

6–13 December 2019

I have been struggling to find an appropriate way of comparing Cocos and Christmas Islands. I loved Christmas. If I had not just been to Cocos, I would rave about it. But it is not Cocos. Christmas is wonderful. Cocos is magic. I loved Christmas Island. I remain in love with Cocos. It is a vibration that still resonates within me, and it will until there is no more me. It is that much a part of me and yet I was only there a week. Cocos is a melody that gratefully, I will always hear. I certainly would not ever want to forget it, even if that were possible.

We landed on Christmas and as you do, we went straight to the grocery. This was a larger grocery than Cocos with a wider selection. It was still not nearly a mainland size grocery, but there were definitely more choices, but still no peanut butter. I will take a small jar in my luggage next time. After our quick shop, we dropped our stuff in our rooms. I was in one of the very nice, shared motel suites. Four of us in three bedrooms with one bath and it was quite comfortable. I had my own room and shared the suite with Richard, Biggles and Glen, a good group.

We went out for a couple of hours that arvo and I saw four of the 'easy' Lifers: Island Thrush (everywhere), Christmas Imperial

A particularly beautiful Christmas Island sunset right out in front of our motel.

Pigeon (everywhere), Christmas Island Swiftlet (everywhere and very fast) and also fairly ubiquitous, the Christmas Frigatebird.

Then we met for a beach cookout with Lisa and staff. As I mentioned, Lisa is the facilitator of these tours. She is the one who sorts all our travel and accommodations and details. And she is very nice.

The next morning, Saturday, 7 December, we met outside the rooms at 5:30am to a beautiful rainbow. I reckon 'beautiful' rainbow is redundant. I do not recall ever seeing an ugly rainbow. The island had been in an awful drought and any rain was considered to be a good thing. It even finally started the Red Crabs migrating, more about them later. I can't really remember exactly where we went during our week there. At least I can check the timestamps on photos and that will give me a chronology for the things that I photographed.

On our way that morning, we stopped and had a look at a beautiful Brown Goshawk. At one time it was considered a separate species, but currently it is a subspecies. It can be a very confiding raptor and this one allowed for photos. It would be cool if it was

Island Thrush on Christmas Island.

Christmas Island subspecies of the Brown Goshawk.

Asian (Common) Emerald Dove male

Asian (Common) Emerald Dove female.

split again in the future. It's the vibe not the number, but like most birders, I do enjoy a nice armchair tick.

Speaking of ticking, I added the gorgeous Common Emerald-Dove to my list. It was split from the also gorgeous Pacific Emerald-Dove. They are a very common sight on the island, and stunning. We looked around the mining areas in hopes of the Purple Heron that Richard had located in November. It would truly be a mega-rarity and a big deal for us. It would be a Lifer for everyone except Richard and Tania. We searched a lot of places without success.

We went to a nesting area of the endangered and wonderfully majestic Abbott's Booby. It is a large booby with very long, tapered wings. It only breeds on Christmas Island. They are stunning to see on their nests and when they fly, their wings appear disproportionately long. Describing them as awkwardly elegant would not be far off the mark. I knew I was going to see them, but still they turned out to be one my favourite birds of the trip.

We returned to our motel home base as a breathtaking sunset poured crimson across the western sky. I was standing on a small

The long-winged, beautiful Abbott's Booby in flight.

A Coconut Crab with a coconut. Yes, they are that big.

island far out in the Indian Ocean. It still doesn't really sink in, so I write. I write so that at least in my words, I relive and re-appreciate these experiences and that is important for me. In remembering and writing, I experience gratitude and that is a stepping-stone toward joy. Yeah, I am working on it and I am grateful.

The next morning, Sunday, 8 December, began clear with a chance of showers, a chance, but not much rain was expected. Three of the four cars were going to an area called the Dales. Jenny said it was an area I shouldn't miss seeing and I do listen to Jenny. It was beautiful and I am very glad I went. On our way into the Dales, we stopped and got up-close looks at a Robber Crab, which is also called a Coconut Crab. It is a massive land crab that can be literally as large as a coconut. And yes, they do crack open, and eat coconuts. They are huge, beautiful land crabs.

We parked and began our hike. It was not a particularly easy hike at my fitness level, but I did okay with some puffing and blowing. There were lots of land crabs around including some very cool small blue ones.

The problem that developed was that the chance of showers became actual downpours. I did not have my fancy, and overly expensive rain sleeve on my camera. I had removed it when I changed the eyepiece back to the regular one. However, at least I had thought (and yes, that can happen) to put a cheap plastic camera cover into one of my cargo pockets. It saved my camera's life. I put my iPhone into Jenny's small waterproof bag. I had also not brought my dry-bag backpack. At the top of one trail, it is possible, and safe, to drink from the Hugh's Dale Waterfall. That is its name and no, I do not know who Hugh was. I filled my water bottle from the waterfall, and I drank from it. Jenny took my photo, and I am grateful that she did. It is a memory I will cherish, always. I drank from a waterfall in a rainforest on an island in the Indian Ocean. Yes, I did that. As we began the hike back up to the cars, the bottom dropped out of the sky and the rain bucketed down.

I filled my waterbottle and drank from a waterfall in a rainforest on an island in the Indian Ocean.

A wet Purple Heron.

We were all drenched to the bone by the time we reached the vehicles. As we were driving out, the crackling CB radio came to life. Through the sounds of the static, broken sentences could be discerned that included the words, 'Purple' and 'Heron'. Glen had found it! Through the sketchy radio communications we established where it was, and Jenny drove us straight there. We were the first to arrive.

The bird was just standing there in the brushy, but fairly open area between the radio domes and the new Detention Centre, which is one creepy, high-tech, prison-looking complex. It looks like a sci-fi movie set. It radiated malice. We stayed away from it. Glen directed us to drive around the backside of the domes and come in behind his vehicle. It is amazing that an almost metre tall heron could blend in as well as it did, but we saw it. And once seen well by all, joy reigned! That expression is particularly appropriate since Joy Tansey was in our car and she had been drenched in rain with the rest of us that morning. Oh yes, puns galore.

We marvelled at the bird. We took photos. We joked. We laughed. We hugged. We fist-bumped. We were in the midst of shared Lifer High. It was shared Mega Lifer High and that is most excellent stuff. It's one of the best Lifer Highs. We all had wanted that bird. As I mentioned, only Tania and Richard had it on their Australian lists and it was this bird from earlier in the year. I think it was only the third record in Australia. It was a magnificent sighting. There were a couple of others who needed to see it, but it was refound the next day in the same general area. There was also an Oriental Pratincole hanging around the puddles by one of radio domes, a cool bird for the island, but one I had seen back in 2012 in Victoria as well as repeatedly around Broome, Western Australia, toward the end of our visit there in 2016. Still a lovely bird to see anytime.

Later that arvo we stopped by a Red-footed Booby nesting area. They are such cool birds with extremely red feet. I loved seeing these awesome birds and I took some photos.

We also did a little sightseeing that afternoon. Christmas Island is truly a beautiful place just about everywhere you look. There was also an almost comical Brown Booby standing around in the rocks on the shore.

Red-footed Booby coming at you.

Back in the settlement, the group had dinner at a very good Chinese restaurant. I attended, but I had eaten earlier as I do. I did taste a few things and I ate there later in the week when we had an earlier dinner one night. It really was very good.

Monday 9 December began with the culmination of a practical joke on me. That is something that I would normally not be keen on, no not if it was ever so. But this was completely good-natured, and I was actually pleased that these people felt comfortable enough to 'mess' with me. It began because I had heard that the birding group on Christmas the week before us had dipped on Java Sparrow. This was true. But Richard and some of the others decided to let me think that the Sparrows were going to be very difficult for us to find as well, and that we might not find them at all. He told me that there had been a family feeding them in the settlement and that is where the birds had traditionally been seen. However, that family had moved away (this part was true as well). That morning after driving around a small neighbourhood building my anticipation, Richard pulled over beside a house with a birdbath in the yard. He got out and spoke with the fellow who lived there.

Brown Booby looking a bit like a Muppet.

The actually quite easy to find, Java Sparrow.

And in a small tree right in front of us were eight or ten beautiful Java Sparrows. Yes, he 'got' me. So it was a good and an enjoyable joke with a very happy ending!

I do not recall the other parts of that morning. I had Java Sparrow Lifer High, and I was also excited because just after noon, we were going to take a little boat ride. We were going sightseeing and snorkelling! It was Richard, Jenny, Joy, Bill Betts and me. This was the regularly scheduled half-day boat trip for Richard's tours. I love snorkelling and very rarely have the chance to do it. So of course, I was excited to be snorkelling in the Indian Ocean off Christmas Island. My excitement was also massively heightened by the fact that we had heard there were Whale Sharks around. They were being seen very regularly just off the island. They are the largest fish in the world and had been a fascination for me since I was a child. That was when I had read *Kon-Tiki*, Thor Heyerdahl's journal about travelling across the Pacific on a balsa raft. As a kid, I would take that book out and sit and stare at the old black-and-white photo plates. I especially would look at the photos of that massive fish. I no longer have that book, nor do I know how it got lost. It

The author and a Whale Shark, an experience I will never forget (photo by William Betts).

should still be amongst my most treasured family possessions, the very few that are left after all the insane moving house that I have done. But sadly, *Kon-Tiki* got away at some point years past. As I write this, I will add that I ordered a copy of the book and read it not long after I had returned from the islands. I am sad that the Whale Shark was mistreated by that expedition. I suppose I had forgotten that part, perhaps on purpose. I was genuinely surprised at how familiar those old black-and-white photos were to me though. I can remember clearly staring at that photo of the spotted back of that massive fish and wishing so much that I could see one. I never really dreamed that one day I would not only do that, but that I would be in the water swimming with one.

We were told by the man driving the boat that if he saw a Whale Shark, he would stop, point to where the shark was swimming, and we should get immediately into the water. Then we should swim as quickly as we could toward it because the sharks can decide to just sink into the depths and disappear. We were holding our masks and fins in anticipation. We were excited. Not more than ten minutes into the trip, he dropped the boat out of gear and literally yelled, "WHALE SHARK!" He pointed off the port side shouting, "There! There! Quick! Quick! Swim! Swim! There!" We were all in the water in seconds and swimming "quick, quick" toward where he had pointed.

And then, there it was. I can still see that first Whale Shark in my mind as it materialised out of the deep, dark blue depths gliding through the water in front of us, massive but graceful. These huge fish swim with seemingly effortless ease and grace. It is as if they are in slow motion. It was everything I had hoped for. I swam along with it and watched it. Time had stopped. I just swam along the surface, propelled by my fins, breathing through my snorkel and gazing down watching the beautiful behemoth before me. Time had stopped. Nothing existed but my breathing and this magnificent creature. Eventually it slowly began sinking into the depths. I watched it until I could no longer distinguish its shape beneath me. Then I swam back to the boat. We were all in a state of amazement. As my dear friend Jenny said, "It was rapturous". And that is not hyperbole. There was certainly a feeling of rapture.

Another with the Whale Shark (photo by William Betts).

We shared a very wet, very heartfelt, very grateful hug.

The boat stopped a couple of times, and we swam with a second Whale Shark as well as snorkelling in another spot with some beautiful reef fish. This is all now a blur in my mind, a wonderful blur of disjointed, joyful memories. However, I will never forget the third and last shark. There is a framed picture of me swimming above it on the wall of my study. I can glance to my left and see it. I am so grateful for that image and the other Whale Shark photos taken by my dear friend Bill Betts. I look at, and I am grateful for that photo every day that I am in my study. I love my memories built of words, but I do treasure that image. I just looked at it again.

We were on our way back in when as he had done twice before, the guy driving the boat yelled, "WHALE SHARK! There! There! Swim! Fast! There!" And once again that is what we did. This fish came closer. I was, for the third time in my life, swimming by, and then above, a Whale Shark.

Sitting here now, I can see it in my mind. I can clearly remember the back of that magnificent creature gliding along beneath me. I remained on the surface breathing through my snorkel as the shark drifted up until it was just beneath me. It was closer to me than I would have chosen to swim to it, but it had come to me. The spotted pattern on its skin looked like a living, moving Aboriginal painting. I can see it clearly in my mind as I write these words. I can feel the water playing along my skin and hear the sound of my breathing through the snorkel. I remember these things all at once and my heart catches for a moment. It is difficult to hold on to. This is why I need to write, because I can reread these experiences and hold onto them for a moment or two longer. And I do have Bill's photos to look at. Thank you again my friend. It is the first photo I have ever framed of myself (not counting the literally hundreds upon hundreds of promotional eight-by-tens in clubs and venues from the years when I was an entertainer. They are a different thing entirely). For the rest of my days, that wonderful photo will hang somewhere wherever I am, so that I can gaze at it

The Christmas Boobook has very yellow eyes.

and relive those magical moments with that majestic, magnificent, massive creature.

That night we went out spotlighting and after a few stops, Richard found us a Christmas Boobook. This was again an example of Richard keeping track of things on Christmas and Cocos. If a bird is not found in one expected location, he knows where to check a second, or third, or fifth. It is his knowledge of his islands that is so key to his, and our, successes. It is what he does.

The next days were spent birding and sightseeing as well as navigating around the crabs. The Christmas Island Red Crab Migration was now fully underway. It is world famous and quite a sight to see. It's a lot of crabs and a lot of closed roads, which can limit accessibility to some parts of the island. Fortunately it really did not impact our birding plans very much, if at all, and it was more than fascinating to see this incredible natural phenomenon taking place. Tens of thousands of the big red crabs all clambering on top of, and over, each other toward the sea. It is a very cool thing to witness. Crab migration, cool.

On our last night we had a group dinner at the nice restaurant

One of the famous Christmas Island Red Crabs.

Christmas Island Red Crab migration underway.

just across the street from the motel. Anyone who had reached a particularly significant number on their Life List was acknowledged and asked to say a few words. I had reached 750 with the Christmas Boobook. I really do not remember what I said. I really don't. I do remember not feeling particularly eloquent. It had been a massive two weeks and I was tired on a deep level. I would call it a good tired, but tired. I was certainly very happy, although I was not keen to leave the island. I would happily have flown back to Cocos and just stayed there. Not necessarily birding or doing anything except absorbing the vibe and listening to the melody of the island. It plays in my heart as I write this. I will return.

On 13 December, we boarded a plane and flew to Perth. There I once again stayed in the unremarkable, but clean and convenient motel near the airport. The next day I flew to Melbourne. My Troopi had patiently waited for over two weeks in the long-term parking. I climbed into that familiar, comfortable seat and drove back to Lara. I had done it. I had been to, and birded, Christmas and Cocos islands and I was glad, grateful and tired.

A portion of Christmas Island coastline.

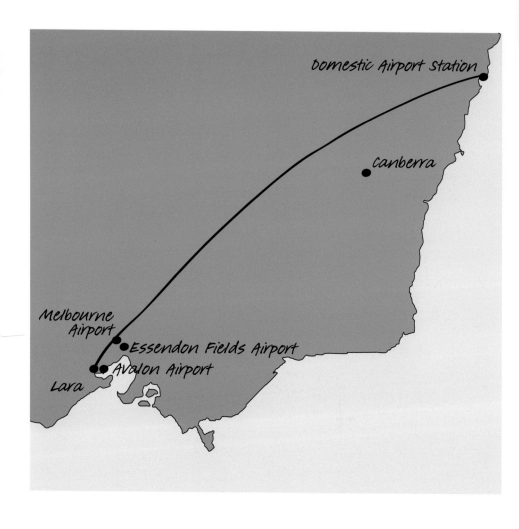

{ 23 }

A Twitch, A Hospital, A Pelagic and the Pandemic

December 2019– March 2020

A Twitch

I was working. I was at my desk writing the blog entries about those two glorious weeks on Cocos and Christmas Islands. I had jokingly, but very accurately, referred to those weeks as 'Richard Baxter's Tour of Abundant Birding Bliss'. That is exactly what they were. Then I read on the 'Australian Twitchers' Facebook page that a Kentish Plover had been reported on a beach in Sydney, but the bird had gone missing. This was on a Wednesday evening.

When I heard that the bird was refound Thursday arvo, I ignored my usual anxieties and booked the first flight Friday morning. That would be a 6am flight. My old pal Robert was going to pick me up at the airport in Sydney. For once I could use the wonderfully close-by Avalon Airport! It is literally five minutes from this house, but it only services direct flights to Sydney. You can go to other destinations, but you will have to connect in Sydney and that can be a huge drag.

I was up at 3am, parked and in the airport before first light. It

271

was an easy flight and I arrived in Sydney in less than an hour and a half. Robert had first collected Christine (a mutual friend from social media) at her Sydney home, then they had come to pick me up at the airport. It was only about 30 minutes from the airport to the spot where the plover was being seen. We arrived there and parked. We followed a path down to, and a couple of hundred metres along, the water's edge. We had arrived just as the tide was the right level and there before us was the Kentish Plover! It was standing around with a few Red-capped Plovers. Joy of a successful twitch!

Then the second-best part of a twitch began, the coming together of the birding tribe. This wondrous joy, as well you know by now that I call Lifer High, flowed to and fro amongst us like the magical energy that it is. It was so palpable that it was almost visible, like a glowing light passing between us. It was the love, the elation. It was friends sharing their passion in the very best way. Robert Shore and I took what must by now be scores of Lifer Selfies that we've taken together. I got to hug the brilliant photographer and long-time social media friend, David Stowe. I had spoken several times with David on the phone, but this was the first time we had met in person. It was also the first time I had met Jenny Stiles as well as Christine in person. Both were friends from social media, but I consider both to be real friends. There were lots of hugs going around. One of my internet friends referred to these close social media friends, as 'e-migos'. I like that. They are real friends and I do have some very good e-migos. I am very grateful for them.

Robert and I went to a cool little local outdoor café suggested by Christine and had some Lifer Pie. I do not recall exactly what I had, but I did return to that café again with other friends after Robert headed off to get some much needed and well-deserved rest. So I know that I had some sort of Lifer Pie there twice.

David and Christine drove me back to the airport. I was able to move my flight ahead and I flew back to Avalon arriving there at 5:40pm in the midst of 45 °C heat in Lara (American friends,

Kentish Plover twitch success.

Red-capped Plover on the left, Lachlan Hall's head in the middle and the Kentish Plover on the right.

David Stowe's wonderful Lifer Selfie for the Kentish Plover. This is the coming together of some of the tribe and the pure, genuine joy of Lifer High on a successful twitch! Left to right: Lachlan Hall, Christine Schulte, David Stowe, Robert Shore and me. I love this photo.

that is 113 °F). I drove the five minutes to the house and collapsed with Lifer High still reverberating through my exhausted body. It continued to echo in my heart in the coming days, like distant thunder recalling the joy of twitch success.

A Hospital

On Tuesday morning, 14 January, I felt some rather intense and familiar pain in my gut. Since my major abdominal surgery in June 1995, I have lived with the possibility of having a small bowel obstruction. I have been hospitalised for it six times and this was to be another. After a couple of nights in hospital, as has happened in the past, gratefully, the obstruction resolved itself without the need for surgery.

I was released Thursday morning. The pain relief was working a charm and I went home feeling good. Looking back, it is all just a fog in my memory. I was drained and tired. But I was back home in my study and grateful to be there. Although I felt like an old, wrung-out, threadbare washrag.

A Pelagic

Just before Christmas, Rohan Clarke had posted the dates of his quarterly Eaglehawk Neck double-header pelagics. I was interested in the February 1-2 trip, hoping for Gould's and possibly Mottled Petrels. I did get a spot, along with James and Alan Stringer. Robert Shore was going as well, but later had to cancel. As I have mentioned, I very much love Eaglehawk Neck and I have done a few trips out of there. Pelagics are the essence of 'a perpetual series of occasions for hope'. You truly never know what you might see out there deep-sea birding.

Saturday began as a lovely morning. However, the winds steadily increased, and the seas built accordingly. It got downright cold, and we were getting knocked about a bit. Of course I was wearing the patch and it did its job. I did not get seasick. Thank goodness for those patches.

Friends on the pelagic, including Paul Brooks in shorts and crocs, Andrew Robinson and Rohan Clarke in extremely red pants.

White-faced and Grey-backed Storm-petrels dancing on a bumpy sea.

We reached the deep water beyond the shelf and began to berley (chum). There were a lot of birds around. The highlights were a Cook's Petrel, a truly gorgeous dark morph Soft-plumaged Petrel and yes, a Lifer for me, a Gould's Petrel. Tick! It was a fast-flying bird, but I saw it well. Thank you, Rohan for first spotting it, and a special thank you to my dear friend, Paul Brooks for bodily pointing me at it when it came in and looped across our stern. I appreciated that my friend. Then the bird flew down the port side of the boat and was gone. No time for photos, just a lifer-look and that was enough.

There were lots of birds around us. We had Wilson's, Grey-backed and White-faced Storm-petrels dancing together on the water behind the boat. We had lots of Albatrosses, Wandering, Southern and Northern Royal, Black-browed, Campbell's, Buller's and scores of Shy. It was indeed rough, one of the rougher pelagics I've done. The ride back in was 'interesting', but just fine. As I have said, John's boat, the *Paulette,* is a very stable, safe boat. I also have complete confidence in his abilities as its captain. The next day, Sunday, was rough as well, but not quite as 'lumpy' and with fewer birds. My hopes for a Mottled Petrel did not come to fruition, but I had gotten my Gould's on Saturday and I was very happy about that.

It was wonderful seeing some of my dear birding friends. These are people I value and feel a connection with, but that I usually only see on the occasional birding trips or twitches. I had not seen Paul Brooks since the Juan Fernandez Petrel trip. Yes, these are some of the best. My dear friend Karen Dick as well as Els, and Rich, and Andy, and Janine, and Nick, and of course Rohan. These are friends, some closer than others, and some that I see more often than others, but all part of that special tribe that 'gets' it. Birders. Those who understand heading out to sea in often uncomfortable conditions, but with hearts alive with hope.

Keeping in contact with these scattered friends is the most important part of social media for me. I can at least follow along with them online even when I do not see them in person for months, or even years, at a time. That is why it is worth 'putting up with' social media to keep those connections going. It gets more difficult as the platforms deteriorate. I use Facebook and have for

Buller's Albatross, because they are beautiful.

Not a bad view from the picnic tables by the food van.

years. Although it has degenerated into a frustrating (and often infuriating) mess. But as I write these words, I am still on there and even have my own groups: 'An Australian Birding Year-The Book' and 'Birder Ink'.

Back on shore, many of the group made the short walk up the hill behind the boat ramp to the food truck. As mentioned earlier, our traditional, after-pelagic meeting spot, the wonderful little café called Havnabite Tucker Spot had gone out of business. It was a wonderful place for friends to visit and share some delicious chips. Gratefully, the food truck had excellent chips as well. They also had very good prawns and scallops. I ate my early dinner there on both days. We sat at the picnic tables overlooking the coast. It gave us a ridiculously gorgeous view of the sea and the rocky shore.

After another nice night's sleep at that familiar comfortable room at Lufra, James, Alan and I had a leisurely drive up to the Hobart Airport. The trip home was gratefully uneventful (as one hopes for travel to be), and James and I collected my old Prius from Long-Term Parking at about 3:15. By 4:30 I was taking a short nap at the house in Lara. The next day, I had a wonderful, quiet and relaxing Lifer Day in celebration of the Gould's Petrel, and I began writing a blog entry about the trip. Then at 5:30 that afternoon, Lynn went with me to Bistro St Jean in Geelong for a delicious Lifer dinner. It was the best Barramundi I have ever eaten, and I have partaken of some very, very good Barramundi. It was literally grilled to perfection and a fitting treat for my 753rd Australian Life Bird. It would be my last Lifer for a while. There was a darkness looming on the horizon of the world.

The Pandemic

It is called COVID-19 and as I write these words it has crushed the USA with well over a half-a-million deaths there alone. My politics are of science, compassion, equality and thought. I will leave it at that.

Here in the state of Victoria we have had competent leadership. And we have done pretty well. Back to the beginning in 2020, most of the coming months were spent in varying degrees of isolation here. Lynn and I stayed at home as much as possible and it was possible for us to stay home a lot. I was ridiculously sedentary for months. I watched a lot of television and spent even more time on the computer than usual. There were houseplants that were more active than I was.

I gained weight that I truly did not need to gain. I had gotten into at least a sort of mediocre shape before going to Cocos and Christmas Islands, but I had lost any of that fitness and more. Months went by like weeks, and soon it was winter in Victoria and my body shape had begun to resemble a giant golf ball on a tee (all belly, skinny legs). Although I reckon I had weighed more, numbers-wise, I was the 'fattest' I had ever been. I did not want to turn into one of those gigantic-bellied old guys, but I had.

There were milestones. On 16 April 2020, I reached 30 years of sobriety. It was certainly a subdued celebration. So subdued that I do not even remember what I did to celebrate it. It was such a significant number that I had looked forward to reaching, and yet it was anticlimactic at best. One day at a time, one day at a time. And time marched on.

I will quickly mention that as I do this last rewrite in December of 2021, I have gotten into much better shape. Over this past year I have modified my eating habits to taking smaller portions and making wiser choices, and I have become a hiker. I started with half-hour walks and progressed to regular 10–15 kilometre hikes in the You Yangs (Wurdi Youang). I've lost over 20 kilos and I had to purchase new jeans and shorts. I have not been a 32 waist in 20 years. It does feel good. I am no longer shaped like a 'golf ball on a tee'.

{ 24 }

A Quick Bit on Ageing and Hope

September 2020

The pandemic continued, and birding and travel was on hold (never fear, there is more coming very soon).

I am at an age where I have lost quite a few friends and loved ones. I've also seen the passing of some of my biggest musical heroes and influences. I was gutted by the losses of Jerry Jeff Walker, Shel Silverstein and John Prine in particular.

Okay, A Little About Ageing (more birding adventures coming soon!)

Ageing is. It just is. Acceptance is a process. Acceptance does not mean surrender, but it does mean accepting some facts because they are facts. Acceptance is indeed similar to surrender, but there is a passivity in the word surrender that I equate with giving up. I believe that acceptance is more proactive than giving up, surrender seems too passive and victim-like. But of course, they are both just words.

For me acceptance means that I must learn to understand that I do have limitations. And I must learn to accept them without (much) resentment, anger or too much grieving. Grieving is a natural part of these ageing changes, whether I acknowledge it or not. As I look back on these last several years, I do grieve. I miss some things that are gone and that will never be again. There is no way around that. I have to accept it, adjust as best I can, and go on living. Living a changed life at times but living my life.

I made a meme once that said, 'Do it now. You never know when too late will happen'. And that is true. The old saying, 'It is never too late to (whatever)', sadly is bullshit. Sometimes it is absolutely too late. There is not a living soul who will not eventually arrive at 'too late'. But I've got stuff to do before then. At this age, I am working toward identifying, and then focusing on, my future as two stacks. These are not unlike the Serenity Prayer in Alcoholics Anonymous: 'To accept the things I cannot change and the courage to change the things I can', which I consider one of the cornerstones for living, regardless of addiction or recovery. Those words are life wisdom. So, I live with these two stacks as follows:

Stack One:
The few things that have become, and must now remain, impossible for me to do anymore. They do exist and they demand graceful acceptance. Not often easy, but I am working on it.

Stack Two:
Things that are now, and can still be, possible for me to do. But they may require more effort and possibly changes in the ways that I do them. But, most importantly, they are still doable. These are the things from which hope can rise. For life to have any quality, this stack needs to be the larger of the two.

Hope is Life. Life is Hope
Hope is one of the most important words for me. It is living. There have been times in my life and these past few years, when I felt like I had lost all hope, or even the ability to have hope. This is called depression.

But now I do have hopes and I have plans. Due to the pandemic and border restrictions and lockdowns, some of those plans had to be postponed or changed in the months since I began writing this account. But things are beginning to get back to normal, Beginning, I hope.

Hopes and dreams are two words that are often put together. I prefer the more solid word 'plan' to the word 'dream' in this context. I am planning some things. Although particularly in today's world, plans need to be fluid and flexible. I have learned how to look forward to something without being completely attached to the outcome. That is the hope I am talking about. Expectations can bring misery. Hope does not. As I am writing, I realise how important my memories are for me. However, I cannot let them replace my hope for future experiences.

Writing has become a massively important part of my life. Writing the first book was done in the largest part to merely preserve my memories of that wonderful year and to realise what we had done. And then it blossomed into a real book that has been enjoyed by a lot of people. Now I am writing this sequel and again I am hoping to preserve precious memories of my experiences that might otherwise get away from me. I do not know how people who don't write manage. I really could not exist without writing. Which brings to mind one of my favourite quotes. It is by Anne Marrow Lindbergh. It is:

'One writes not to be read but to breathe … one writes to think, to pray, to analyse. One writes to clear one's mind, to dissipate one's fears, to face one's doubts, to look at one's mistakes – in order to retrieve them. One writes to capture and crystallise one's joy, but also to disperse one's gloom. Like prayer – you go to it in sorrow more than joy, for help, a road back to 'grace'.'

Ms Lindbergh related to writing in the same ways that I do. Writing helps to give me perspective and to better understand my life and who I am. A while ago, I received a nice compliment and Lynn said sweetly, "You should be proud of yourself." Without even thinking I responded, "I don't know how to do that." And that is absolutely true. However, I can write about it and in that way I can at least try to realise it by reading my own words. Maybe on occasion, I can be genuinely proud of myself. I know that sometimes I deserve to be. We all do.

Now let's go birding!

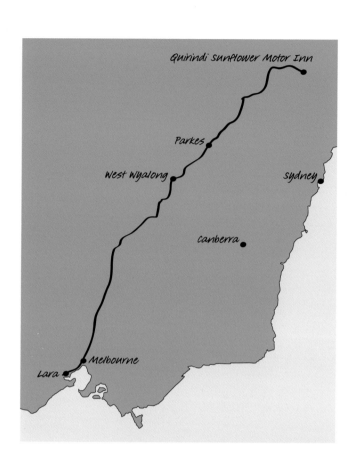

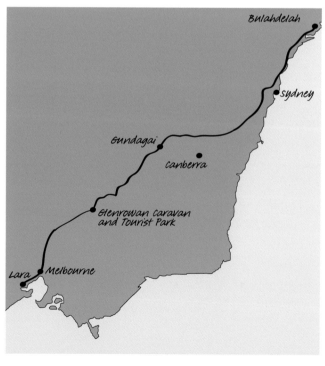

{ 25 }

Two Button-quail Tales (Futton-bucking-quail No More!) New South Wales

14 December 2020 and 4 February 2021

First: Red-chested Button-quail
I found Lifer joy in a place called Warrah Ridge, New South Wales. As has often been the case over the years, it was somewhere I had never heard of until I needed to go there to see a bird.

It took four days, 27 hours of driving and approximately 2,400 kilometres travelled to finally added a new Life Bird to my Aussie list. The Red-chested Button-quail. Yes, a button-quail. It was my first Lifer since the pandemic came to Oz. The long year of the virus had eliminated my travelling birding adventures. And once again, it was my old friend Robert Shore who alerted, then encouraged me, to go after a bird. No surprises there. Also, once again, my birding buddy, James Cornelious went with me. Yes, Team Troopi would ride again but this time we were wearing masks. I mean, indoors.

Beautiful light under an angry sky making the hay look golden.

We did not wear them riding along in Troopi.

Robert had been on a trip to Mount Kaputar National Park in New South Wales and had gone to the Grundy Fire Tower near Nowendoc looking for lizards. He was driving back home to Parkes by way of unsealed roads and had heard about the Button-quails. Since it was only a bit off his route, he diverted to check them out. After having a look around, he stopped to chat with another birder. It turned out that this birder had gotten some terrific photographs of the Red-chested Button-quail. He and Robert walked up the shoulder of the road and flushed several of them.

Then they waited until dark and spotlighted for the birds hoping to possibly get better photos. Using a torch, they managed to find several RCBQs, including a mother with five or six chicks. They took a few quick photos, then left them alone. As Robert was leaving the area, he stopped and rang me. He knew it was a bird I needed and there was actually a place where this often-difficult bird was being seen in numbers! That is so not normally a button-quail kind of thing, quite the contrary, but they were there. He had photos. I knew that I had to go and try to see them. I also knew that I needed get up there as soon as possible. So Sunday morning Team Troopi was on the way to New South Wales.

James and I left Lara at 9:20am and drove to Robert and Judy Shore's comfortable home in Parkes. We arrived there about 6:30pm. That's after over 750 kilometres and about nine and a half Troopi hours. We had a lovely visit with the Shores. They are certainly both people who I would like to see more often. Many of my dearer friends are spread too far out across this country (as well as across the globe) to see on any sort of regular basis.

As we do, we went to sleep fairly early and were up and on the road by 6am. After an easy drive, we arrived at Cattle Lane in Warrah Ridge, New South Wales, at about 11am filled with anticipation and yes, hope. This would normally not be thought of as ideal Button-quail birding time. But then again, this situation wasn't exactly normal. So we gave it a go and to our surprise, within only ten minutes we had seen one! We had beheld an actual Red-chested Button-quail. There was much joy! And it was only the beginning.

Another bird flushed. It flew, or jumped, only a couple of metres.

Red-chested Button-quail in Warrah Ridge, New South Wales.

Red-chested Button-quail standing tall.

And it hopped up on the low scrub and just stood there right in front of us! It gave us both wonderful lifer-looks for perhaps three seconds before dropping down into the brush and into invisibility.

We continued walking up and down the shoulders of that road and we saw, or flushed, at least a dozen birds including a young bird that seemingly had gotten stuck upside down after trying to fly away. James carefully helped it up and safely on its way. I am not sure what had happened with that bird, but it seemed fine after James rescued it.

A couple hundred metres away, a combine tractor was harvesting the hay in a large paddock. It seemed possible that as they harvested, they were driving these Button-quail from the paddock out to the shoulders of the road on this side of the fence. It is a good theory anyway. We spent several hours out there before going into the closest town which was Quirindi and only about 20 minutes away.

Around mid-afternoon, we checked into the very nice little Sun-flower Motor Inn. I was as exhausted as I have ever been. Trudging up and down the shoulders of the road, often through thick and tangled brush was tiresome. And my fitness level at that time was perhaps the lowest it has ever been. The long drives had also taken a toll. Without exaggeration, I staggered like a drunk person as I approached the reception desk. I could not even remember my mobile number. I was that exhausted. But on the inside, I was very, very happy. Lifer High!

I collapsed in the room and took about a two-hour nap before we went back over to the Cattle Lane site around 7:30pm. We bumped into friends Jeff Jones and Bruce Watts who were also there for the Button-quail. The late arvo light was beautiful under the grey, cloudy skies as we waited for darkness to look for the RCBQ's. We hoped to see them out more in the open and get some photos in our torch lights. We were successful. We had two particularly co-operative birds. And I will add a big thank you to Jeff for holding his torch as we photographed one of the ones that he and Bruce located. After we had taken a few pictures, we let them be. As I say, those little birds owed me nothing more. I had seen them so well and even had photos. I will never again refer to that family of birds as 'Bucking-futton-quail'.

The next morning, we left the Sunflower Motor Inn and drove down to West Wyalong, New South Wales. As we passed through Parkes, James reckoned he had seen a Ground Cuckoo-shrike on the grounds of the hospital. Granted, he also reckoned he had seen a Channel-billed Cuckoo a few days ago on the way up to Parkes. That bird had turned out to be a Little Pied Cormorant perching rather uncharacteristically at the top of a tall tree. But this time, he was so sure that I turned Troopi around and drove back to check. And to my surprise we were definitely looking at a Ground Cuckoo-shrike hopping happily about the neatly mown grass of the hospital grounds. This was a bird that in the first book, Lynn and I had quite a difficult time finding. Now here was one in Parkes right by the hospital. James called Robert to let him know about this pretty unusual sighting in his town.

We continued on to West Wyalong and spent the night in a

comfortable and reasonable cabin. I had stayed there twice in the past camping in Troopi. It is a good stop-over going north and I reckon I might use their cabins again some time. I am glad I did this time. I was tired. Happy as, but tired as. I managed a short nap again while James wandered about the neighbourhood birding. There were Major Mitchell's Cockatoos right beside our cabin. They are always a treat to see.

The next morning I was up silly-early, and we were on the road by 6am, arriving back in Lara in the early arvo. I was still riding that Lifer High that I so often write about. As I have said, it can reverberate through me for days. It is a lovely feeling of accomplishment, appreciation, gratitude and satisfaction. I was tired but I did have a new Lifer. I am truly not as attached to the total number anymore, but I love getting a Lifer, a new bird experienced! And I do keep track. RCBQ was number 754 on my Australian list and I wasn't finished with button-quail.

Second: Red-backed Button-quail

Okay, I love button-quail. That is not a sentence I ever expected to write. My joy of finally seeing a Black-breasted Button-quail was told in chapter 7 of this book.

On Thursday night, 28 January, I saw a Facebook post by Bruce Watts and Jeff Jones regarding seeing, and even taking some gorgeous photos of, a Red-backed Button-quail. This was up near Nabiac, New South Wales, the night before. I contacted Jeff and he shared the location and details with me. Of course I really wanted that bird. I knew it was a long shot. It was also my granddaughter, Delilah's, birthday on Saturday and James was out of town for the weekend. So I made plans to leave Monday arvo. It was about 1,350 kilometres to the birding site.

James arrived at noon and after we had bought a few groceries, we headed up to stay a night at Glenrowan Caravan Park, the Turquoise Parrots caravan park. We rolled in about 4pm and set Troopi up to camp in a beautiful area under a tree out the back where I had parked in the past. And yes indeed, we saw Turquoise Parrots as I always have there. I was also quite flattered that the park owner, Kylee, came over to Troopi and asked me to autograph her copy of *An Australian Birding Year*. I told her that I was writing the second book and that she would be in it! And yes indeed, here she is. Hi Kylee!

Yes Kylee, I love your caravan park. We had an excellent and peaceful night's sleep inside Troopi. It was the first time I had slept in her in for about two years. It is not as easy for me to get in and out of, nor to move around inside the back of Troopi as it had been. I have never been a limber person, but with age and weight gain had come even more limited flexibility. Some of my joints just did not seem to work as well as they used to.

Speaking of which, my left fibula will 'pop' out of my knee joint if I am not careful with it. This first happened in January 2016 and is recalled in chapter 14 of the first book. It amazes doctors. My GP here said that in over 30 years' practice, he had never seen

James behind Troopi in her favourite spot at Glenrowan Caravan Park.

anything like it. I can cause it to happen, but it hurts when it does. I have been told by doctors never to do it. So I only ever do it on purpose if I need to show it to a new doctor. It occasionally pops out on its own. To pop it back into place, I have to be able to sit up and swing my leg out straight. It makes an audible 'clunk' when it goes back. It hurts while it's out and it remains tender for a while afterwards. I have been warned that one day, it just won't go back into place. That would be hugely unpleasant. I reckon I would have to get myself to an emergency room somehow. I sure hope it never happens. Like much of life, it just is what it is until it isn't.

The next morning we drove on to stay the night again at Robert and Judy Shore's in Parkes. We arrived in the later arvo, but a full three hours earlier than the last time. Lara to Parkes is an uncomfortably long drive in Troopi hours. We had a delicious dinner and another wonderful visit with the Shores. As I said before, I really do wish they lived closer. They are good friends and enjoyable, comfortable company.

Wednesday morning we headed over and up toward Nabiac, New South Wales. We checked into one of my favourite motels in Australia. We arrived in the early arvo at the Mount View Motel in Bulahdelah where I had reserved a room. We would be using Troopi as transport, not accommodation. The rooms there are excellent and very reasonably priced. Our lovely, air-conditioned suite with two beds and a kitchenette was only a hundred dollars, almost unheard of in Australia. Not knowing how long our quest might take, I asked if it was possible to keep it for an additional couple of nights if necessary. It was.

James also took a very cool photo of me there. In front of the motel is a big Koala. You can go in through the back and then stand up and it appears that it has its arms around you. So of course I did this, and as I said, James took my photo. I was able to grab a short nap before we drove the 40 minutes to the area near Nabiac where Jeff Jones our friend and our Red-backed Button-quail connection in New South Wales, was meeting us at 7pm. Just a few kilometres

The big Koala and me in front of Mount View Motel in Bulahdelah, New South Wales (photo by James Cornelious).

from the coordinates where we were meeting him, our passing in Troopi flushed an RBBQ off the shoulder of the road.

We arrived where Jeff and Bruce had seen the birds on the 27th and soon Jeff joined us. After parking, we saw a few Brown Quail and flushed what could have been a Button-quail. In a later examination of James' photos, we had indeed seen an RBBQ crossing the road near where we had parked.

Jeff arrived (he lives an hour or so from the spot) and we went to where he and Bruce had seen them, and the birds were calling! Even I could hear the deep, loud, distinctive, ascending, *oom, oom, oom, oom, oom* call. It was not far from us either. We heard at least three separate birds in there, but not one of them was interested in coming out and being seen. After it became full dark, they stopped calling. We did not hear another sound out of them. We trudged about in the very wet brush in hopes of flushing one without success. We bid Jeff farewell and he went home. We went back our motel.

I got into my comfortable bed just before 11pm and as I checked my phone, I saw that Victoria had gotten a locally acquired case of COVID and new restrictions were coming into effect. Damn. I managed to go to sleep but when I awoke at 2am, I remembered the virus news and anxiety shot through me like an electric shock. And that was that for any more sleep. Less than three hours, just damn. I finally woke James up at five and we drove up to Nabiac for first light. We went back to the same spot and soon heard them calling again! But even though one sounded quite close, we still could not get a look at it. We moved about trying to locate it as it got later in the morning. It was not showing itself, but it continued calling.

We headed out to the road and as we trudged back to Troopi, I suggested that James walk into the grass on the shoulder a bit to see if one might flush. In literally a matter of seconds, a Red-backed Button-quail erupted at his feet and flew across the road in front of us. It was a flight view, but it was without a doubt, an RBBQ! It dropped down on the other side of the road and disappeared into the thick bush.

We heard more calling and we walked down the road toward the calls. There was a track going in that was covered in water (there was a lot of standing water everywhere). We stood by the gate of that track and clearly heard the calling again. It really sounded close. Then, less than ten metres in front of us, she flew diagonally across the track. It was a beautifully coloured female; they are the more colourful of the two. We both had heartstopping, gorgeous, full-on side views of that RBBQ. The sun was behind us, and I will never forget that beautiful bird and how brightly her colours showed as she flew across the open area of the track. She landed in the scrub somewhere on the other side and as they do, disappeared. We had experienced beautiful views of a Red-backed Button-quail. Rejoice dear hearts, rejoice.

We stood around and listened as that bird called sporadically for a while before we walked back to Troopi. We were both soaked from the thighs down from walking through the very wet brush. I got into the back of Troopi and decided to change into dry pants. As I was doing that, James saw 'something' run cross the road in front of our vehicle in the same spot where he had flushed the RBBQ on the shoulder of the road earlier. He walked around in front of

Red-backed Button-quail in Nabiac, New South Wales. Joy! (photo by James Cornelious).

Troopi to have a look and saw that a Red-backed Button-quail had crossed the road and stopped for just a moment in the grass. And in that moment, James was able to get a photo! Joy, joy, joy. As James and I say after a successful twitch, "We did it!" We actually continued to say this many times over the coming days because we did! The Button-quail were still calling as we were leaving. It was close to 10am. I always thought of them as being more cre-puscular, if not actually nocturnal, but these certainly were most active during the daylight hours.

The Lifer High was wonderful, but even Button-quail Lifer High could not overcome three hours of sleep for too long. I was happy but stupid-tired as we drove back to the motel. We spent a couple of hours there and then I took a much-needed nap. When I got up, we headed north again to a spot where my buddy, Liam Murphy, had given us the coordinates for Mangrove Gerygone. That would be a Lifer for James. After a little over an hour's drive, I parked Troopi across from the Manning River in Harrington, NSW. We walked over to the edge of the bush along the river and literally in seconds, a little bird flew in right in front of us. It was a Mangrove Gerygone.

As I have mentioned lots of times, it is better for me to eat early. So just after 5:00pm, I made a sandwich in the back of Troopi while James had a wander around. I was sitting in a carpark of a large bowling club, and I had a lovely view of the water. Life in the back of Troopi can be sweet. I enjoyed that sandwich although I did get a few looks from the punters parking and going into the club. I will note that there were not any 'parking only for…' types of signs there or I would not have parked. I do obey signs almost all of the time.

We drove back to the motel and had a very good night's sleep. The next morning we were on our way back to Victoria. We drove the most direct route. This took us by Sydney using the truly amaz-ing new tunnel. I don't know what the toll price was, but it was worth it (I have a device that pays tolls electronically). With this

James inside Troopi watching the sun setting under storm clouds.

new miracle of engineering, one drives into a tube in the ground on the north edge of Sydney and comes out nine kilometres later on the other side of the worst of the congestion. It makes the drive through that part of Sydney a breeze. I used to avoid that route, when at all possible, now I no longer need to avoid it. That is brilliant. As we know, it is not often that I am grateful for change, but this one? It is a very positive change. Thank you, National Transport Network (I looked that up online).

We headed on to Gundagai, the home of the 'Dog on a Tucker Box'. It is a famous Australian poem about a dog loyally guarding its owner's tucker box (a large lunchbox). There are various interpretations of the original poem or song. The actual meaning seems to be lost to time, but it is a well-known monument. There is a statue of the dog sitting on a tucker box there. This has been a tourist attraction since the early 1930s. I have stopped at that statue, and I have stayed in Gundagai a few other times as well.

There were some very severe thunderstorms rolling around the

James' photo of lightning over Troopi in Gundagai, New South Wales.

area and we took a room at the Tuckerbox Motor Inn. It is a very nice and convenient (but a bit dear) motel just off the highway. We watched the thunderstorms booming about and James even got some photos of lightning using his phone. I do love a good storm, and it stormed and thundered most of the night. The next morning we drove on to Lara, arriving in the early afternoon. Yes, in time for a nap. We did it. A Lifer Day would be coming soon.

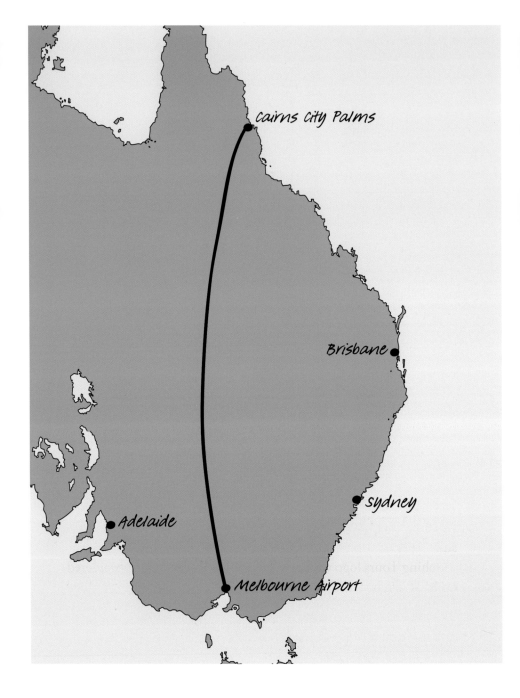

{ 26 }

Serendipity and Alexander von Nordmann's Greenshank, Cairns and FNQ

11–15 February 2021

It All Began with a New Shirt

My dear friends David and Janet Mead sent me a beautiful polo shirt. It is my only polo shirt. It has their Great Northern Birdwatching Tours logo with a Yellow-billed Kingfisher embroidered on it! It is now my go-to, nice but still casual, shirt. I really liked and appreciated it. I contacted David on Tuesday 9 February to thank him. We chatted a bit and then he invited me to come to Cairns and twitch the Nordmann's Greenshank and then make a day trip up to Cooktown (Janet's and his old hometown) to try and find me a Black-winged Monarch. I could add that mega-rarity Greenshank that had seemingly taken up residence for over a month in Cairns, as well as possibly another Lifer. I contacted James and not unsurprisingly, he was keen to go with me. I booked

The shirt that started it all. Thank you Janet and David.

flights for us for Thursday morning. I was finally going to go for that extremely rare wader. The world population of the Nordmann's Greenshank is estimated only to be about 500 to 1000 individuals. A rare rarity indeed.

James' mother and my dear friend, Jill, generously drove us to the airport. Our direct flight to Cairns was on time and all was good. Except for non-mask wearers. It was a requirement to wear masks on all flights. They announced this through the airport intercom as well as in the plane before we took off. But still, some people did not wear them or wore them under their noses and that did make me a bit nervous. So did the constantly yelling toddler in the row right beside us (not crying, just yelling, shouting at his 'screen' as he banged on it). Evidently his young mommy was utterly unaware of the existence of other human beings on the flight. Honestly, she was probably unaware of a lot of things.

We arrived in Cairns at quarter to noon where David collected us and took us straight down to the Esplanade to look for Nordy, that is the twitcher nickname for this visiting Greenshank. The tide was perfect, but despite several hours of careful scanning, we did not find it. It had been seen there the evening before as well as every day back to the first of January when Adrian Walsh originally found and identified it. We went back and gave it another good try in the later arvo/early evening, but Nordy was not around.

The next morning, we were back at 6am. We spent several hours intently scanning the flats for the bird with no joy. So we decided to make the drive up to Cooktown and see if we could find a Black-winged Monarch. They are normally only seen further north in the Iron Range in the summer wet season. But they can occasionally be found as far south as Cooktown, if you know where to look. David used to live in Cooktown, and he knew where to look.

On the way up, we birded briefly in a few spots, bearing in mind

Looking out from the Cairns Esplanade.

Torresian Kingfisher on the Esplanade.

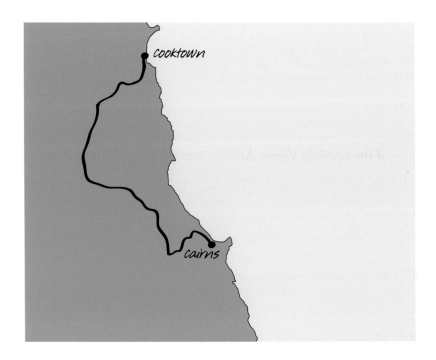

that it's about an eight-hour trip to Cooktown and back. Without too much effort or time, we were able to find James a few Lifers: Crimson Finch, Tawny Grassbird, Northern Fantail and a brief, but unmistakable look at a Pale-vented Bush-hen. So including Black-necked Storks, that made five Lifers for him so far on this trip. He had already seen my Cooktown target bird, Black-winged Monarch in the Iron Range a couple years ago.

We arrived in Cooktown and went to a road in his old neighbourhood where David had seen BW Monarchs before. After a few hours of wandering up and down this little dirt road in the heat and heaps of humidity, we rested in the shade by a small stream. We were just waiting and watching. Then silently, a beautiful Black-winged Monarch flew in and landed on a branch right above us! We all saw it well. Then it called a couple of times and flew off. I had great views, but my old camera had issues with the intense humidity and would not 'fire'. Later in the day, it functioned fine again. This has happened a couple of times in the past when in extreme humidity. But once again, thank goodness James got a few recording shots. I had jokingly said that he was becoming the official photographer of our expeditions, but it was not completely a joke. He is faster and has better eyes than I do. He usually gets a photo, and he definitely has an artistic eye.

We drove around a bit in Cooktown to show James the pretty little town. As we arrived there, I had mobile reception, and I got one of the horrible Virgin Airlines texts that begins with 'Virgin-Aus apologises'. This message said that our Saturday flight 'may have changed'. We were thinking that this had happened in relation to a new COVID outbreak in Victoria. A full-on lockdown had been implemented down there from Friday at midnight to the next Wednesday. Scary. Virgin's text suggested calling their customer service number. I did that and I even got through! I asked if flight VA1294 had been cancelled. The person just began reading the details of my original itinerary to me. I stopped her and said that I had that information. I was asking specifically if that flight had

My Lifer Black-winged Monarch in Cooktown (photo by James Cornelious).

been cancelled. She said (in an unmistakeably snide tone of voice), "I think I just explained that to you." I tried again to ask about the status of that flight. She began again, unbelievably, to read me my original flight information. I gave up and hung up. A few hours later, I received the 'VirginAus apologises' text saying that the flight had indeed been cancelled. They again suggested contacting the service number. I tried, but due to high caller volume it was impossible to get through. My anxiety was building.

Later I found that the flight had been cancelled only because too many people had cancelled their reservations on that flight to Melbourne due to the COVID lockdown in Victoria. The flight had been cancelled because the airline needed more people to prevent them from losing money on that one flight. Short rant coming.

Dear Virgin, if your services are the same, or worse, than an 'economy airline', I should merely switch to an actual economy airline. I was willing to pay a bit more for quality and service, but both of these were completely lacking regarding this issue. Rant over for now. And in full disclosure, since I first wrote this, I have booked flights again on Virgin. Acceptance? Or surrender? Incompetence in all things is just taken for granted these days. That's not a good thing. I have always liked Virgin and I did remain a customer regardless of this experience.

We headed back to Cairns and tried for Nordy again the next morning without a lot of hope and with no success. After that, David took us to his house so we could say hello to Janet and so that they could wash a couple things for us. At that time, we had no idea how long we might be staying in Cairns. Neither of us had checked a bag and had almost no extra clothes. Janet saw my anxiety about the flights and wanted to help. She jumped on her computer was able to figure out a bit more of what was going on and helped to sort it for us. We found out that Virgin had indeed re-booked us to leave at noon Monday on a flight connecting in Brisbane. It was not a direct flight like our original flight had been, and that was a drag, but we were going back. I cannot adequately put into words how grateful I was for Janet's calming assistance.

Along the water in Cooktown, Queensland.

James (the king of squatting) and David Mead of Great Northern Tours scanning for Nordy.

My anxiety dropped from around a 9 to a much more manageable 6 or so.

I extended our motel booking for the additional two nights. I highly recommend the Cairns City Palms Motel. The staff could not have been more helpful or friendly, and the rooms are very reasonable and very nice. My bed had an excellent mattress. I had no complaints about our stay there and I am sure I will return someday. We went back to the Esplanade for the late arvo tide and again we did a lot of intense looking and again no joy.

Sunday, David had some stuff to do, and I slept in. I did not get out of bed until 6:45am. That is late for me during a birding trip. I had gotten almost eight hours on that lovely mattress. Yes, a long and good sleep for me. I needed it. Later in the arvo, I even took a nap too. Good stuff.

Then I got a message from David that the Nordmann's had been seen again! It had been there, but very far out on the flats after we had left late Saturday evening. And importantly, it had been spotted by a reliable birder, who is a guide and friend of David's. This man is known for always going barefooted. When I met him, I looked at his feet and marvelled. They were amazing. It is my understanding that he is about 70 years old, and that he never, ever wears shoes. He also does not carry a mobile phone, nor does he do any sort of social media. David happened to bump into him at the market and that is how he learned that Nordy was back. So, even though the tide was already way too far out, we went down to the Esplanade that evening. We gave it a good go, but no Nordmann's.

Monday morning, we were back down there at 6:30am. The tide was still pretty far out but it was rising. With some genuine hope in our hearts, we began scanning as we had so many times before. About 7am, David had a distant greenshank that he thought looked like a possibility. Then James said he thought that it looked good too, and then for what it was worth, I stared through the scope and thought it did as well. And it was! We had found Nordy. Huge joy.

I rang Dick Jenkin, a new birder friend who I had exchanged mobile numbers with the day before in case of either of us found

Twitch success! Nordmann's Greenshank or Nordy as it was known.

I love this photo by the man who originally found Nordy, Adrian Walsh (photo by Adrian Walsh).

the bird before the other. That morning he had gone toward the north end of the Esplanade, but he came back quickly and joined us in watching the bird. As the tide rose, Nordy and the various other waders came slowly closer as they do. Soon the Nordmann's Whisperer himself, Adrian Walsh, rocked up. He did not know that the bird had been refound. We got to share that joyous news with the man who originally found this bird. He had thought it was gone for good as well.

At this point, it was David, James, me, Dick Jenkin and Martin Cachard and now Adrian was with us as well. We were all looking at, and rejoicing in, 'his' Greenshank. It was a genuine pleasure meeting him and we remain in touch. I took some recording shots, but it was still quite a distance for my old 100-400mm lens to capture anything very impressive, but make no mistake, I am extremely happy and very grateful for the shots I got.

We left Nordy and went to poke around a couple of local birdy places before heading to the airport. And then I got another of the dreaded 'VirginAus apologises' texts. This was telling me that our

Nordy strutting about.

flight departure was being delayed an hour. That would be tricky to say the least, since we only had 40 minutes between our connecting flights in Brisbane. To make a long and stressful story short, the situation was that there were 27 other passengers that needed to make that connection, so they just held the Brisbane plane for us. We went straight from one full plane to another, almost full plane, and more non-mask wearing nitwits. But two hours later, we arrived in Melbourne where James and I both had arranged for taxis to collect us. My ride was quite dear because of the distance, but absolutely worth it. I arrived back in Lara at 7:30pm. Phew!

So, on Friday as the flight chaos began, I had gotten pummelled in what is probably my most vulnerable anxiety spot. My flight was cancelled, and Victoria was going into lockdown. I had no idea what was going to happen. I had 'being trapped away from home' separation anxiety. It is a very primal fear for me and the reason I hated the movie, 'The Wizard of Oz' as a child. I was steeping in anxiety. Yes, my 'buttons' were being pushed to the extreme. But thanks to a bit of personal growth, and some wonderful friends, especially Janet Mead, things had gotten mostly sorted. And as has always been the case in all things, I ended up being okay.

The amazing serendipity is that we had dipped on the Nordmann's Greenshank on Thursday, Friday, Saturday and Sunday. The bird that had been seen consistently every day since Adrian had first found it and identified it on 1 January. And the day we arrived; it had gone missing for the first time since then. Most birders (including me) thought that Nordy had 'left the building' (an Elvis reference). If my original flight had not been cancelled and rescheduled at noon Monday, I would not have seen this truly special and very rare bird.

Serendipity. How often does this sort of thing happen? Really, quite often. Repeatedly in my life, the seemingly 'bad thing' ends up leading to something good or even wonderful. I am not saying that it is painless or easy, often quite the contrary, but I am saying that it is usually worth it. It does sometimes take a while. Serendipity has its own timing.

After tense travel difficulties the author is back in his study and writing will begin.

I will include here one of my favourite Joseph Campbell quotes. It is: 'The cave you fear to enter holds the treasure that you seek.'

That has been very true for me so many times. If I do not work at it, if I do not force myself to do things, my comfort zones would become prisons. I must continue to break through the walls of anxiety, and get out and seek that treasure. For me, seeking that treasure, and then writing and sharing my experiences is living. This book is me living. It ain't always pretty. It ain't always easy, but I do it. And often it brings me joy.

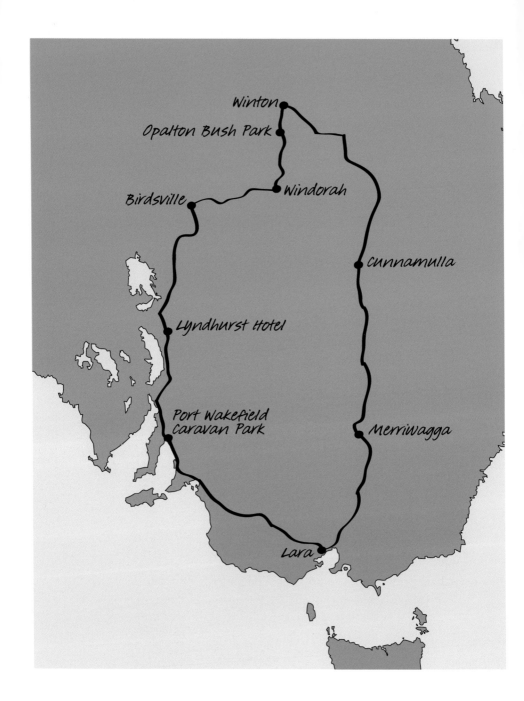

Winton

Opalton Bush Park

Birdsville

Windorah

Cunnamulla

Lyndhurst Hotel

Port Wakefield
Caravan Park

Merriwagga

Lara

{ 27 }

The Great Grasswren Expedition, Opalton, Queensland and the Birdsville Track

28 April-9 May 2021

The Great Grasswren Expedition: Part One

It had been about a year since the IOC first gave the Rusty Grasswren full species status and renamed it the Opalton Grasswren. It had previously been a subspecies of the Striated Grasswren, and it was only found in the (well, duh) Opalton area of western Queensland. I thought I'd be able to get up there in a couple of months as soon as this 'virus thing' settled down. Little did I know... Over the coming months, I planned a few trips that ended up getting cancelled. In the autumn of 2021, I was finally able to make a solid plan for a trip up there with my buddy James. We were to leave the end of April and were going to be joined on the expedition by our dear friends, Alan Stringer and David Adam. It seemed like this time I was really going to get there.

As you know, James and I are Team Troopi. In a spirit of fun, Alan and David in Alan's Subaru Outback became Team Subi (pronounced 'soo-bee'). I like that. We left on Wednesday 28 April and travelled north to our first overnight at Merriwagga, New South Wales. It was a nice, old caravan park. I will return sometime. Next, we were planning to stay at a park just south of the Queensland border. We arrived there and none of us had any useable mobile reception, even though the WikiCamps app listed the park as having Telstra. It was still fairly early, so we decided to continue a little over an hour further north to one of my favourite caravan parks in Oz, the Warrego Riverside Tourist Park in Cunnamulla, Queensland. I really do love that park. It is beautiful there as well as being very birdy.

Alan and David picked up a Lifer or two walking around the park. It is a great place for birders. Thanks to James, I even got a Lifer frog, the Red Tree Frog. Now I keep little lists of reptiles, amphibians and mammals, but my main focus remains on birds. Speaking of birds, on the entire expedition Alan added 19 Lifers

David Adam, Alan Stringer and James Cornelious at the caravan park in Merriwagga, New South Wales.

David and Alan were following us and David took this photo of Troopi rolling along with a little cloud above her (photo by David Adam).

and David picked up seven. David said he would like to come back and spend a few days there. Everything about that park is first rate.

The next morning, we rolled along to Tambo, Queensland, and took rooms at a nice little motel with beautiful bottle trees around it. I wanted an easy, comfortable night's sleep. We would be leaving very early, and we thought, going 'straight' over to the Opalton Bush Camp. We were soon to discover that Robert Shore had been correct in his warning that navigation devices were incorrect between Longreach and the bush camp. We wandered around for hours and never did find a route that went through. Even though all of our various devices and apps indicated that several did just that.

However, at one point far down yet another track that did not connect to the seemingly mythical Opalton Road, we pulled into a picturesque little spot to discuss our options. And then David noticed a couple of Opalton Grasswrens! Just like that, there they were. Yes! We were all quickly out of our vehicles and taking photos of the main target bird of the trip, and my only Lifer target of the expedition. We had accidentally found them where no-one else

Two Opalton Grasswrens Joy!

The lovely Rufous-crowned Emu-wren (photo by James Cornelious).

A pair of Opalton Grasswrens dancing.

Opalton Grasswren in a tree.

had reported them before (that we know of anyway). I am not sure exactly where we were, but as best I know, the coordinates were 23.4952161, 142.8355741. Somewhere out there we also saw a group of babblers and they were Hall's Babblers! Those were a hoped-for target for James and the others as well.

We may have been on private land. There was a gate involved but it was not signed. We merely closed it, since it was closed when we had gotten to it. That is the rule for gates in the outback. If it is closed, reclose it. If it is open, leave it open.

We rejoiced in the grasswrens, but we continued to try and find some route up to the bush camp. We never did. We decided to drive all the way back to Longreach. We arrived there just before dark and stayed at a truly rundown caravan park run by a literally loony anti-vaxxer lady. I did not have to talk with her. I just paid her and moved quickly along. David and Alan were not as lucky,

Signpost near the Bush Park (photo by James Cornelious).

The little building that James and I called the vampire house in Opalton Bush Park (photo by James Cornelious).

and they got an earful about pig DNA and other crazy conspiracy talk. She said that the vaccine could cause mutations. Later I told the guys that at my age, almost any mutation would probably be an improvement anyway.

The next morning, we drove north to Winton and came down to the Opalton Bush Camp (or Bush Park, it gets referred to as both). The road is unsealed and occasionally rough, but most importantly, it exists. It was really not bad at all. We arrived at the camp in the early arvo. We found a nice spot to set up next to a little one-room building that James and I called the 'vampire house'. We had joked earlier in the week about there being vampires in Queensland. I mean, not really, but it was funny at the time. We had decided that there are no vampires in Victoria, South Australia, Western Australia or New South Wales. The jury is still out on the Northern Territory though. They are quite possibly up there as well as in Queensland.

We went just across the road to bird an area recommended to us by several people who had been out there recently. It was along the track into Glenn's house. Glenn is basically the local of that area and a nice guy. James and I drove out to his place and had a short visit with him. When we returned, we discovered that David and Alan had found numerous Rufous-crowned Emu-wrens. We saw them as well, marvelled at their coolness and took photos. We had not yet seen the Opalton Grasswrens in their official area though.

We decided to try a spot for the grasswrens five or so kilometres down the track to the west. We still did not find them, but we did see a Spinifexbird. Yet another target for the guys. As the day faded, we headed back to our camp by the vampire shack.

After one of the best night's sleep that I had on the expedition, we went back across the track again and quite quickly we did indeed find those beautiful grasswrens. Several years ago, for various reasons, I stopped taking tons of bird photos. I used to occasionally shoot over a thousand in a day. That was maybe eight or ten years ago. I took quite a few photos of the Opalton Grasswren and the Rufous-crowned EW, but certainly not a thousand and that is the way I prefer it.

Alan Stringer, David Adam and me looking for Grasswrens and Emu-wrens.

Rufous-crowned Emu-wren in the spinifex looking cool (Emu-wrens are cool full stop).

The Great Grasswren Expedition: Part Two

We left the Opalton Bush Camp with very specific instructions provided by a knowledgeable local. He made us a 'mud map' with written directions to get to the track that goes up to Lark Quarry to the north, and to Windorah to the south. This route worked without a hitch, and we arrived, safe and dusty in Windorah later that arvo. Before long we heard from Team Subi. They had driven up to Lark Quarry, had seen the resident Grey Falcon on its tower and then decided to just come on down to Windorah.

Originally, James and I had planned to stay in the caravan park there where we had stayed back in chapter 12. It was inexpensive and okay. The weather was borderline hot, upper 30s and sunny. Unfortunately, the park was pretty full and there was only one small spot that promised a bit of shade in the afternoon. As I was backing Troopi into this site I had some misgivings. There was a caravan parked close by with its big awning out and a radio on. I loathe radios (or televisions) playing in shared spaces. There was a rotund, older guy sitting in a camp chair reading a newspaper. He

Troopi and me as the sun was going down in Opalton (photo by James Cornelious).

Driving down to Windorah from Opalton, no idea where exactly, there is a lot of this view out there. I do genuinely love it (photo by James Cornelious).

did not even look up. As I got out of the vehicle to begin setting up Troopi, his little dog (it was on a lead tied to his steps) bolted out from under the caravan steps barking (or coughing or choking. It was a loud and wet sound). I adore dogs, but small barky-types do not necessarily make good neighbours in a park.

Before we got started setting up, we decided to drive to the store. I told the dog guy we were going to run an errand and asked if he would mind watching our spot. He did not look up. He just mumbled, "first in, best dressed" (an Aussie version of "first come, first served"). We know my hearing is poor. I asked politely what he had said, and he repeated it louder, pointedly not looking up from his paper. My request was being rejected and I was being dismissed. I decided then and there that I did not want to camp next to this jerk, his dog and his radio. We left, and James and I ended up very happily staying in a comfortable accommodation just around the corner at Cooper Cabins. All good, truly.

The two teams left for Birdsville the next morning. Team Subi did a bit of birding on the way and picked up Eyrean Grasswren in the same spot James and I had gotten our Lifers in May 2018. Team Troopi drove on to the Birdsville Bakery in hopes of curried camel pie (priorities are important). We did arrive before their early closing time of 2:30pm, but still it was not to be. They would not have any camel until 10 May (it was 4 May). Instead we had kangaroo pies and they were pretty delicious.

Then we booked into the Birdsville Caravan Park. There was a surprisingly long queue to register, and the flies were intense (see the photo of me and the queue wearing a fly head-net. Don't laugh, they work). After over a half an hour, I secured us a powered site in partial shade up the front. The weather was delightful. It can easily be in the upper 30s or higher out there in early May, but it was in the low 20s. We slept well and, in the morning, both teams were off at first light to the Grey Grasswren site 92 kilometres south of Birdsville. It is a well-known spot to many birders.

As told in chapter 12 of this book, it is where I saw my 700th

Feel free to laugh but fly-nets work.

Australian bird. It is a very special place to me. I saw that bird only because of James' ears. As I have said, I cannot hear grasswrens at all. According to an audiologist, I have severe hearing loss in my right ear and moderate hearing loss in my left and that was three years ago. My hearing has gone further downhill since then. A lot of loud rock 'n' roll and hundreds upon hundreds of live shows with amplification over the years has definitely taken a toll. I used to turn my right ear to the monitors, and I reckon that is why there is more hearing loss on that side. But as you know, I had my hearing-ear boy with me.

    We pulled off onto the side of the track by the same spot where we had parked Troopi on 15 May 2018. We were able to drive off the track and onto a small open area to park back then, but now there is a ditch preventing that. It did not matter; we were in the right place. We began birding and by birding, I mean that James, David and Alan were listening, and I was following them around looking. Soon we were looking at a large lignum bush in which the others could hear the grasswrens. I took their words for it, and we stared at that bush.

And then David saw a Grey Grasswren moving about inside the bush. Now we knew for sure it was in there. We stared some more and other tiny glimpses were achieved, but that was all. They were hearing other GGWs behind us as well and we changed lignum bushes. By now my back was screaming at me. Standing

Me doing some easy birding. I did see a Grey Grasswren and took its photo (photo by James Cornelious).

around makes my back ache. It has done this for years (possibly from having such poor posture). I walked over to Troopi and got my old camp chair and returned to watching the bush. The others were now on camp chairs too, except James. I have called James the 'squat king' because he can squat down comfortably for hours. I can no longer squat. My knees just don't do that anymore. And if I did manage to squat, I do not reckon I could un-squat without some kind of assistance.

We stared at that lignum bush. I was sitting. I was wearing a fly-net. I was comfortable. It was pretty easy birding. Then I glimpsed the Grasswren moving about inside the bush. And then several moments later astonishingly, it stuck its head out and dropped down to the ground. I could hardly believe my eyes! That is an expression I have used and often heard, but rarely experienced so vividly. I could hardly believe I was seeing a Grey Grasswren out in the open! It was moving quickly, but there it was! And I even got some recording shots. It was quite a thrill for me to see my 700th bird again and even take its photo. I was very pleased. I reckon the Grey Grasswren is my favourite grasswren. They are

The amazing, wondrous Grey Grasswren.

Gibberbird in the gibber, as they do.

incredibly beautiful and very difficult to see. Those are things that birders tend to like. I know I certainly do.

We had decided to only go as far as Mungerannie and camp there. It is an unpowered camp, but they do have showers and toilets. I called and spoke to the owner, Phil, the day before. I had met him the afternoon after seeing the Grey Grasswren in 2018, so admittedly I had been in the best state of Lifer High at the time. Regardless, I remembered it is a very cool place. I chatted with Phil and told him we were coming there the next day and even asked if a bit of power might be sorted. He said, "Yeah, come on down. We'll figure out something." Cool, it was all set. So we took our time getting down there.

After a few stops, which included looking at and photograph-ing a cute-as Gibberbird, we arrived at Mungerannie. As James finished topping off Troopi's main tank I had gone in to see Phil. However, he wasn't there. He was, and I quote, "not seeing people". The seemingly disinterested lady behind the bar further said, "Phil is not the best version of Phil today." She really said that whatever that might mean. I told her I had spoken to him the day before and she said she knew nothing about any of that. Then she told me that their water was broken, and the showers and toilets did not work at all. At this point, James came in to pay for the diesel on his card. He does not carry cash. She said their Eftpos machine wasn't working. In the meantime, in what I remembered from three years ago as a very friendly place, the punters at the bar were eyeing us like they were extras from the old film 'Deliverance'. The vibe in there that afternoon was actually creepy. Except that it would have been in an Aussie accent, I half expected to hear something like, "You ain't from around here, are you boy?"

The lady then said that Marree, which had the only possible next accommodations of any kind, was only two hundred kilometres down the track. She also mentioned that the track was in good shape between there and Mungerannie. I got the feeling that we weren't really welcome. And my friends, I must say that is a very unusual feeling for me. I did not care for it. It was the exact opposite of the vibe I had gotten on my first visit there. Also bear in mind that by now it was only about an hour to sunset. When team Subi arrived we all decided to leave for Marree. We would

Inland Dotterel chick on the Birdsville Track.

not get there until at least 7pm which is a bit late for me to eat, so I had two muesli/protein bars as I drove. No worries.

About a half an hour before we got to the town, James and I unexpectedly saw a family of Inland Dotterels standing on the track. I hit the brakes and James got another Lifer. There were six birds, including a very cute chick that we made sure was safely away from the track before we left. We also took its picture. Alan and David saw the chick as well. It was also a Lifer for Alan. As we reached our first mobile reception since Birdsville, we began trying to contact either of the two caravan parks in Marree. As is sometimes the case, neither park could be bothered to answer their phone. Over the radio (we did have radio communication between the vehicles) David said that a few years ago he had stayed at the old hotel there. It was a historic building constructed in 1883. I rang them and the very helpful and very friendly young lady, two qualities that had been completely lacking back up the road, said that she could provide us rooms, although they were quite full. There were tour groups rolling in. These were tourist tour groups, not birding tours. There is a difference.

This was the beginning of the time of year when some people (yes, about my age) will gather together and hire someone to take them out and show them stuff. Their 'adventures' are looking at the things that we see on our way to see birds. The birds lead us into awesome and I am grateful that they do. These tour groups also do heaps of eating and drinking. The restaurant at the motel was a madhouse and it took us ages just to get checked in. I was glad I had eaten those muesli bars a few hours earlier. Our rooms were expensive and not particularly nice, but they were mostly clean, and the mattress wasn't uncomfortable. And I do not think it was haunted and there were no vampires. We were in South Australia.

We all left the next morning bidding a very fond farewell to our dear friends of Team Subi. It had been a very successful expedition. Sadly, Alan had discovered a flat tyre on his Subi. It must have been a slow leak as they did not notice anything amiss as they were

Sunset view in front of Port Germein Caravan Park (photo by James Cornelious).

driving in the night before. He had merely noticed the car leaning at an odd angle where it was parked in front of the hotel. They headed for a tyre repair down the road. James and I headed south for the Arid Lands Park just north of Port Augusta.

But first we called in to the Lyndhurst Hotel. I really like that place. We had stayed there on that wonderful day in May 2018 as told in chapter 12. It was as friendly and welcoming this time as it had been the first time. Laurie Kalms is the owner and in both my visits there, made me feel very welcome. I like him. I will also mention that their diesel was quite reasonable for the outback. He even pumped our fuel while he was chatting with us, a nice guy indeed.

Continuing south, we arrived around midday at the Australian Arid Lands Botanic Garden just north of Port Augusta. Our friend Sam Gordon who lives in Adelaide, had given us suggestions to help James find a Chirruping Wedgebill. They suggested the scrub along the entrance road, particularly near the track over to the lookout. After maybe 15 minutes looking around near that track, even I heard it chirruping. Soon we were both looking at this small, loud, grey bird with a crest. James added another Lifer. It stubbornly moved about inside the large bush and did not co-operate for photos, but it gave James some good Lifer views. Sweet.

We headed south to Port Germein and took a site at yet another of my favourite caravan parks. As I was checking in, I told Des, the owner, about his park being in my book. He wanted to see the book and I showed him. He was pleased. He ended up trading us a powered site for the copy. That was kind of cool. I autographed it to him. I had an excellent night's sleep there. That is one of the bittersweet memory places for me.

The next day I discovered what was to become another favourite caravan park. The Port Wakefield Caravan Park was excellent, and our reasonably priced, powered site backed onto a gorgeous lagoon. We had a wonderful view out of our 'backdoors'. My friend, Michael Greenshields, came to the park and collected us to take us in search of a Grey Plover for James. There had been a couple

Troopi set up at the caravan park in Port Wakefield, South Australia. It's definitely one of my favourites now.

That beautiful sunset at our Troopi's back doors, Port Wakefield, South Australia.

of those waders being seen at two beaches near Port Wakefield. Michael lives close by and knows the area. I had thoroughly enjoyed being a guest on his podcast, The Birder's Guide, a few months previously. We had a great time birding with him, although those plovers were just not around.

We returned to the caravan park and experienced a beautiful sunset right behind Troopi. It truly was stunning. James took a photo of me just gazing at it. I plan to use his picture as the back cover of this book. It has now become one of my very favourite photos. Even though it is of the back of my head, it still captures me, an old long-haired hippie standing there drinking-in the sunset. That is who I am. It is a good photo of my life at present. Yes, I will always appreciate sunsets and sunrises. I deeply appreciate my dear friend James' company on our trips and I appreciate his artistic eye for 'seeing' this photo and taking it. He was behind me and asked me to just stand there for a moment as he took that photo. It is a wonderful capture, thank you my buddy.

The next day we looked briefly around Adelaide for a Barbary Dove for James, but it began to pour, and I mean pour, rain. We will see that bird another time. We drove on to the Keith Caravan Park where I had reserved one of their very comfortable and yet very inexpensive cabins. We stayed there in chapter 13 and I am sure I will stay there again. We headed back to Lara the next day. The sun had set on the Great Grasswren Expedition. It was time to leave the outback, at least physically. I would soon be back at my old desk remembering and writing about it.

Yes, I might leave the outback, but the outback never leaves me. I can 'hear' it as I sit here doing this rewrite. It's not a sound that everyone can, or wants to hear but for those of us who do, it is a lovely vibe. It's in our very core. It resonates inside like the drone of a digeridoo. No hyperbole, it is part of the beating of my heart.

James and Troopi in front of the cabin at the caravan park in Keith, South Australia.

{ 28 }

A Longer Dedication Remembering Unk

June 2021

This book is dedicated to Unk, George R Massenburg, Jr, my mother's brother. Even though he lived to be 93 years of age, he always kept the "Jr" at the end of his name. I asked him once why he kept it. He said that it had always been part of his name. And that was that. I never knew his dad. He died a few years before I was born. Many of the men in my family died on the younger side. Unk did not, and I hope that some of those genes were passed along through my mom's side of the family. The older I get, the more I realise how much I am like him, and that is a positive thing.

Most importantly for this book, more than anyone else, Unk inspired me to become a birder. He inspired and nurtured my love of the sea and of nature in general. He used to point out birds to me before I even cared what they were. He often used the antiquated names for them such as English Sparrow for House Sparrow, or Redbird for Cardinal, or Soldier-winged Blackbird for Red-winged Blackbird.

I sit here at this over-100-year-old desk that came from his father, and to my right, beside my bed is his antique box-compass as well as his old walking stick. I treasure them both. I have a few

I love this photo of Unk and Lynn. This was on his last birthday in August 2009. He was 93.

other things of his, but that stick in particular was so much a part him. I do not know how old it is. He had it as far back as I can remember. I reckon it's older than I am. Sometimes I will just pick it up and hold it. Seriously. It is like being able to take his hand. I find comfort in that. I truly do. He used it in his later years when he walked, but he had also used it since I was a child to look for softcrabs. The rest of us used crab nets and yet Unk could out-crab anyone in the family with his stick and his bare hands.

I grew up softcrabbing. When a Blue Crab moults, it backs out of its shell and is about a third larger than it was, and its shell is soft. This is when you need to catch it. Then you take it home to eat. Left in the saltwater, in a few hours the shell will begin to harden. In about twelve hours it becomes what is called a 'papershell' and is not edible. One prepares the crab by removing a few parts, dredging it in flour with a bit of salt and then frying it. Softcrabs are my favourite food. I have eaten them all my life. They are a part of who I am.

I am from the city of Hampton, Virginia. That whole area was called Tidewater. My hometown as I remember it no longer exists. It was 'developed' out of existence. It had been a beautiful little saltwater fishing village literally built on oyster shells. Many of the roads were 'paved' with oyster shells, one was named Shell Road. It was a seafood town. It was inseparable from Hampton Roads Harbour and the Chesapeake Bay. That Tidewater is gone, but still remains safe in my memories and even in the memories that were passed on to me from Unk.

Unk also believed in my creativity, in my music and art. I did not understand that, nor how much he did until our later life together. We became closer during his last years. He lived with us

Unk's old box compass beside my bed here in my study.

in Fredericksburg, Virginia. We added a first-floor bedroom and bathroom on our big, beautiful old house for him. I am so very grateful for those years with him. He died there, at home in his room as he had wanted. And as far as I know, he never felt afraid.

That was the most important thing to me. My only wish for his last days was that he would never have to be afraid. I honestly don't think that he ever was. I was with him to the end. He was loved as he departed peacefully and he knew it. I cannot imagine any better ending to a life. He deserved that.

He was a father figure for me. He and Nana lived next door. They were as much my family as my mother and father. The property was originally my maternal grandfather's. My parents had built a small three bedroom house on the back of the lot behind the old two-story house that my grandfather built in 1917. When I was about eight, we traded houses, and Nana and Unk moved into the smaller house, and we moved into the old two-storey house. It was my mother, father, brother and me.

I tore that old kitchen in Hampton back to the studs myself. Then Unk built us tons of open shelving.

An old photo of softcrabs frying. They are one of the very, very few things that I can cook.

My trips to Florida with Unk and Nana were without question the best memories of my childhood. We first went there in the later 1950s and continued through the 1960s. We'd spend two weeks there on holiday every June. We'd stay one week on Sanibel Island at the High Tide Cottages right on the Gulf of Mexico, then we would spend one week travelling around to the Keys, Everglades and other areas. We also always went sailfishing out of Stuart on the sportfishing boats of the Whitaker Fleet. Truly, those memories remain some of my very best, not only of my childhood but of my entire life. I am so grateful for them.

The Florida that I carry in my heart is the most magical place I have ever been. I know that it no longer exists. It has been destroyed by development as well. I went back to Sanibel almost 20 years ago, and it had become mostly a nightmare of condos, golf courses and 'McMansions'. But if you stood on the beach and looked out into the gulf, then it could seem the same. I have my memories and I have old slides. I will find a way to get them digitised before they are lost forever. Florida was wondrous back then. I adored it. When

Bluefishing on the Outer Banks.

Unk installing jalousie windows (or louvre windows depending where you live) at our cottage porch-room in Nags Head, NC. They were very 'tropical' and reminded him of Florida.

A true piece of my uncle, his walking stick. It stays here with me in my study.

I compared Cocos to Sanibel in chapter 20, that is the highest praise I could give to a place. I cherish my memories of Sanibel. I owe that all to Unk. The way that I am able to love Cocos I owe to Unk. I dedicate this book, as well as much of the remainder of my life to him. Unk, I thank you with all my heart. You had more to do with the good parts of who I am now than you can ever know. Or maybe you can. That would be nice indeed.

In closing, I'd like to tell y'all a little story about something that happened less than a week before Unk died. He was pretty far along at that point and one of the lovely hospice workers was sitting by his bed just talking to him. She noticed the nautical things in his room and asked him about boats. He said that he had always loved the water and boats. She asked if he had a preference, sailboats or power boats? He said that he liked and had had both. But then he paused and said softly, "But I stuck with sail".

Unk had not owned a sailboat in well over 70 years, but that is how I imagine him now, sailing in the Hampton Roads harbour as it was when he was a young man. I scattered his ashes in the water along the shore where he and I both grew up softcrabbing.

{ 29 }

A Birding Epilogue, The Hudwel Twitch

November 2021

The progress on this book had taken a couple of months longer than I expected. At the end of November my publisher had not begun the editing, so after communicating with my dear friend, supporter and inspiration Kenn Kaufman, I decided to sail into a fairly comprehensive rewrite in early December. I am very pleased with the changes that I made to the telling of these tales of my journey. It is made up of many trips, adventures and experiences, but it is all my journey. Now this has become the book that I want to share with you all. Yes, a book about travelling, birding and living in Australia written from the heart.

So what would make an excellent last chapter birding epilogue? I suppose that a successful twitch of an Australian First right here in Victoria would fill the bill.

Over the years there had been a few reports of Hudsonian Whimbrel in Australia, but no record had ever been confirmed. So when a 'possible' Hudsonian Whimbrel was first reported in Toora, Victoria, I was interested but not overly excited. Of course I did follow the discussion about the bird on the Facebook Australian Twitcher's page.

In the months since I wrote the last birding chapter, I had been getting into shape. I had continued to, and I quote me, "Eat smaller portions and make wiser choices". I had dropped about ten kilos. Then I added in walking regularly. I gradually increased those walks. A half hour walk soon grew to an hour and an hour to an hour and a half and so on. Now as I write this, I have lost 20 kilos and I am regularly doing ten-plus kilometre hikes in the You Yangs (Wurdi Youang) only ten minutes from the house. I love it out there. It takes me about two or three hours to do these hikes and I can go up steep trails without getting winded. That is amazing to me. I can do it and I enjoy it. I had reached the top of one portion of my hike that is called the Saddle on the morning of Monday 22 November. I happened to check the Facebook Twitcher's page as I paused for a drink of water and saw that the discussion had come to a conclusion. By those who have the knowledge about such things, the bird had been definitively determined to be a Hudsonian Whimbrel. This would be the first record of it in Australia. Now I was excited.

The heavy-hitters had weighed in and they all agreed. Yay! There were several determining factors in this consensus. It had a dark rump/lower back area, although that is not considered definitive it was still a very good sign. Around the world, Whimbrel rumps can be quite variable. However, this one did look good. The factor that turned the most expert heads was the buffy-ness of the auxiliaries in the stripes of the 'armpit' area of the bird. They were buffy compared to the flanks. There was also a difference in size, with the Hudsonian being slightly, but often noticeably, larger. And there was also a white dot in its 'eyebrow' stripe above its lores that helped in identifying it. I do not think that was necessarily a field mark of all Hudsonian Whimbrels, but it was noticeable on this bird and through the scope, it was a good way to pick it out when just the head was poking up out of the mangroves.

In Australia, names and phrases often get shortened. And bird names are no different. As I mentioned in chapter 8 for example, the

Bar-tailed Godwit is called a Barwit and the Hudsonian Godwit a Hudwit. But there was no shortened version of Hudsonian Whimbrel until my friend Carolyn said "Hudwel". Sweet. From then on, at least to me, the Hudsonian Whimbrel became the Hudwel.

I was an hour away from where I had parked and I hiked back down the trail. Our dear friend and birder Carolyn Edwards lives just a few blocks from us. I contacted her to see if she was interested in going for the bird. She was and she could be ready by 1pm. That gave me an hour to get it together. Toora was four 'Troopi hours' away and the bird was being seen. The twitch was on.

I had not dashed off on a twitch in many months, nor had I gone on any sort of trip for that matter. This was only over into Gippsland but the old Prius is getting very long in the tooth. She is still ticking along (literally ticking, and that is the potential problem), so I am a bit uncomfortable driving her very far. I decided to take Troopi. I still had to organise myself for an overnight journey and as I said, it had been a while since I had done that. I am grateful (and lucky) that I did not forget anything.

We were going to have to drive through Melbourne. It was not even close to rush hour, but as far as I am concerned there is no 'good' time to drive through the city. True to form, there had been a serious incident on the Westgate Bridge that turned traffic into a crawling carpark adding about 45 minutes to the drive.

I had posted in the thread on the Twitcher's page that I was going to be over there later that afternoon. As we got closer to Toora, I heard from my friend Geoff Glare, a great guy who I have run into on more than a few birding occasions. He and John Alan, another great guy in our birding community along with another birder named Ron had located the bird and were there looking at it as we spoke. They said that they would stay on it until we arrived. I did not catch Ron's surname, but he was in on the finding and watching over the bird with John and Geoff. I deeply thank them all. Carolyn and I would be there by five. Geoff would met us in the carpark beside the bird hide and the area where the Hudwel

'Our' Hudsonian Whimbrel in flight (photo by Geoff Glare).

And again with its wings up showing the buffy-coloured flanks (photo by Geoff Glare).

was being seen. This was going well.

Carolyn and I rocked up in Troopi, met Geoff and parked in a spot at the end of the road by the carpark. We were overlooking the area where they had the Hudwel staked out. We could see them looking at it. I wasted no time in dashing over and not immediately, but in a several minutes or so, I had acceptable and tickable views of the bird through the scope. Sweet.

The Hudwel moved a few times and we followed it. I never did get any decent photos, but I had good scope and binocular views. After a couple of hours we headed to the caravan park in Waratah Bay where I had reserved a two-bedroom cabin. This is the same spot where James and I had stayed in chapter 15. The view there is lovely. You can see Wilson's Promontory in the distance. We settled in and had a good night's sleep. In case you're wondering where James was, he had gone over to Toora with some friends on Sunday and had already seen the bird basically one day before it was confirmed. So for once, James wasn't on the twitch with me.

The gorgeous view from the cabin at Waratah Bay. That is Wilson's Promontory across the water.

The following morning we went back to have another look and we saw the Hudwel again. Oddly, we were the only ones there, but having seen it the evening before, we soon picked it out ourselves. The light was atrocious for photos, but again I had some very good views though the scope. About midmorning we headed back home and gratefully, there were no traffic incidents. We arrived in Lara in the early afternoon of the twenty-third.

On the 20th November Lynn and I had enjoyed a Thanksgiving dinner with our children and grandchildren. A part of the desserts with that dinner was a pecan pie that Lynn had made. It is my favourite sweet pie. So on the 24th November while I was having my Hudwel Lifer Day, I had a piece of true, proper, perfect Lifer Pie (à la mode of course). I cannot think of a better ending to the twitch or to this book. Lifer Pie: the edible affirmation of hope. I love me some 'hope à la mode.'

The author beaming with Lifer High.

Lifer Pie in the form of pecan pie and ice cream.

THE END

Author's Australian Life List Additions

January 2017 to May 2021

672   Buff-breasted Sandpiper, 20/01/2017, Lake Murdeduke, VIC

673   Painted Button-quail, 17/02/2017, Mangalore Reserve, VIC

674   Pacific Swift, 26/02/2017, Distillery Creek Picnic Ground, VIC

675   Parasitic Jaeger, 5/03/2017, Port Fairy pelagic, VIC

676   Long-tailed Jaeger, 5/03/2017, Port Fairy pelagic, VIC

677   Letter-winged Kite, 27/04/2017, Terrick Terrick NP, VIC

678   Wandering Albatross, 14/05/2017, Port Fairy pelagic, VIC

679   Antipodean Albatross, 14/05/2017, Port Fairy pelagic, VIC

680   Northern Royal Albatross, 14/05/2017, Port Fairy pelagic, VIC

681   Antarctic Prion, 14/05/2017, Port Fairy pelagic, VIC

682   Cape Petrel, 14/05/2017, Port Fairy pelagic, VIC

683   Arctic Tern, 14/05/2017, Port Fairy pelagic, VIC

684   Westland Petrel, 14/05/2017, Port Fairy pelagic, VIC

685   Red-lored Whistler, 24/05/2017, Murray Sunset NP, VIC

686   Striated Grasswren, 25/05/2017, Pink Lakes, VIC

687   South Island Oystercatcher, 19/06/2017, Stockyard Point, VIC

688   Little Stint, 26/06/2017, Stockyard Point, VIC

689   Northern Shoveler, 31/07/2017, Tilley Swamp, SA

690   King Quail, 9/11/2017, Postmans Track, QLD

691   Black-breasted Button-quail, 10/11/2017, Noosa, QLD

692   Hudsonian Godwit, 19/11/2017, Reef Island, VIC

693   Aleutian Tern, 12/12/2017, Old Bar, NSW

694   Providence Petrel, 14/01/2018, Eaglehawk Neck, TAS

695   Black-bellied Storm petrel, 14/01/2018, Eaglehawk Neck, TAS

696   Juan Fernandez Petrel, 14/01/2018, Eaglehawk Neck, TAS

697   Purple-backed Fairywren, 12/10/2012, Gluepot, SA

698	Thick-billed Grasswren, 9/04/2018, Coober Pedy, SA
699	Yellow-rumped Mannikin, 11/04/2018, Katherine, NT
700	Eyrean Grasswren, 13/05/2018, East of Birdsville, QLD
701	Grey Grasswren, 15/05/2018, Birdsville Track, SA
702	Copperback Quail-thrush, 16/05/2018, Lake Gilles Conservation, SA
703	Naretha Bluebonnet, 24/06/2018, Nullarbor Plain NP, SA
704	Princess Parrot, 26/09/2018, Jupiter Well, WA
705	Tasmanian Boobook (Morepork), 8/10/2018, Cape Liptrap, VIC
706	Citrine Wagtail, 29/12/2018, Whyalla Wetlands, SA
707	Tufted Duck, 3/01/2019, WTP (T-Section), VIC
708	Spotted Scrubwren, 21/02/2016, Cheynes Beach, WA
709	Rufous Grasswren, 11/06/2016, Uluru, NT
710	Common Diving-petrel, 26/01/2019, Eaglehawk Neck pelagic, TAS
711	Cook's Petrel, 26/01/2019, Eaglehawk Neck pelagic, TAS
712	Buller's Shearwater, 27/01/2019, Eaglehawk Neck pelagic, TAS
713	Tahiti Petrel, 22/03/2019, South West Rocks pelagic, NSW
714	Rufous Scrubbird, 23/03/2019, Brushy Mt Campground, NSW
715	Gull-billed Tern, 26/06/2017, Jam Jerrup, VIC
716	Southern Fulmar, 1/06/2019, Eaglehawk Neck pelagic, TAS
717	Blue Petrel, 1/06/2019, Eaglehawk Neck pelagic, TAS
718	Grey Petrel, 1/06/2019, Eaglehawk Neck pelagic, TAS
719	Sooty Albatross, 1/06/2019, Eaglehawk Neck pelagic, TAS
720	Great Shearwater, 2/06/2019, Eaglehawk Neck pelagic TAS
721	Soft-plumaged Petrel, 18/06/2019, Eaglehawk Neck pelagic, TAS
722	Salvin's Albatross, 4/09/2019, Eaglehawk Neck pelagic, TAS
723	Western Fieldwren, 7/09/2019, Cape Arid NP, WA
724	Black-throated Whipbird, 14/09/2019, Cheynes Beach, WA
725	Green Junglefowl, 29/11/2019, Cocos Island, WA
726	White-breasted Waterhen, 29/11/2019, Cocos Island, WA
727	Javan Pond Heron, 29/11/2019, Cocos Island, WA
728	Saunders's Tern, 30/11/2019, Cocos Island, WA
729	Western Reef Heron, 30/11/2019, Cocos Island, WA

730	Chinese Pond Heron, 1/12/2019, Cocos Island, WA
731	Oriental Cuckoo, 1/12/2019, Cocos Island, WA
732	Blue-and-white Flycatcher, 2/12/2019, Home Island, WA
733	Asian Koel, 2/12/2019, Home Island, WA
734	Arctic Warbler, 1/12/2019, Cocos Island, WA
735	Red-footed Booby, 4/12/2019, Horsbugh Island, WA
736	Christmas White-eye, 4/12/2019, Horsbugh Island, WA
737	Northern Pintail, 4/12/2019, Horsbugh Island, WA
738	Japanese Sparrowhawk, 4/12/2019, Horsbugh Island, WA
739	Graceful Honeyeater, 10/10/2015, Mt Toser, QLD
740	Mugimaki Flycatcher, 5/12/2019, Cocos Island, WA
741	Narcissus Flycatcher, 6/12/2019, Cocos Island, WA
742	Eyebrowed Thrush, 6/12/2019, Cocos Island, WA
743	Christmas Imperial Pigeon, 6/12/2019, Christmas Island, WA
744	Christmas Island Swiftlet, 6/12/2019, Christmas Island, WA
745	Christmas Frigatebird, 6/12/2019, Christmas Island, WA
746	Island Thrush, 6/12/2019, Christmas Island, WA
747	Common Emerald Dove, 7/12/2019, Christmas Island, WA
748	Abbott's Booby, 7/12/2019, Christmas Island, WA
749	Purple Heron, 8/12/2019, Christmas Island, WA
750	Java Sparrow, 9/12/2019, Christmas Island, WA
751	Christmas Boobook, 9/12/2019, Christmas Island, WA
752	Kentish Plover, 19/12/2012, "Bonna point, Kurnell", NSW
753	Gould's Petrel, 1/02/2020, Eaglehawk Neck pelagic, TAS
754	Red-chested Button-quail, 14/12/2020, Warrah Ridge, NSW
755	Red-backed Button-quail, 4/02/2021, Nabiac, NSW
756	Black-winged Monarch, 13/02/2021, Cooktown, QLD
757	Nordmann's Greenshank, 15/02/2021, Cairns, QLD
758	Opalton Grasswren, 1/05/2021, Opalton, QLD
759	Hudsonian Whimbrel, 22/11/2021, Toora, VIC

Glossary

Predominantly for my American and non-Aussie readers, this is a list of words and phrases used in Australia, as well as a few birding terms for the non-birders. I have either used these in the book or I have heard them often enough that I thought I would mention them here.

Ablutions: Another name for the toilet block/showers in a caravan park. This word is seemingly used mostly in the west.

Amenities: Toilet block/showers in a caravan park. This word is used across Australia.

Armchair tick: When a subspecies is split into its own species and you have already seen it. You do not have to go see it again, you can sit in your armchair and add a 'tick' to your life list.

Arvo: Afternoon. I use this word a lot.

Avo: Avocado I do not use this word a lot.

Backpackers: Young, foreign tourists travelling around the country as inexpensively as possible.

Barra: Short for Barramundi, a delicious white, flaky fish.

Bench or Bench top: Kitchen counter.

Berley: Also known as chum. It is cut or ground bait and oil dumped into the water to attract birds when pelagic birding.

Bin: Trash can.

Bins: Short for binoculars.

Bird: The verb, to go birdwatching.

Birding: Called birdwatching by some. I think that much too passive.

Billabong: Pool formed when the course of a creek or river changed.

Blokey-bloke: Stereotypical, white Aussie male, a man's man of rather limited interests. "He likes his footy and he likes his beer." As I am sure you are aware, I am not a blokey-bloke.

Bogan: Redneck-like, but Australian.

Bottle shop: Liquor, beer and wine store.

Brekkie: Breakfast.

Call in: To go to. "You should call in at those wetlands when you are up there."

Chockers: Short for 'chock-a-block' meaning full. "The morning train was chockers with footy fans."

Chook: A chicken, or a demeaning word referring to a bird that some consider overly common. Sometimes used jokingly between birders who have seen a bird for those who haven't.

Chemist: Pharmacy or drug store.

Chuffed: Pleased and happy.

Chum: see Berley.

Crook: Sickly, feeling unwell.

Cuppa: Hot tea or coffee.

Dam: A pond, usually manmade.

Dinky-Di: Genuine. Usually used in reference to a Dinky-Di Aussie.

Dip: To fail to see a bird that you have gone looking for, it is the birding word for missing out.

Dodgy: Iffy, questionable in a bad way.

Doona: Comforter.

Drop toilet: A non-flushing outdoor toilet, i.e. outhouse.

Dunny: Toilet, often one that is outdoors.

eBird: An online, citizen-science, avian database run by the Cornell Lab of Ornithology.

Ensuite: A bathroom connected to a bedroom.

Esky: A cooler.

Fair dinkum: Genuine. I have only heard really old-school Aussies use this expression, but I have heard it.

Feral: Wild but also applied to people that are a bit out of control. "The place was over-run with feral children."

FNQ: Far North Queensland, pronounced Efin' Cue.

Fortnight: Two weeks (this is used very often in Australia).

Gas: LPG not gasoline.

Gen: Information, "He gave me the gen on the button-quail location."

Greeny: Environmentally conscious person, most likely a member of the political Green Party.

Gripped: To be very jealous of another birder's sighting.

Gumboots: Below-the-knee waterproof boots.

Hotel: Usually, a restaurant. Sometimes there are rooms available; often it is just a restaurant or pub.

Home patch: Area near where a birder lives with which they are very familiar.

Hungry Jacks: The fast-food chain Burger King in Australia.

Kettle: Usually an electric kettle. There is one in every motel room, cabin or camp kitchen. For making a cuppa.

Life Bird: See Lifer.

Lifer: A new bird on your list. The first time you have seen that bird in your life.

Lifer Day: My extension of, but also including, Lifer Pie treat(s). It is a whole day to relax and appreciate the Lifer High.

Lifer High: The euphoria that most birders feel after seeing a Lifer. It can reverberate through you for days.

Lifer Pie: The self-indulgent celebratory treat for a Lifer. It can be anything that brings you joy, but it is still referred to as your Lifer Pie.

Maccas: what Aussies call the fast-food chain, McDonalds.

Mega: Short for mega-rarity. A very rare bird for where it is being seen. It is a bird that could be common in Europe, but if it visited Australia, it would be a mega.

Parma: A popular pub meal of chicken parmigiana served with chips and salad.

Pelagic: Deep-sea birdwatching. "We went on a pelagic off Eaglehawk Neck, Tasmania."

Petrol: Gasoline.

Plastic: In relation to birds, a plastic is an introduced species that although looked down upon by some but is still tickable on your list.

Pot: A small glass of beer at a pub, about a half pint.

Poms: What some Aussies call British people.

Pudding: Can mean any type of dessert. This can be confusing to Americans. Also, a dish, sweet or savoury, that's cooked by being boiled or steamed in something.

Prawn: Shrimp. Although the advertisement was popular, no Aussie puts 'shrimp on the Barbie'. They are called prawns.

Rego: Vehicle registration number (licence plate).

Road train: A truck with as many as four trailer sections. You learn to get out of their way.

Rock up: To arrive. "We rocked up just as they spotted the bird."

Rubbish: Trash or garbage.

Servo: A service station.

Shout: To pay for. "Come on in mate. I'll shout you a beer."

Sorted: Arranged, figured out, organized.

Stubby: A bottle of beer as well as men's shorts (stubbies) that are really much shorter than they should be.

Stubby-holder: The insulated drink holder that helps keep a drink cool. Sometimes called 'huggies' and 'coozies' in the US.

Tassie: Tasmania, of course.

Tea: Not only a beverage, but can also refer to the meal taken at dinnertime (evening). (This also can really confuse Americans.)

Tick: A new bird, a Lifer on your list.

Tickable: A bird that qualifies to be on your list and be ticked.

Tinnie: A small aluminum boat.

Twitch: *verb*, To pursue a rare bird that has turned up somewhere.

Twitch: *noun*, The adventure of the pursuit of that rare bird.

Twitcher: Sometimes used for birders in general, but specifically for those who chase rare-bird sightings.

Whinge: To complain.

Whinger: Complainer.

Woolies: Woolworth's grocery stores.

Yabby: Freshwater crayfish, eaten just like crayfish (mudbugs in Louisiana, US).

Who's To Bless and Who's To Blame

I have sometimes thought when reading acknowledgements in other books that the first person thanked should be the author themself. So, I thank me. I could not have done it without me. All joking aside, it is difficult for me to thank myself at all for anything. If you have read this book, you might understand some of why that would be. But I am the main person that I need to thank. For my personal growth, my hours upon hours of working with these words, and my continuing determination to (at least sometimes) be the me that I want to be, even when I do not feel like it. So, I thank me.

I will also mention as in the first book that I am putting these acknowledgements in the back of the book. I have always thought that is where they should go in books. Then theoretically, you will have read the book and know whether or not anyone deserves to be thanked (haha).

Next, I will thank Robert Shore and James Cornelious. Robert has been my biggest encourager toward getting out amongst it, going after birds and just doing it. As I have said before, he is like family to me. James has become my regular birding companion, as well as a true buddy in general. He is the other half of Team Troopi and is also very much like family. I mentioned his excellent 'birding ears' in the book but he also has good eyes and as much heart as anyone I have ever known.

And I want to thank my wonderful friend Kenn Kaufman. His inspiration, his encouragement and his enthusiasm for my writing means the world to me. With his thoughts and suggestions as a compass, I sailed confidently into the rewrite that became this book. And Kim Kaufman and her wonderful Black Swamp Bird Observatory (my BSBO hoodie is truly a part of my birding life). And my stepson, Josh for his love, patience and assistance with technology. And my Stepson Michael Johnson for his invaluable assistance on my website.

Huge thanks to John Beaufoy publisher, Rosemary Wilkinson editor and my friend Sarah the publicist for their tireless efforts to share my words with the world.

I want to thank Richard Baxter for his amazing leadership and knowledge, Jenny Spry for being like a Yoda for me in the islands and while I am there, Joy Tansey, Darryel Biggles Binns, Tania Ireton and Glen Pacey. As I said, I was birding with legends.

Always a thank you to my yabok, Denise Lawungkurr Good-fellow and my mamma Una Thompson, who adopted me into the Ngalanbali clan of the Kunwinjku people ten years ago in Gunbalana, Arnhem Land, NT.

David Adam for his friendship and for his brilliant cover photo of our Opalton Grasswren. Bill Betts for taking and sharing his wonderful photos of the Whale Shark (and other photos). Karen Dick for her dear friendship, her organizational skills and patience with sorting Eaglehawk Neck Pelagics. Alan Stringer for his friendship and patience as a valued birding companion. Kay Parkin for her advice and friendship, Mark Carter for sharing his knowledge, friendship and enthusiasm, David and Janet Mead of Great Northern Tours for their friendship (and that cool shirt). Laurie Ross for sharing his information and knowledge (and cool shirt too), Steve Davidson the Melbourne Birder for years of sharing his knowledge (and another cool T-shirt of mine as well), Rebekah Abela and her mom, Norma Abela for their support, and my wonderful grandchildren who continue to fill my heart even when we have necessarily spent way too much time apart during these Covid years.

More thank yous to my dear friend Dez Hughes the Wader Whisperer, brilliant pelagic birder Peter Vaughn, Jenn Stephens, Nigel and Jaime Jackett, Murray and Charlie Scott, Jillian

Cornelious, Jeff Jones, Bruce Watts, Marie Tarrant, Marc Gardner, Anne Collins, Tim Doby, Ruth Woodrow, Paul Dodd, Tony Palliser, Paul Brooks, John Young, Mike Carter, Tom Tarrant, Alan McBride, Dean Ingwersen, Neil Macumber, Anita Flynn, Adrian Welsh, David Harper, Ross Jones, John Tongue, Kylee Cleal, Damian Baxter, Alan Gillanders, Maarten Hulzebosch, Geoff Glare and John Alan.

And to everyone whose name I forgot to write. Remember that I have a very ADHD brain and if I forgot you it does not mean that I am not grateful for you. And lastly but very importantly, I want to thank everyone across this wondrous land who was willing to joke for a moment, return a smile, share some information or just touch lives in a genuine way. There were so many of y'all and I love you.

The author hiking in Wurdi Youang (the You Yangs). He considers this his neighbourhood.

From the Author

Performing as R. Bruce, I made my living as an internationally touring singer/songwriter and comedian. I released three albums of original songs that are still available through digital distribution and receive airplay on satellite radio in North America.

I live in Lara, Victoria, Australia with my wife Lynn. This puts me near my stepchildren and grandchildren who live in the Melbourne region. I am writing this in December 2021 in this changed COVID world. My birding travels have been curtailed to say the least. However, my Troopi waits patiently in the driveway. I trust we will eventually go off again.

At this point I have seen 759 birds in Australia. But as we know, my birding is not about the number. It is truly about the vibe and the journey. My journey will continue, and I will always write about it. I need to write for me, but I am very pleased to discover that others also enjoy my words. I do love to share. For me, sharing is an integral part of living. That is genuine. This is genuine. This is me. If you've read this book, you have pretty much met me. I do hope you enjoyed it.

Sending love from the Land Down Under.
Cheers for now,
rb